Language and the City

Language and Globalization

Series Editors: **Sue Wright**, University of Portsmouth, UK and **Helen Kelly-Holmes**, University of Limerick, Ireland.

In the context of current political and social developments, where the national group is not so clearly defined and delineated, the state language not so clearly dominant in every domain, and cross-border flows and transfers affect more than a small elite, new patterns of language use will develop. The series aims to provide a framework for reporting on and analysing the linguistic outcomes of globalization and localization.

Titles include:

David Block
MULTILINGUAL IDENTITIES IN A GLOBAL CITY
London Stories

Diarmait Mac Giolla Chríost
LANGUAGE AND THE CITY

Julian Edge (*editor*)
(RE)LOCATING TESOL IN AN AGE OF EMPIRE

Roxy Harris
NEW ETHNICITIES AND LANGUAGE USE

Clare Mar-Molinero and Patrick Stevenson (*editors*)
LANGUAGE IDEOLOGIES, POLICIES AND PRACTICES
Language and the Future of Europe

Clare Mar-Molinero and Miranda Stewart (*editors*)
GLOBALIZATION AND LANGUAGE IN THE SPANISH-SPEAKING WORLD
Macro and Micro Perspectives

Ulrike Hanna Meinhof and Dariusz Galasinski
THE LANGUAGE OF BELONGING

Leigh Oakes and Jane Warren
LANGUAGE, CITIZENSHIP AND IDENTITY IN QUEBEC

Forthcoming titles:

John Edwards
LANGUAGE AND SOCIAL LIFE

Colin Williams
LINGUISTIC MINORITIES IN DEMOCRATIC CONTEXT

**Language and Globalization
Series Standing Order ISBN 1–4039–9731–4**
(*outside North America only*)

You can receive future titles in this series as they are published by placing a standing order. Please contact your bookseller or, in case of difficulty, write to us at the address below with your name and address, the title of the series and the ISBN quoted above.

Customer Services Department, Macmillan Distribution Ltd, Houndmills, Basingstoke, Hampshire RG21 6XS, England

Language and the City

Diarmait Mac Giolla Chríost
Lecturer, School of Welsh, Cardiff University

First published 2007 by
PALGRAVE MACMILLAN
Houndmills, Basingstoke, Hampshire RG21 6XS and
175 Fifth Avenue, New York, N.Y. 10010
Companies and representatives throughout the world

PALGRAVE MACMILLAN is the global academic imprint of the Palgrave Macmillan division of St. Martin's Press, LLC and of Palgrave Macmillan Ltd. Macmillan® is a registered trademark in the United States, United Kingdom and other countries. Palgrave is a registered trademark in the European Union and other countries.

ISBN-13: 978-0-230-01878-5   hardback
ISBN-10: 0-230-01878-5   hardback

This book is printed on paper suitable for recycling and made from fully managed and sustained forest sources. Logging, pulping and manufacturing processes are expected to conform to the environmental regulations of the country of origin.

A catalogue record for this book is available from the British Library.

A catalog record for this book is available from the Library of Congress.

10 9 8 7 6 5 4 3 2 1
16 15 14 13 12 11 10 09 08 07

Printed and bound in Great Britain by
Antony Rowe Ltd, Chippenham and Eastbourne

for Niamh Elain

Contents

List of Photographs

List of Figures

List of Tables

Acknowledgements

I owe several debts of thanks in the writing of this book. I am grateful to Jill Lake of Palgrave Macmillan for her initial interest in the work and her patience in bringing it to press. I am also grateful to Professor Sue Wright for her interest in the work and, in addition, her invaluable suggestions and insights regarding various aspects of the book. Also, I would like to record my thanks to other colleagues, who shall remain nameless, for their different promptings, encouragement and constructive criticism. The final version of the work, however, with all its faults, is my responsibility alone. As usual, my greatest debt is to Ema. Please note that all translations in the text are by the author, unless otherwise stated.

I would like to thank the following for permission to use copyright material in this book: Figures 4.2, 'A schematic view of a national language planning situation'; 4.3, 'The pull of political, linguistic and social forces on language planning'; 4.4, 'Forces at work in a linguistic ecosystem'; 4.5, 'Effect of time on a linguistic ecosystem'; and 4.6, 'Effect of an ecological perspective on a language planning activity', are from Robert Kaplan and Richard Baldauf (1997), *Language Planning from Practice to Theory*, and are reproduced here with permission of Multilingual Matters. Figures 5.1, 'Chicago Hispanic tracts 1990–2000'; 5.2, 'New York Hispanic tracts 1990–2000'; and 5.3, 'Los Angeles – Riverside – Orange County CMSA Hispanic tracts 1990–2000', are from Roberto Suro and Sonya Tafoya (2004), *Dispersal and Concentration: Patterns of Latino Residential Settlement*, and are reproduced with permission of Pew Hispanic Center, a Pew Research Center project. Figures 5.4, 'Dominant language in Cape Town 1991', and 5.5, 'Language shift in Cape Town 1980–1991', are from Colin H. Williams and Izak Van der Merwe (1996), 'Mapping the multilingual city: A research agenda for urban geolinguistics', *Journal of Multilingual and Multicultural Development*, and are reproduced here with permission of Multilingual Matters. Every effort has been made to contact all copyright holders. Any rights not acknowledged here will be acknowledged in subsequent printings if notice is given to the publisher.

1
Introduction

Preliminaries

The impact of the city on language is varied; it is often far-reaching and is, occasionally, revolutionary. One example of the impact of urbanisation on language is the relationship between the appearance of the first cities in the world and the independent innovation of writing in a number of different parts of the globe – Mesoamerica, Ancient Egypt, Sumeria and China. Then, in the European context for the first time, the evolution of writing, literature, philosophy and the full range of language-centred activity associated with the rise of the city-state in Ancient and Classical Greece. In the contemporary world, the city is becoming increasingly important in economic, political, social hand economic terms, in particular due to the specific nature of the current form of globalisation. Their significance may be measured simply in terms of population. For example, Castells noted in 1996 that there were 13 cities in the world with populations in excess of 10 million people and that before long there would be a number of cities with populations of over 20 million (Castells, 1996). Also, the United Nations (UN) recently estimated that the majority of the world population, for the first time in history, will be living in urban centres by the end of this decade (UN, 1999 & 2001). More recently, in 2004, it was calculated that there were 20 cities in the world with a population in excess of 10 million (15 of which were located in the so-called developing world) and that by the year 2015 there will be over 20 cities with a population in excess of 10 million, comprising around 5% of the total world population (UNPF, 2004). Awareness of the significance of this for language is beginning to emerge. For example, Fischer noted some years ago that

> One major cause (of linguistic change) of the past 200 years has been unprecedented urbanization. In 1790, only one in twenty Americans lived in a town; in 1900, only one in 40 lived on a farm. The Third World is now experiencing a similar urban revolution, eradicating not only languages but entire language families. The inversion of traditional human settlement patterns brings about innumerable linguistic upheavals, a *punctuation* causing innovation, dialect levelling and even language replacement.
>
> (Fischer, 1999: 173)

Thus, the city is the birthplace of the most outstanding linguistic innovation but it is also a cemetery for languages. How might this contradiction be understood?

The intellectual concerns central to the work are set in relation to scholarly debates regarding language in city contexts, drawing from the areas of cultural and urban geography and the sociology of language in particular. In the text it is shown how the contemporary form of globalisation has certain effects on language in social context and the city is identified as the most important site for the realisation of these effects. Also, it is shown that from this arise a number of important questions to which the text responds: Is the discipline of sociolinguistics necessarily urban? Is cultural diversity inherent to the city? Is linguistic diversity sustainable in urban context? Is language change forged by the city, or is it the product of mobility? What are the implications for language planning and policy? The book challenges a set of assumptions that hold sustainable linguistic diversity to be inherently non-urban and regard the city as an unproblematic site understanding the social function of language. Also, the book argues that language is central to understanding how the city works and that the nature of the global connections and disconnections between cities and other places are crucial to understanding how language is changing in the contemporary world. While the globalisation of the English language and its translation into various local practices exemplifies some of the contradictory impacts of the relationship between language and the city, the study of other languages can be enormously illuminative. The case of global English is a striking phenomenon, one which has merited very considerable scrutiny (e.g. Crystal, 2003; Kachru, 1992; Mair, 2003; McArthur, 2003), but here the focus is on linguistic diversity in the urban context. The normative statements challenged by this book are implied in fields of study beyond the sociology of language and so this work is a contribution to a number of disciplines.

By way of introduction the term 'globalisation' requires some clarification at this point. This term is often associated with the various and rapid changes the world is experiencing at present. Its meaning relates to a number of issues, including increasingly extensive global interconnections, the transformation of interactions across local and global processes, and the organisation and operation of power at levels above and below the nation-state. Globalisation can be described as a multidimensional process that encompasses all social relations – cultural, economic and political – and, as a result, its effects may be perceived in every aspect of society. According to Cochrane and Pain (2000), the principal features of globalisation are as follows:

- Stretched social relations – that is, the existence of cultural, economic and political networks of global connection. These transcend the borders of the nation-state and they are especially obvious in the phenomenon of regionalisation; that is, the increasing interconnection between states that share borders. Also, the individual is located within such networks so that local actions might have global implications.
- Intensification of flows and interactions – this stretching of social relations appears to relate to an increase in the intensity of global interactions, suggesting in turn that the effects of actions are greater than before. The intensity of contemporary communications connects distant actions, decisions, people and events within a shared immediate social space, a space that is virtual rather than physically or territorially real.
- Increasing interpenetration of global and local social processes – distant, as understood in conventional geographical terms, cultures and societies meet at the local level increasingly often and with greater intensity than before. This interpenetration of local and global geographies creates cultural variation and hybridity.
- Development of a transnational, global infrastructure – that is, the formal and informal institutional organisation that is necessary to the workings of the global networks. This includes transnational and global organisations of political and economic governance. These are expressed as interconnections that transcend nation-state borders and operate beyond its systems of management and regulation.

There is considerable difference of opinion on the significance of globalisation. Crudely speaking, three contrasting perspectives may be identified (Cochrane & Pain, 2000):

- The traditionalist perspective – that globalisation and its impact is greatly overstated. Proponents argue, for example, that the nation-state remains the key polity although its will to act has been diminished by the rhetoric of globalisation. Critics point out, however, that regionalisation, as within the European Union (EU), and proliferation of transnational corporations suggest some sort of basic qualitative, if not quantitative, change.
- The globalist perspective – that globalisation has transformed the world in a thoroughly revolutionary manner. Proponents argue, for example, that the nation-state has been overtaken by the transnational, business community, described by some as a global cosmocracy. Power is the property of global capital, isolating the nation-state as a polity that is simultaneously too small (to control global capital) and too big (to engage with individual citizens). Critics point out, however, that the technologies associated with the information and communications revolution that is central to globalisation are equally accessible in all societies and in all parts of the world. This suggests that there are limits to globalisation.
- The transformationalist perspective – this perspective draws upon the other two in adopting the position that globalisation is being driven by epistemic communities, NGOs and social movements. Power is conceived of as circulating between the state, business corporations and people and is a response to the fact that the power of the traditional nation-state has been eroded. If phenomena such as multilayered governance are accepted as evidence of globalisation, then it follows that this process and its impacts are clearest in Europe.

The city plays a critical role in the process of globalisation. Whether one concurs with Sassen – in that cities are key sites in a hierarchy of urban centres and that they possess and are empowered by important expert services located within institutions (1991) or with Castells – who argues that cities are critical nodes in a space of flows and that the city is a process where the extent of its power, derived from the global economic networks, is related to the levels of access to these networks that are possessed by the groups of experts that are resident in the city (1989; 1996 & 1997), it is the case that most of the important commentators

on the city in globalisation agree that the network as the strategic architecture and that the exact location of a city in the network is a matter
of power, dependent upon the ability of the city to negotiate its position with other players.

How does one read all of this with regard to the question of language
and, in particular, linguistic diversity and minority languages? A profound duality is held as a central assumption to this text – globalisation
is a threat to local cultures and identities but it is the case that they can
be transformed and renewed through globalisation. Calvet recently
published (2002), in French, a paper with the title 'Sociolinguistics and
Cities: Hazard or Necessity?' Given the contemporary form of globalisation and the centrality of cities to it, the response seems quite clear. The
challenge of understanding the relationship between sociolinguistics
and cities is a necessity, hazardous perhaps, but essential. Moreover, if
Crystal (e.g. 1987 & 2001), Fischer (1999) and others are correct in
regarding the current historical juncture as a language extinction hori-
zon then it is a necessity of the most pressing kind.

Thus, the central purpose of the text is set out, which is to construct
a fresh conceptual framework for understanding language–city relationships that brings together critical literatures in human geography, language planning and urban planning while also drawing from material
in sociology, anthropology, sociolinguistics and cultural studies. The
various aims of the text are as follows:

- To provide the first comprehensive treatment of language–city
  relationships, illuminating the workings of language within the
  urban context
- To illustrate and to explain how cities function as the sites of linguistic diversity and innovation
- To illustrate and to explain how cities function as the sites of language change, language shift and language death
- To indicate ways in which language planning and policy might
  address these functions of the city in the interests of sustainable
  linguistic diversity
- To propose a conceptual framework for understanding language–city
  relationships through critical reference to cutting-edge research on
  the geography and sociology of the city and on the sociology of
  language, drawing upon relational and radical perspectives on the
  city and upon an ecological view of language
- To consider the extent to which the discipline of sociolinguistics is
  necessarily urban

- To counter a simplistic biodiversity = linguistic diversity formulation in identifying cities as significant sites of linguistic diversity and innovation, as well as being the sites of language change, language shift and language death
- To situate sociolinguistics, in general, and language planning, in particular, in relation to the theorisation of the contemporary form of globalisation
- To present original research on the language in city contexts from a global perspective, drawing upon sites from around the world
- To relate conceptions of the city to ecological perspectives on language.

The main body of the text is divided into two parts. In Part One, entitled 'The Intellectual Inheritance' and comprising Chapters Two, Three and Four, three interrelated sets of literature are critically reviewed. These are, in Chapter Two, the geography, history and sociology of the city; in Chapter Three, the development and practice of sociolinguistics, or the sociology of language, in urban contexts; and in Chapter Four, modern and contemporary theory and practice in the field of language planning in relation to linguistic diversity in the city. Part Two of the text, entitled 'Towards a New Conceptual Terrain' and comprising Chapters Five, Six and Seven, develops a number of themes that are crucial to understanding the relationship between language and the city, namely place, identity and power. Much of the original research will be presented in this part of the book. The final chapter of the book, Chapter Eight, draws together the various main points of the text. Also, directions for future empirical research are indicated.

Part I The Intellectual Inheritance

2
The City

Introduction

The city has been subjected to sustained interrogation in a number of disciplines in recent years. Here, certain key insights are highlighted as they have significant implications for the way in which language–city relationships are to be understood. The various social, economic and environmental aspects of city life are interrelated in complex ways within the city, between cities and between the city and other forms of spatially arranged polities. The spatial patterning of the city, in which contrasting worlds are juxtaposed in close physical proximity and distant social propinquity and where multiple and contested senses of place are negotiated, is understood to have generative effects. Arising from this are various urban tensions relating to community and difference, movement and settlement and order and disorder. In the context of the peculiar intensity of the social relations that define city life, these tensions are often manifest in ways which are paradoxical. The diverse social geometry of urban space is cross-cut by issues of power and its asymmetric circulation. A cue is taken from Castells in that 'Ultimately, the meaning of cities depends on the governance of cities' (Castells, 2002: 557). Thus, the significance of language in governance and the centrality of the craft of language policy and planning in understanding the meaning of language–city relationships are underlined. These various issues are examined here through a number of themes – connection and internal differentiation, the 'stranger' and difference, rhythms, social and spatial division, marginalised groups and resistance and, in conclusion, order and disorder. This chapter borrows heavily from the relational perspective on the city, as articulated by a set of geographers associated with the Open University in the UK. Of course, this is not the only approach to the city but it is one in which sufficient scope is given to the social and cultural. It is, as a result, more immediately accessible to sociolinguists and language planners who, naturally, may be rather unfamiliar with the vast range of literature in the field of urban planning and the study of the city more generally. This view of the city is, therefore, the starting point.

Connection and internal differentiation

The traditional approach to the city, characterised as evolutionary or historical, offers an attractively simple but superficial and ultimately inadequate model for understanding the dynamics of the city. Implicit to this approach is the view that all cities broadly conform to the same linear mode of development, in which cities are relatively homogeneous entities with regard to their internal organisation and, finally, that spatial relationships between cities and urban–rural relationships are of limited significance with regard to understanding the nature of the city (Massey, 1999). Some contemporary features of the geographies within and between cities challenge this approach. For example, of the 13 cities with populations in excess of 10 million, as noted by Castells (1996) for the year 1992, only Tokyo, New York and Los Angeles are found in what may be described as the core rich countries of the world. None of the cities listed are located in Europe. If current trends continue it is likely that, before long, there will exist a number of cities with populations in excess of 20 million, and all of these, other than Tokyo, will be located outside of the core rich countries (Pinch, 2000). On the other hand, it is clear that cities in the core rich countries are characterised by a mosaic of polarised geographies of wealth, social status, health, ethnicity and gender and that the forces of globalisation are throwing these features into increasingly stark relief (e.g. Castells, 1989; Sassen, 1991). Given this challenge, an alternative conceptual framework is necessary, and in this rethinking of cities connections and internal differentiation are crucial points of reference.

The case of the city of Chicago can be turned to in order, in the first place, to consider how cities in general are connected and, secondly, to explore how they are internally differentiated. Pile (1999a: 20–32) shows how Chicago came to be situated at the centre of a network of connections that facilitated the cross-cutting of various markets, goods and resources. Importantly for the development of Chicago, as the mere fact of location is not sufficient to make a vibrant city, this intersection was actively made to work by a number of agents. This included, for example, the operation of transport links by railways companies, the implementation of commodities regulation by the Board of Trade of the city and the regulation of land and natural resources by the federal government. Also, power is a feature of this complex weave of inter-connections. Patterns in the organisation of labour as well as the shape of the relationship between nature and the city indicate as much.

Chi-goug was, in the 18th century, a modest trading settlement of a few dispersed buildings on the edge of Lake Michigan. In less than a century this place would become the city of Chicago. The active par-ticipation of very many agents in the construction and maintenance of a network of interconnections was a central feature to this. Up until the mid-19th century the site was gravely restricted by the fact that the passage of traffic along its lines of transportation was not without severe difficulty at different times of the year. For example, the streets within the site and the road between Chicago and other settlements were blocked by mud and snow during the rainy season and in winter, respectively. In the summer the harbour was inaccessible to ships as water levels were not high enough to enable docking. From 1848 a number of actions resolved these issues. In the first place, and in a period of some 20 years, the street levels of the whole site were gradu-ally raised by up to 14 feet (Pile, 1999a: 23). Thus, the internal connec-tions were secured all year round. Also in 1848, the matter of external connections was addressed. In March of that year the first railroad was built in Chicago, rapidly followed by many others (Pile, 1999a: 24). Moreover, Chicago quickly became a point of intersection for a network of railroads. As Pile notes, 'these developments in the transport network both within and beyond the city changed the way in which people and goods travelled in the region' (Pile, 1999a: 24). The final innovation to Chicago in 1848 was the telegraph. Given that telegraph lines tended to follow railroads, there was a tendency also for the telegraph to employ Chicago as a hugely important point of intersection. The combination of greatly improved internal infrastructure, fast and efficient external connections to numerous other places and the ease of access to reliable and prompt sources of information meant that Chicago became an essential juncture in the movement of people, the exchange of com-modities and capital, the provision of services, and the meeting of cul-tural diversity. Many other agents took further advantage of these flows through the construction of warehouses, factories and other enterprises. Thus, Chicago came to possess a certain intensity that defines cities, not only with regard to its sheer size, including in terms of both the built physical environment and population, but also regarding its capacity to compress both time and space. At this point, information, capital, commodities and people now moved to and through Chicago in greater volumes, with greater speed and from across greater distances then ever before. Importantly, for Chicago, the density of industry in the city enabled it to adapt and thrive, as the network of connections based upon the railroad subsequently shifted and changed to the extent that by the end of the 19th-century Chicago was not a focal point.

Conceiving of the city as a complex geographic plexus does not tell the whole story. Chicago is not a homogeneous social entity but, instead, is characterised by a diversity that defines cities. Pile's (1999a: 35–41) critique of the work of the Chicago School of Sociology during the 1920s and 1930s on the internal social patterning of Chicago is a useful point of access for examining the notion of internal differentiation in cities. While, as Pile recognises, the work is conceptually flawed in a number of respects, what it offers that is of value is a description of the social and spatial organisation of Chicago during the first quarter of the 20th century. For example, Pile notes that Burgess constructed an analytical model for the social structuring of Chicago comprising a series of concentric zones occupied by increasingly wealthier residents the further one moved from the centre of the city. However, what is of greater value in the model, argues Pile (1999a: 38), is that these concentric zones (which only seem to work as an overlay upon Lake Michigan and not upon the city) are cross-cut by a number of districts. It is through this relationship between the concentric zones and the districts that Pile is able to read more closely the social complexity of the city. The cross-cutting of the zones by the districts raises questions regarding the distribution of people by socio-economic class, ethnicity and gender and also the interrelationships between these matters. Thereby, Chicago is redrawn by Pile to better illuminate these complexities.

Zorbaugh, another member of the school, explored the various districts identified by Burgess in detail. According to Pile (1999a: 38–41), Zorbaugh makes a number of points that add further depth to understanding the diversity of Chicago. In his study of the 'Gold Coast' area of the city he concluded that while the rich and poor of the city occupied a physical juxtaposition, their lived worlds were far removed, that is to say that despite spatial proximity no intimate social propinquity existed. Thus, the poor, while frequenting the beach in the summer, might gaze upon the waterfront houses of the wealthy, but there is no significant social interaction between the classes. In his study of the 'Roomers' district, an area that Zorbaugh regarded as rather bohemian, he noted that many young and single individuals were drawn to live in this district. He also noted that while the area was much animated by the activities of radical clubs, theatres, studios, tea rooms and so forth, it was quite deserted for the greater part of the day as many of the residents pursued work as clerks, waitresses, shop assistants, entertainers and other different forms of employment. Zorbaugh concluded that, despite the precarious socio-economic positions of many of these individuals, Chicago presented many and varied opportunities that were uniquely available in cities. Finally, in his study of the 'Underworld', he noted that crime and violence were ever present. And although many different migrant groups lived in very close proximity, for some groups the horizons of their worlds might not often overlap but, for others, they would violently collide. For Zorbaugh, this sense of uncertainty and danger is a characteristic feature of the street life of Chicago.

Early 20th-century Chicago was a cosmopolitan city. It has drawn in migrant groups from across the USA and much further afield. It is a home to African-Americans, Germans, Italians, Irish, Greeks, Persians, Poles and Slavs. Their complex distribution within the city, in Pile's words, 'evokes the different histories and geographies of migration into the city – and, more than this, the social dramas of people living in Chicago' (Pile, 1999a: 41). The enormous range of social, economic, cultural, ethnic and other contrasts that Chicago is a home to define it as a city but, and perhaps more significantly, the city serves to exaggerate these contrasts. It is in this quality that the definitive feature of the city may be identified – its intensity. As Pile (1999a: 43–8) notes from the work of Wirth, the city in its sheer size, density and heterogeneity creates something new – new kinds of social interaction, new forms of difference and new opportunities in lifestyle. The novelty of the city, however, is also inherently paradoxical. For example, moving to the city may enable an escape from the ties that bind many typical rural communities together within a rigid set of values to which conformity is highly valued but it may also entail the loss of the sense of social intimacy that such a community often affords. City life, by contrast, can provide ready social familiarity but of a form that is largely superficial and quite anonymous.

The unique intensity of cities is the product of both connections and internal differentiation. They ought not to be considered as simple discrete subjects but rather as interrelated phenomena. The case of migration to the city of Chicago illustrates the point. Through this complex process, early European adventurers arrived at the shores of the Great Lakes of the North American subcontinent and subsequently displaced the First Nation Americans from the place that was Chi-goug. As a result of this it was possible to establish the European notion of the legal ownership and disposal of land as individual property in relation to this place. Presented with this opportunity, white colonisers conceived of the possibilities for their own socio-economic advancement that would flow from the successful development of the site as an urban centre of significance. In seeking to realise the metropolis of their imaginations they actively set about improving the connections that linked Chicago with other places. In this respect, the most important innovation for 19th-century Chicago was the railroad. The fact of the construction and expansion of the rail network, and the location of Chicago as a key intersection, enabled people to travel to Chicago with greater ease than ever before. It is also the case that the strategic position of the city meant that many travellers, migrants or otherwise, had no choice but to make their journey via Chicago. Migrants were, doubtless, attracted to Chicago by the socio-economic opportunities they believed to exist there. Indeed, as the industrial base of Chicago expanded along with the railroads and other connections, such opportunities multiplied at a rapid rate of growth during the second half of the 19th and early 20th centuries. Thus, migrants were attracted to Chicago from across the USA, Europe and further afield. Upon their arrival and settlement in the city, these peoples made a home of Chicago; as a result, the social and physical fabric of the city came to comprise that which Pinch describes as 'an intricate variety of social and built environment' (Pinch, 2000: 31). In this respect, as both Allen (1999a & 1999b) and Massey (1999) show, other processes function in a manner similar to that of migration. This includes social, economic, environmental, cultural and political processes, together with associated flows of information, commodities, services, capital and ideas. As they also show, this is the case for cities across the globe. Paris, Jakarta, New York and São Paolo all exhibit this complex interrelation of connection and differentiation.

It can be concluded that cities are the focal points of social relations and that the vigour of this focus is central to their vitality. However, cities are more than simple social foci. Through interrogating the city as both connected and internally differentiated it is possible to illuminate that which is socially and conceptually distinctive about cities and their social relationships. That distinction is to be drawn in an intense quality of time and space and being. That quality is the product of the complex interrelationships of connection and differentiation. In this way, the idea of the city is best understood.

The 'stranger' and difference

The 'stranger' is central to an understanding of urban life. The key features of the open intensity that defines urban life – cities as sites of proximity and co-presence, as multiplicities of space-times and as meeting places – turn, in many ways, upon the notion of 'strangeness'. Through examining the place of the social and natural 'other participants' in urban life, to paraphrase Hannerz (in Allen, Massey & Pryke, 1999: 40), the physical spaces that are cities can be shown to be the sites of multilayered and complex relational webs. Working within a relational perspective on cities, it is also noted that there is a bond between the known self and the strange other. The 'stranger' is not a wholly ephemeral or transient presence – there can be no potential sense of excitement of discovery nor sense of threat of the unknown in a temporary acquaintance – but is instead an 'intimate stranger' – the embodiment of the ambivalent tension of the recognisable or familiar unknown and, as such, an intrinsic feature of that which defines urban life. This encounter with 'strangeness' may be energising and liberating in enabling the forging of new identities but, as is further noted, this intimate encounter is not innocent of questions of inequality and domination. In this sense, negotiating difference and identity is also a matter of power.

The idea of the 'stranger' as an intimate outsider may be illustrated from the work of Wirth. According to Wirth, 'a city may be defined as a relatively large, dense, and permanent settlement of *socially heterogeneous individuals*'[my italics] (Wirth in Pile, 1999a: 43). A city, therefore, comprises the following:

• Large numbers of people
• Density of settlement
• Heterogeneity of individuals and of group life.

An examination of these features can help begin to locate the 'stranger' in urban life. Large numbers of people in cities affect the ways in which people interact because of the greater range of variation between individuals, the greater numbers of social interactions and the greater potential for differentiation among people. This, according to Wirth, 'should give rise to the spatial segregation of individuals according to colour, ethnic heritage, economic and social status, tastes and preferences' (Wirth in Pile, 1999a: 43). Wirth, however, does not explain why spatial segregation should arise nor does he describe the social processes underlying either spatial segregation or social differentiation. It is significant, however, that it is noted that the large numbers of people allow for new kinds of social interaction that do not rely upon kinship ties, neighbourliness, communal sentiment, tradition and folk attitudes characteristic of rural life. In this sense, the density of urban population is socially liberating. However, a note of caution should be drawn, as according to Wirth, 'the contrasts of the city may indeed be face to face, but they are nevertheless impersonal, superficial, transitory, and segmental. The reserve, the indifference, and the blasé outlook which urbanites manifest in their relationships may thus be regarded as devices for immunizing themselves against the personal claims and expectations of others' (Wirth in Pile, 1999a: 44). The social interaction of urban life is ambivalent, therefore as, for example, contacts may at the same time be superficial and anonymous while also releasing individuals from the obligations or expectations that pertain to the more immediate and rigid framework of rural communities. Also, while urban-dwellers are released from such traditions, ties and constraints, they become alienated from participation in communal life and do not relate to other people as if they were part of a community. In this sense, cities disorganise social life as previous forms of social organisation are undermined and replaced by social relations whose organisation is based on indifference, superficiality and individualistic materialism. This is also, of course, one of the paradoxes that seem to define urban life – the embodiment of elements that are seemingly opposed and their intensification and concentration in the city.

The intensity and concentration characteristic of cities are crucial in understanding the social production of difference in urban space. The concentration of people leads to forms of distancing as the city contains the possibility for individuals to differentiate themselves from others, and also the opportunity for like-minded individuals to form new associations. According to Wirth (drawing on Simmel), 'the close physical contact of numerous individuals (which) necessarily produces a shift in the medium through which we orient ourselves to the urban milieu ... our physical contacts are close but our social contacts are distant ... we tend to acquire and develop sensitivity to a world of artefacts and become progressively further removed from the world of nature'. (Wirth in Pile, 1999a: 45). Thus, as the city intertwines and amasses people and concentrates the coexistence of differences, an exactness of co-ordination and organisation is required. For Wirth and Simmel, therefore, through the resultant differentiation of urban space, the city comes 'to resemble a mosaic of social worlds' (Pile, 1999a: 47) where juxtapositions between one piece of the mosaic and another are abrupt and clear-cut.

Pile, however, modifies this vision of difference in the city. He notes that while the former rigidities of identity begin to break down in the encounters between different people, differences become much more nuanced. Moreover, the social stratification of cities is difficult to determine, as people are continually bridging and crossing social hierarchies. The status of individuals changes from context to context, and over time, there is an inherent instability and insecurity in urban identities. The metaphor of the mosaic is thus reworked:

> Because urban identities are exposed as social fictions, individuals are freed to identify, affiliate and associate with divergent groups. The consequences of this are not just personal, however. Urban spaces, like urban social hierarchies, are liable to be fluid, unstable and contain people with allegiances and affiliations to multiple groups. It would, therefore, be a mistake to characterise the city as having a stable pattern of differences – like a mosaic of coloured ceramic tiles cemented to the earth. Instead, the surfaces of the mosaic are liable to shift, to slide over or between one another, even to change pattern.
>
> (Pile, 1999a: 48)

The spatial expression of heterogeneity in urban life is most clearly manifest in the meeting of different peoples in public spaces. The 'strangers' pushed and pulled by various forces of migration to the city do not relate to each other as immediate and necessary companions in a coherent community possessing a singular and fixed notion of its sense of place in the world but rather are bonded by common civic values, realised through the institutions of urban citizenship. McDowell puts it in the following terms:

> The ties that link urban strangers ... are the ties of the polity. The bonds between urban residents are not the close personal and intimate ties based on the private relationships between kith and kin and close personal friends. The urban crowd, the multitude of strangers, is instead united through the rights and obligations of common citizenship and through participation in the public life of a city.
>
> (McDowell, 1999: 97)

Accessibility to public space, both literal and metaphorical, is a key issue for the equal expression of diversity and the negotiation of

difference. Two important points flow from this – firstly, that the production of social differences between people affects who may or may
not move within and between the public spaces of a city; and secondly,
that people can and do become fixed or trapped in urban space. This
is another of those city paradoxes, dynamism and stasis – the city, on
the one hand, as a 'fluid collection of people' and, on the other hand,
the city as a set of 'urban villages' (McDowell, 1999: 96).

The introduction of a temporal perspective at this point may help to
better illuminate the issue. According to Sennett, public space became
much more important in social relations in urban context than private
space during the 19th century in Western European and North
American cities. The term 'public' is both spatially and socially significant. Sennett argues that with the expansion of the bourgeoisie from
the 18th century, and the lessening of concern with social origins,
more and more diverse groups increasingly interacted in the growing
urban centres. In Sennett's words, the term 'public' came to mean 'the
region of social life located apart from the realm of family and close
friends, but also that this public realm of acquaintances and strangers
included a relatively wide diversity of people' (Sennett quoted in
McDowell, 1999: 103). By the beginning of the 19th century new
'networks of sociability' or 'places where strangers might regularly meet'
emerged, including, for example, urban parks, coffeehouses, coaching
inns, theatre and opera (Sennett quoted in McDowell, 1999: 103).
Thus, this urban spatial realm afforded the individual the freedom to
'roam the newly built streets and highways and to enter public spaces
like cafés and drinking houses' (McDowell, 1999: 101) as well as creating new opportunities for the making of novel and diverse forms of
public association between 'strangers.' McDowell notes (1999: 101–2)
that the cultural critic Williams, for example, related the rise of the
artistic movement of modernism – in art, music, photography, the
novel and poetry – to the rapid urbanisation in late 19th and early
20th-century Western Europe and North America and the social diversity brought about as a result. Sennett traces other, less positive, trends.
According to Sennett, as cities grew with the ever greater numbers of
'strangers' drawn to them, accompanied by the socio-economic trau-
mas of capitalism, urbanisation and industrialisation, and, also, as the
dynamics of mass production and mass consumption brought about
increasing uniformity in many ways, the term 'public' became more
closely associated with vice and the private sphere of the idealised
family became associated with virtue. As a result, the public realm is

one in which the relative 'strangeness' of others becomes something which it is desirable to maintain. Sennett puts it as follows:

> Out in the public was where moral violation occurred and was tolerated; in public one could break the laws of respectability. If the private was a refuge from the terrors of society as a whole, a refuge created by idealizing the family, one could escape the burdens of this ideal by a special kind of experience, one passed among strangers or, more importantly, people determined to remain strangers to each other.
>
> (Sennett quoted in McDowell, 1999: 103–4)

The nature of this 'special kind of experience' requires, however, that it be problematised. As McDowell points out with regard to two particular groups, women and gay men (McDowell, 1999: 105–8), the particular social characteristics of these groups have a differential impact on their access to public places. Also, spatial location can be important in differentiating among 'strangers' in that certain spaces are identified with particular social attributes and, under certain circumstances, individuals may acquire the social attributes of the space that they enter. That is to say that the social identity of an individual may be read from the nature of the space they occupy. Hence, assumed associations between women in particular public spaces at certain given times and certain forms of sexual morality or the identification of discrete areas in cities as gay villages.

There is a relationship between the public space and the polity. Put simply, in democratic societies all citizens are equal *de jure*. Theory, however, does not translate into practice in a straightforward manner, and in the urban public space the same rights are not enjoyed by all *de facto*. As McDowell points out, some peoples (variously women, children, the working class, non-natives, the mob, young people) are 'less welcome' than others in the public space, a domain which is regarded by the empowered sections of urban society as the realm of 'decent' citizens (middle-class males, generally speaking) (McDowell, 1999: 109). As illustrated by McDowell (1999: 114–24) for Los Angeles (following Sennett) and for Paris (following Maspero & Frantz), this is reflected in the restriction of access not only to physical civic space but also to the civic spaces that are the public institutions of urban life and to citizenship itself. In short, anxiety regarding the uninhibited, public association of 'strangers' is a constant feature of urban life and central to this anxiety is a contestation over rights of legitimate access to public space, and therefore to the benefits that flow from that as a result. The question arises, therefore, as to how might the 'stranger' be accommodated to urban life – how might diversity be negotiated, conflict resolved and social and political institutions tolerant of difference be created and sustained.

According to Iris Marion Young, the notion of 'unassimilated otherness' is central to the successful negotiation of urban diversity. McDowell (1999: 127) indicates the general thrust of her position as follows: 'that if we accept diversity between people, then we must reject the liberal view that all individuals are equal and construct a new, group-based notion of social justice. She [Young] also suggests, however, that we must reject the notion of community'. The problem, as Young sees it (from McDowell, 1999: 128–9), is that the socio-political action necessary for the positive transformation of cities appears to operate from the premise that the community is the ideal unit around which such action should be based. This, Young argues from her study of local action in Balsall Heath in Birmingham, is based upon a false presumption of commonality of interest among the citizens of a bounded area and denies the diversity that is a feature of all cities and their inhabitants. The solution, according to Young, is to abandon the concept of community as

> Identification as a member of a community often occurs as an oppositional differentiation from other groups, who are feared or at best devalued. Persons identify only with some other persons, feel in community only with those, and fear the difference others confront them with because they identify with a different culture, history, and point of view on the world.
>
> (Young quoted in McDowell, 1999: 129)

The 'new, group-based notion of social justice' that Young argues for would comprise 'social relations without domination in which persons live together in relations of mediation among strangers with whom they are not in community' (Young quoted in McDowell, 1999: 129). It is not of especial interest here as to whether there exists the potential for the practical realisation of this but rather to note the centrality of the tension between the urban 'stranger' and 'community'. More to the point again, it is largely in the notion of 'stranger' that Young invests her utopian vision of urban transformation, celebrating the variety, heterogeneity, publicity and eroticism of the city. Attaining the 'unassimilated difference' that will allow for the 'strangers' to negotiate their diversity in the city will, according to Young, depend upon 'mutual forms of distancing' (Allen, 1999b: 92), creating the time and space to mediate difference (Young, 1989 & 1990). And while their respective views on the trajectory of diversity in urban life are markedly different, this mutual distancing between 'strangers' is something that both Young and Sennett share.

The notion of the 'stranger' in urban life can be extended to natural strangers. Hinchliffe (1999) argues that cities are also characterised by environmental diversity and that, as such, 'cities contain the possibility for some exciting changes to human relations with nature' (Hinchliffe, 1999: 138). Hinchliffe challenges what he describes as common-sense ideas of the city–nature divide through describing the extent of nature in the city in the 'varieties of spaces, movements and changes that occur and are produced in ... cities' (1999: 139). These city–nature formations have their own rhythms and, as Hinchliffe shows (1999: 156–64, they may interfere with the dominant, social rhythms of urban life. In the case of the conservation struggle surrounding Rainham Marshes in London, an idealised landscape of nature as a static form was being promoted by the developers as an improvement on the less than picturesque marsh-lands which comprised the development site. Similarly, the cases of the street pigeon and the Canadian goose are deployed by Hinchliffe to show how these species have been enormously successful in adapting to urban dwelling, but as they are regarded respectively as pests and non-native to the UK, they are subject to quite extensive culls. One could add a number of other natural 'strangers' to this repertoire – the fox, the rat, the hedgehog, and not to mention urban plant life, the variety of which appears to increase with city size (Hinchliffe, 1999: 148–9).

Just as the spatial expression of social diversity is a matter of substance for urban life, Hinchliffe suggests that 'If cities are places where not only all manner of different people live in close proximity but also all manner of animals, plants and eco-social relations, then interspecies negotiation of urban space will be a matter of everyday importance' (Hinchliffe, 1999: 165). This demands that our vision of cities be reformulated so that cities are seen not simply as social products but that it is recognised that they are also shaped by city–nature formations. This, it is argued, may be accomplished through a transpecies urban theory. Moreover, it is suggested that this perspective on the city may be a resource for bringing about more sustainable forms of urban living (Hinchliffe, 1999: 170). In this way the extension of the notion of the 'stranger' in urban life to include natural 'strangers' is of value in generating new insights into the city.

Toni Morrison, in an impressionistic (*chez* Hannerz, 1990 & 1996) account of 1920s Harlem, described the place as 'thriftless, warm, scary and *full of amiable strangers'* [my italics] (Morrison quoted in Massey, Allen & Pile, 1999: 54). Perhaps the adjective is not quite right, but the perception of the urban scene and the place of the 'stranger' in it holds true for the city in general. The conception of the 'stranger' plays a central role in understanding cities as sites of open intensity, of connection and disconnection, and as a series of overlays, where some movements and relationships come into full view while others are partially obscured. Yet, as Allen (1999a & 1999b) puts it, as the overlays shift, different groups of people and their worlds come into proximity. Hence, 'Cities are evocative places, places where people are drawn into all kinds of proximate relationships, often by chance, often fleetingly and often on an unequal basis' (Allen, 1999a: 85). Issues of power also pertain to locating the 'stranger' in the city. While cities have the potential to empower and liberate, the encounters between 'strangers' are not of necessity a 'genuine cultural interchange' for, as Amin and Graham (1999: 34) put it, 'Change intermeshes with the highly unequal relations of social and economic power which tie together as well as disconnect, the diverse groups living in cities ... Contemporary urban landscapes ... are thus etched with highly uneven social and power relations. ... Every aspect of the social fluidity and cultural dynamism of cities leads to complex asymmetries of power and enablement, and constraint and domination'. Application of the notion of the 'stranger' to urban life throws the complex nature of cities into relief, revealing aspects of the city that would otherwise be less completely comprehended.

Rhythms

An examination of what may be described as the rhythms of cities reveals that they are profoundly shaped but not wholly determined by a limited number of empowered, global cities. It can also be seen that the power of these global cities arises from a complex arrangement of factors relating to the networks of which they are a part. However, there are indications that their power is not overwhelming and that the rhythms of cities are also shaped in other ways and by other forces. This insight suggests that there is a case for moving beyond the existing conceptual framework within which city rhythms are currently largely understood.

While the focus here is upon economic rhythms, as they have been most extensively researched, it should be noted from the outset that the notion of city rhythms encompasses a patterning of behaviours from the full range of social activity at all levels. Allen puts it as follows:

> By city rhythms, we mean anything from the regular comings and goings of people about the city to the vast range of repetitive activities, sounds and even smells that punctuate life in the city and which give many of those who live and work there a sense of time and location.
>
> (Allen, 1999b: 56)

And alternatively, city rhythms are the 'regular beats and repetitive flows which mould it [city] in different ways at different times' (Allen, 1999b: 63). A city is characterised by a set of separate but related rhythms. However, this patterning of rhythms within a city can be disrupted – 'city spaces are constructed in a discontinuous fashion ... [they] are not simply given: they are produced through many movements and interactions coming together in ways that often disrupt existing rhythms and relationships across cities' (Allen, 1999b: 66). Some rhythms may become dominant, others be submerged; new rhythms may cut across existing rhythms; disruptions may come from beyond the city as well as from 'below the surface' (Allen, 1999b: 71 & 73).

The critical issue in this brief study is not the existence of such rhythms but rather the understanding of how such rhythms pass, or flow, between cities, the role certain cities play in shaping these flows and the extent to which certain cities can be said to be powerful, global agents in relation to other cities. The works of both Sassen (e.g. 1991) and Castells (e.g. 1996) are important keys to developing such an understanding. Both Sassen and Castells focus upon economic issues in their work. Rhythms of this type include both formal and informal economic activities such as, for example, the rush hour, housing market patterns, shopping behaviours and the black, or underground, economy.

Sassen and Castells represent two different, but related, perspectives on this question. They are both concerned with the nature of connections between cities and the function of networks in the global economy. For both, the flows of investment finance via the connections of new information and communications technologies comprise an especially significant network. While such flows are extremely dynamic they are not anarchic. They are partly defined by the technology but are also shaped by laws, regulations, institutions and states. Such organising elements operate at all levels, micro and macro. It is upon the manner of the organising, that is, the question of the locus of power in these global economic flows, that Sassen and Castells may be said to diverge. This difference is crucial in developing an understanding of the extent to which the rhythms of cities are determined by a small number of powerful, global cities.

For Sassen, certain powerful cities may be said to run the global networks of economic production and finance. As such, power is located in these cities and, in this sense, the global networks arise from the fact of the power of these specific sites – the global city powers the network. Sassen builds upon the work of Friedmann (Allen, 1999a: 192–4) in her conception of a global hierarchy of cities. For Sassen, the intensity, complexity and scale of global economic connections mean that the emergence of an elite club of powerful cities with a global influence is inevitable. Cities such as New York, London and Tokyo occupy key locations in the global economy and exercise substantial control over it because of their agglomeration of various important specialist activities. Their global capacity is produced through the acquisition of expertise – financial analysts, lawyers, managers, bankers etc. – and, taken together, this critical mass of financial services professionals constructs the economic power of the cities. The global economy, which is the domain of such individuals, is not so much an arena into which they and others might venture, but rather, it is something which is embedded in the institutions of which they are a part. And, it is through the practices of these institutions that the global flows of economic activity are regulated, or, as Allen puts it, 'stabilised':

> The production of a global capability in this context stems from the possibility of attracting from elsewhere best practice in managing and settling a greater proportion of the economic flows and transactions worldwide. In short, the greater the concentration of flows stabilized, the more intense the power that is said to radiate from it.
>
> (Allen, 1999a: 198)

In this way, the cities of New York, London and Tokyo, interconnected by the new information and communication technologies, dominate the global economy.

In contrast, Castells's relational view sees a 'space of flows' as the locus of power and, in this way, the power of certain cities is a product of the nature of the flow of global networks – global networks mobilise specific cities. Castells argues that global cities are best understood as a process rather than a series of discrete places. According to Castells, the power of certain cities as hubs or nodes in the global economy also relates to the élite personnel of the financial services but not as a result of their particular city-base. Instead, Castells sees their power as being derived from their particular point of attachment to the global economic flows. It is in this 'space of flows' and not in the global cities as discrete sites that power resides. Hence, the power that cities exercise is drawn from the networks of the global economy in accordance with the level of access their resident professional élite have to these networks. As Allen puts it, 'city powers are mobilized through networks; it is what flows through the networks which empowers particular groups and generates certain cities as sites of power' (Allen, 1999a: 199). Indeed, according to Castells, these 'particular groups' are in closer social and cultural proximity to others who have similar access to the networks of the global economy than to other different groups who, while they may reside in the same city, occupy contrasting social, cultural and economic spaces. Global cities as process displace a hierarchy of sites with a network of flows punctuated by hubs through which they are directed.

That said, the differences between the two might be somewhat overstated. For example, Castells would probably concur with Sassen in her assertion that with regard to the global economy 'the network is the strategic architecture' (Sassen, 1999). Moving beyond a simple dichotomy between Sassen and Castells through developing a relational view of the city that includes connection with, for example, the contemporary nation-state and its current trajectory on a global scale, as Castells (1997) begins to trace in his work on Catalonia, and as Gilbert notes (1999: 267) for Bogotá, seems essential. Equally, the task of more closely identifying the significance of transnational flows other than the economic, something Sassen hints at through reference to immigrant populations in global cities, appears vital.

At present, however, most commentators can agree that the dominant economic rhythms of the global economy are related, in some way, to certain global cities. Pryke summarises the centrality of their role as follows:

> Global cities are the centres of webs of financialized information; they are the control centres for the growing financial flows which operate in simultaneous time, empowered by the new information communication technologies which link markets in different time-zones and serve to integrate national and 'global' financial markets.
>
> (Pryke, 1999a: 245)

Further explanation should be offered on a number of key points. The global cities described by Pryke are not only hosts to the financial services experts but also to institutions such as the World Bank and the IMF. The macroeconomic management practices of these players, applied to the economy through intervention on matters of rates of interest, wage levels, taxation thresholds and the other component parts of economic flows, enable the exercise of some control over these flows. Moreover, such practices are not localised events in terms of their impact; their reach is much greater. One reason for this is that the global economic network is a dynamic and ideology-laden process. The most powerful interconnected cities of the global economy share a set of values on economic policy, ideologised as neo-liberalism. There is no serious, global competitor to neo-liberal economic ideology; resistance, where it exists, is local. The exposure of other cities in various parts of the world to this empowered process shapes the local context of urbanisation within a global framework.

Neo-liberal values are shared also by the international and multilateral financial agencies, such as the World Bank and the IMF, that have proliferated since the 1970s and are headquartered in cities like New York and London. Their role in extending various forms of financing to the developing world allows for these values to be imposed upon, or otherwise negotiated, others as best practice in macroeconomic management. In order to address the debt crisis of the 1980s, developing countries have been obliged to stabilise their debts through structural adjustments to economic policy that conforms to neo-liberal principles. A shift from official government finance to private sector finance, coupled with a policy steer towards export-led growth (Pryke, 1999a: 240), exposes these countries further to the forces of globalisation. The particular effects of the dominant economic rhythms produced by a few powerful, global cities, the reach of which is extended through certain international financial organisations, can be seen in many cities across the developing world (Pryke, 1999a: 252–6). In Harare (Zimbabwe) the effect of such exposure was large rises in the cost of living and multiple closures of small, local companies. For the city of Dar es Salaam (Tanzania) it meant severe decline in large-scale industry, increased unemployment and lower wages.

Pryke, however, also notes the salience of alternative networks, of local innovations and resistances – the rhythms of the global cities may be 'compelling' (Pryke, 1999a: 247) but they are not completely deterministic. For example, the women of Dar es Salaam have responded to exposure to economic globalisation through beginning their own economic enterprises, adopting roles as key income generators for their families and constructing their specific networks of opportunity, information and support. Similarly, the architectural rhythms of Kuala Lumpur and Singapore conform to the neo-liberal template of contemporary global capital but, at the same time, the local idiom is also projected. For example, illustrations from the cityscape of Kuala Lumpur comprise such juxtapositions. Also, the case of Bogotá (Colombia), where the impact of exposure with global economic flows appears to have been less inimical than other places, shows that specific context of this exposure is a critical factor in shaping the particular outcomes of that unequal encounter. Whether the operation of neo-liberal economic policies in Bogotá has been a success or not remains unresolved (Gilbert, 1999), but that it has had a profound impact is beyond question.

The uneven nature of the impact of the economic rhythms of certain global cities would suggest that their reach, while remarkably extensive, is not thoroughly overwhelming. The limitations to their reach are not easily explained by either a straightforward hierarchical view of global cities or by a simple relational position. The current conceptual framework needs to be extended. Allen, drawing upon both Sassen and Castells, suggests as much through asserting that the power of a city 'is best understood as something which is continuously produced in various settled formations through its networked relations, and not as some locatable 'reserve' (Allen, 1999a: 185). Thus, it is in the dynamic interaction of cities and a globalising economy that the rhythms of certain global cities exert a powerful influence over other cities. But, the rhythms of cities are also shaped locally and informally, from underground. In this way, the rhythms of cities are defined by both context and flow.

Social and spatial division

According to Pile, the complexity of the social divisions, that is the classification of people and their activities according to social, racial, economic or other features, and spatial divisions, that is the classification of places according to their having particular features, that characterises the city is more than a matter of the zoned organisation of social space *chez* Burgess and the Chicago school (Pile, 1999a: 35–41). Rather, the relationship between social and spatial divisions turns upon the negotiation and management of difference and its peculiar intensity in urban context; 'urban spaces are produced through the negotiation of heterogeneity ... heterogeneity creates distinctive urban spaces that are constituted by the ways people negotiate relationships with others, the city's spatial relationships (inside and out), and the tensions of its life' (Pile, 1999b: 12). Such negotiations are complex, uneven and unequal and, as others have pointed out; their resolutions may be paradoxical (Sennett, 2002: 47). It is argued here that a relational perspective on social and spatial divisions within cities best reveals the nature of the responses aimed at managing the special intensity of difference associated with cities and the ambiguous consequences of these attempts to de-intensify difference in the context of the inherent openness of urban life.

The production of differentiated urban spaces relates to social divisions in complex ways. These diverse spaces are not simply discrete and homogeneous social containers, in the geographical sense, but rather they are also characterised by their connectedness and heterogeneity. As Pile (1999b: 38–9) shows, this paradox arises from the uneven and unequal nature of the connections and disconnections both within and beyond the city. Also, it is the product of the response of people to the intensity and diversity of social differences and relations both within and beyond the city. It is in the cross-cutting of these features that the variegated urban spaces of the city are constructed. For example, the inner-city spaces of Harlem in New York (from 1918 to 1929) and Sophiatown in Johannesburg (from 1955 to 1960) are shown to be characteristically ambiguous and paradoxical urban spaces (Pile, 1999b: 19–27):

> Harlem and Sophiatown were both havens and hells; both were cities within a city; both established wider connections, yet both were marginal, disconnected; both came to symbolize black people's place in the city, yet both were sites where black subjectivities were being contested and transformed.
>
> (Pile, 1999b: 26)

Pile extends the argument noting that, in this respect, suburban sites have much in common with such inner cities. They are also both homogeneous and heterogeneous, connected and disconnected. For example, Pile (1999b: 35–7) traces the origins of the bungalow, that icon of suburbanisation, to the colonial cities of Madras and Calcutta from the 17th century onwards. In this sense the suburb is the product of complex historical and geographical encounters. Also on the matter of connection and disconnection, both Pile (1999b: 30–4) and Chambers (1999) note how women, in response to their isolation in 20th-century suburbia, created their own networks of connection that transcended the physical and social confines of the suburb.

The desires for specifically designed urban spaces so as to create particular social environments that are manifest in planned processes of suburbanisation are based upon an assumption that overstates the distinction between order and disorder. As Mooney (1999: 59) states, order cannot be unambiguously and simplistically contrasted with disorder. Mooney (1999: 54–92) argues that conceptions of order and disorder are value-laden. That is to say that matters of order and disorder are grounded in issues of power and legitimacy. Order and disorder hold very different meanings for different groups. The perception, organisation and use of urban space is, therefore, subject to contestation. Moreover, as is clear from his exploration of these issues in sites in the UK such as Manchester and Glasgow, this contestation is shaped by unequal social relations. Because of this certain social groups are associated with urban disorder and, as a result, their relationship with the urban environment may be denied legitimacy. The consequences of this can be the formulation of policies which marginalise, segregate or displace. The case of post-1945 Glasgow illustrates the point (Mooney, 1999: 76–80). The massive housing estates constructed on the peripheries of the city were designed to solve the problems identified with the industrial slums of the Clydeside but quickly became associated with unemployment, poverty, racism and violence. Similar contradictions and contestations can be seen in cities elsewhere in the UK, Europe and further afield. Efforts by a socio-economic élite to transform the city of Istanbul into a global city at the expense of the squatter settlements (*gecekondus*) of the urban poor are revealing in this respect. For example, while the residents of the *gecekondus* have been associated with criminality, poverty, ignorance and religious extremism (Mooney, 1999: 66–70) they are also central to the identity of Istanbul. It is with some irony that Mooney (1999: 70) points out that the projection of Istanbul as a global city has, in itself, been a major source of disorder, thus confounding the rhetoric of order espoused by the socio-economic élite. Order and disorder, therefore, are best described as relational and interconnected in complex ways. Their various forms are subject to constant contestation and reconfiguration and are manifest in the interweave of social and spatial divisions in urban context.

The place of power in this interplay of social and spatial divisions is highlighted by Mooney in the following terms:

> The existence of places of extreme wealth and affluence and the ghetto and the shanty town represent the coming together of disparate groups of people, working to sometimes very different rhythms in segregated spaces within the city. Here we have, once again, the

intensification of difference, underpinned by unequal power, class and social relations.

(Mooney, 1999: 87)

A number of historical and contemporary responses to this intensification of difference may be noted. McLaughlin and Muncie (1999) identify a modernist approach and a postmodernist approach, as well as an approach described as intensified circuits of policing and surveillance. According to McLaughlin and Muncie, the modernist approach, as exemplified by the reworking of the streetscape of Paris by Baron Haussmann during the late 19th century, is defined by the replacement of a complexity of tight, narrow streets with a largely medieval city centre by a network of wide, straight boulevards with large pavements. This reordering of the city created a city of spaces in the image of the bourgeoisie. As a result of their desire to de-intensify social relations, in particular to increase their distance from the working class, Paris was transformed by 'delineating concentrations of commercial, business, manufacturing, administrative and entertainment areas; socially segregating residential neighbourhoods; and replacing integrated, semi-public space with privatized ones (McLaughlin & Muncie, 1999: 112)'. For example, the development of arcades and department stores – 'interior streets' – to cater to the shopping habits of the bourgeoisie served also to exclude the urban poor. This modernist approach was applied widely, with some local variations. For example, while socio-economic class and gender were significant features of the pattern of boulevardisation in Paris, the issue of race or ethnicity also featured in the case of Rio de Janeiro.

The postmodern approach to such segregation and displacement has taken form, from the 1980s, with the emergence of gated enclaves or communities. McLaughlin and Muncie (1999: 117) describe this as voluntary ghettoisation or self-segregation. These take various forms – 'lifestyle gated communities', 'prestige gated communities' and 'security zone gated communities'. Some commentators claim that these entities have a positive impact (McLaughlin & Muncie, 1999: 120–1). They contend that such gated communities draw residents together, creating a sense of space and place that is expressed in a particularly localised form of politics that is 'owned' by the residents. They also suggest that such communities are the most effective means of accommodating the tensions arising from the very great social, economic, cultural and ethnic differences that are a feature of contemporary cities. In addition, they assert that gated communities assure the safety of residents in their urban environment and, given this sense of security, the residents are able to develop new social networks with other like-minded people. Critics of gated communities argue that these enclaves are a negative phenomenon (McLaughlin & Muncie, 1999: 121–2). They see in the gated communities the enclosure and privatisation of public space. Moreover, they argue that this closing down of space exacerbates tensions of difference rather than relieving them. McLaughlin and Muncie underscore some of the key concerns regarding the aggressive territorialisation represented by gated communities, claiming that they produce

> A narrowing or breaking of traditional notions of urban citizenship and governance; … extreme forms of insular subjectivity; … a less balanced view of trust and risk and fewer opportunities to cross boundaries; … a paranoid attitude towards strangers where cloistered communities define themselves by what they are against, and sanction racist discourses of 'outsiders' and the 'criminal other.
>
> (McLaughlin & Muncie, 1999: 122)

The intensified circuits of policing and surveillance comprise a third key response aimed at reordering the city. According to McLaughlin and Muncie (1999: 126–30), the emergence of a novel and proactive form of urban policing was, along with the urban architecture of Hausmann, one of the most significant and radical reforms in 19th-century governance. The policing that was first pioneered on a large scale in London with the creation of the Metropolitan Police was, in effect, the spatialisation of panoptism. This concept, derived from the work of the philosopher Jeremy Bentham, relates to the surveillance of the criminal in such a manner that its effect in imposing the will of the law upon them would be permanent. According to Bentham (McLaughlin & Muncie, 1999: 126–7), this was possible through placing the inmates in a space in which they would feel themselves to be, potentially, under perpetual gaze. In inducing a state of conscious and constant visibility in those incarcerated, the automatic functioning of power would be assured. The 'beat' of police officers, including the 'zero tolerance' policing of contemporary New York, imitates this concept. The introduction of new forms of surveillance, such as CCTV cameras, in many UK cities may be read as an extension of this principle. McLaughlin and Muncie (1999: 130–4) note that scholarly opinion is divided as to whether it is an intensification of the panoptic gaze – a hyper-panoptism driven by new technologies, following the work of Corbett and Marx (McLaughlin & Muncie, 1999: 130–3) – or, that it is instead more paradoxical, on the

basis that there is no necessary relationship between the new surveillance infrastructure and authoritarian forms of urban control. This
post-panoptic perspective, following the work of Lyon (McLaughlin &
Muncie, 1999: 133–4), is based upon a number of assumptions, including that the potential to contest power always exists and that technology is never complete in its application and always has unintended
consequences. However, as Davis (1994) illustrates, the fact of this surveillance, while beneficial in part, contributes to what he describes as an
'ecology of fear' in that the perpetual and widespread presence of the
electronic gaze further displaces and alienates the urban stranger, thus
reinforcing those characteristics that make this figure an object of fear
in the first place.

As we have seen with regard to various cities across the globe, the
various mechanisms (Robinson, 1999) for shaping the differentiation of
city spaces, such as the functioning of the land use market and its management by the state through planning policies and processes, and the
actions of powerful groups or institutions in society or particular strategies for 'improving' urban life contribute to the segregation of space in
social terms. The mapping of race in late 20th-century Johannesburg
illustrates the possible impact of the determined operation of such
mechanisms to the specific purpose of apartheid. However, it is also
the case that these divisions are not wholly clear-cut. A deeper racial
geography would have to account for the different meanings such
divisions hold for the various actors involved. It would also have to
trace the connections between the different social groups in the various
parts of the city and the nature of the border crossings undertaken by
many. In this way, and as Robinson (1999: 188) asserts, the social and
spatial divisions within cities can also be conceived of as positively
facilitating novel connections, and through this the possibility for
new kinds of urban spaces begins to open up afresh.

Marginalised groups and resistance

Urban regimes, charged as they are with the responsibility of imposing
order on urban space, are confronted with a particular set of tensions.
On one level, the imposition of order in cities relates to the effective
realisation of the dominant orderings of global capital, set within a
neo-liberal economic discourse, in local context and in partnership
with local capital and local governance (Allen, Massey & Pryke, 1999).
Within the city this ordering operates through networks of influence –
social, economic, cultural and political – and, in this way, a city can be

successfully navigated through the ebbs and flows of the global economic system. On another level, however, such imposition of order is counter to the very nature of the city itself, as a city is defined by the heightened nature of its openness, diversity and intensity (Mooney, Pile & Brook, 1999) – its 'anarchy'. In this tension resides the crux of the relationship between urban regimes and their task to impose order and the various groups that comprise city life, for in each act of ordering arises a question of values – whose order (Allen, 1999a & 1999b)? In all such determinations of relative values some values, and the groups who espouse them, are more equal than others. It is upon this that notions of marginalisation and resistance turn.

The notion of marginalisation relates to distance from power. This can be presented in a number of ways. For example, the task of defining the nature of urban problems in the UK in the recent past has often been undertaken by parties at a distant remove – in social, economic, cultural and political terms – from the problem in hand. Specific cases include, by way of example, the Victorian period, in which such parties comprised various philanthropists and social reformers of the upper middle class and the aristocracy; urban planners and civil servants fulfilled a similar role post-1945. Those people most directly affected by 'the problem' as such were not a part of the process by which it was to be addressed – they were marginal to the identification of the issue, its management and its resolution. It could be argued that the cases above are simply benign, patrician and technocratic but it is the case that the ability to define a problem and to intervene in it is limited to those in authority, those with expertise and those with capital. Marginalisation can also be related to questions of status. It is a *sine qua non* that those who possess the power to have their views voiced, represented and responded to are connected to these networks of influence, be they bureaucratic, professional and/or economic, while not necessarily being in themselves authorities upon, experts in or economically engaged with the particular problem-solving process in hand. Individuals and groups who are not engaged with such networks of influence are thereby marginal. It is also the case, however, that a group that is routinely a part of a network of influence might become marginal when their particular interests run counter to other interests that are considered to be more prevalent. Marginalisation, therefore, should not be considered to be a domain occupied only by those for whom the networks of influence are largely inaccessible. Groups who normally wield power can be isolated within ordering processes under circumstances where discrete and exclusive priorities can be set and enforced. As such, marginalisation should not be regarded as a simplistic function of hier-archy but rather as an expression of the diverse circulation of power.

It is in the context of the diffuse arrangement of power that various forms of resistance are possible. And it is in this context that resistance can be defined as the means and ability to negotiate the imposition of order. Resistance takes many forms. It may be informal or formal, banal or sublime, progressive or regressive and its very nature is shaped by and contingent upon a complex 'nexus of powers and exclusions' (Watson, 1999: 211) that operates on multiple levels and across various arenas. For example, according to de Certeau (in Pile, 1999a), the city of New York appears immobilised upon viewing it from the height of its tallest buildings but upon descent into the canyons one can discern people and their myriad activities at odds with the prior semblance of rigid order and uniformity. Thus, 'the city contains a world of possibilities' (Pile, 1999a: 8) and from these possibilities the banal resistances of indi-vidual citizens arise. Similarly, the development of informal economies in sub-Saharan Africa (e.g. Pryke, 1999a) and alternative networks of association (e.g. Tripp, 1999) may be read as resistances to the ordering imperatives of neo-liberal global capital. Equally so, the variegated street-life of Kuala Lumpur contrasts with the architecture of the Petrona Towers and the rhetoric of the Multimedia Super Corridor (Watson, 1999: 206–15) – both signatures of participation in a globalis-ing economy. Also, that resistance is not confined to any particular socio-economic section of urban society can be seen in the case of Wythenshawe in Cheshire, where the resident middle class sought to frustrate housing development in the area (Massey extract in Watson, 1999: 212–3). As Allen (1999a: 214) notes, beyond the caricature of wholly powerless marginalisation, resistance is commonly manifest in many forms in urban contexts.

Watson (1999: 202–5) usefully arranges resistance into a number of discrete types, based upon the understanding that the everyday politics of urban life around which resistance is focused relate to struggles over a particular set of economic and cultural issues – governance and administration, distribution of resources, and ownership of and access to public space. These key types of resistance may be explored briefly in turn. To begin with, community politics (Watson, 1999: 221–8), with their emphasis upon mutual co-operation, local empowerment and independence from the state, have had, according to Watson, a profound impact upon cities. This particular form of resistance has been central to raising public awareness regarding a range of issues which would otherwise have been ignored. Given the rather organic nature of community politics the agenda with regard to this type of action tends to shift quite significantly according to local and tactical concerns, in contrast to the more deeply embedded strategic interests of institutionalised politics. Watson notes (drawing from Castells) that from this type of resistance various city-based political alliances have arisen – Castells's term is 'urban social movements'. Some such movements are global in their nature, having connections across the world which draw together like-minded groups in disparate cities.

Watson defines a second type of resistance in terms of the politics of identity, meaning and representation (Watson, 1999: 228–36). This type of resistance is characterised by an understanding of identity as something that is shifting, multiple, fluid and complex; it is a politics of difference in which differences of race, gender, sexuality and class are driving issues. According to Watson it is this type of resistance that has increasingly come to define the urban political agenda, as it is in cities in particular that such differences, and the social relationships inherent to them, are especially intense. As such, the places and spaces of the city are critical sites for the expression of difference and the articulation of the politics related to the recognition and accommodation of difference. Thus, Aboriginal Australians are increasingly vocal and assertive in their particular claims upon the sites of and sites within cities like Sydney (Watson, 1999: 229). Similarly, the Gay Mardi Gras of Sydney animates a very different set of concerns and in a manner that connects with groups that share those concerns in places such as San Francisco, Amsterdam and New York (Watson, 1999: 234–6). In this way, resistance is both local and global.

The final type of resistance is a phenomenon popularly understood as Nimbyism, derived from the acronym NIMBY, meaning Not In My Back Yard (Watson, 1999: 216–20). As a form of resistance, it adopts the guise of a single episode or an event. It is, almost invariably, concerned with a very local matter and, while it may not be expansive, it tends to generate passionate interactions. It arises in sites of 'intense juxtaposition of people' (Watson, 1999: 221) where their conflicting needs, aspirations and fears centre upon contrasting positions on possible land use. As it is at least partly based upon fear – fear of the other or fear of the unknown. Nimbyism is ambiguous; it can be either regressive or progressive as a form of resistance. Watson (1999: 218–9) again turns to Sydney by way of exemplification. The reaction of residents to the possible construction of non-Christian buildings of worship is contrasted with their likely very different reaction to the locating of a new McDonald's outlet in the area, despite the fact that according to any objective measure the latter is more likely to bring greater disruption to their environment in terms of increased traffic, for example, than the former.

With regard to the extent to which marginalised groups might effectively resist the imposition of order by urban regimes, this largely depends on how forceful the regime is prepared to be. In the case of some societies, such as apartheid South Africa or communist Eastern Europe, the regimes were very prepared indeed to impose their will, and even in these settings some resistance was possible. According to Cochrane (1999: 328–30), however, there is an increasing recognition that urban regimes function more effectively through processes of negotiation and partnership arrangements. According to a number of commentators, regime theory provides the conceptual framework for transcending this apparent dichotomy between order and disorder, based upon the understanding that disorder is internal to order. In this context, therefore, resistance is a part of the dynamics of urban governance. Cochrane puts it as follows: 'At the heart of the debates about urban administration and governance is a tension between attempts to achieve fixity and to work or manage fluidity' (Cochrane, 1999: 328). Moving beyond traditional notions, *viz* hierarchical, technocratic and managerial, of what constitutes the urban regime, Massey and others (Cochrane, 1999: 328) identify an alternative approach. This, in part, derives the concerns of regime theory with realising more inclusive forms of urban politics and policy/planning processes (Stoker, 1995 & 2000). The term 'associative democracy' has been coined to give expression to a coalition of interest, capacity and shared ownership of the urban domain that is based upon an understanding of society in the city as a 'plurality of associations' (Cochrane, 1999: 329). By extension, as epitomised in the work of Jacobs, the necessary diversity of a city may be sustained not only through the particular culture of its socio-political institutions and processes but also by a sympathetic physical infrastructure. According to Jacobs (1999: 340), the latter should comprise city districts that each have varied socio-economic functions, short blocks of buildings so that streets have frequent turnings and junctions enabling interaction, a range of buildings of different ages and condition and thereby of varying economic output and a dense concentration of people, including residents. In this way planning processes will better reflect the organic nature of city life.

It is recognised (Cochrane, 1999) that such approaches to the social problems of city life do not easily incorporate the real social tensions that exist in cities. It is the case that the plurality of associations in any given city is also cross-cut by unequal and uneven power relationships. If a resolution resides in a radical reworking of civic leadership

(Cochrane, 1999) then that must be premised on the recognition of the endemic nature of disorder in city life. In this way, the resolution of social problems in cities does not lie in the replacement of disorder by order but is instead to be approached through an understanding of order that positively accommodates disorder. The intense diversity that defines urban life is almost inevitably manifest in contestations of the purpose and meaning of city spaces – to paraphrase Sennett (1996), disorder, or the anarchy of resistance, is a necessary, even desirable, feature of the social function of urban space; 'conflict (i.e. disorder) ... [is the] ... desirable product of people seeking to govern themselves' (Sennett, 1996: 198). Moreover, Sennett asserts that social problems can only be addressed by allowing for conflict and disorder:

> When conflict is permitted in the public sphere, when the bureau-cratic routines become socialized, the product of disorder will be a greater sensitivity in public life to the problems of connecting public services to the urban clientele.
>
> (Sennett, 1996: 198)

Thus, the multilayered and multi-textured space that is the city cannot be triangulated by simplistic geometries of order. Neither is disorder wholly anarchic, the source of urban social problems. It is instead a feature consistent with the very nature of city life. Disorder conforms to the cultural logic of the city itself as an open and diverse entity defined by an intensity that is, in and of itself, inherently disordering. Therefore, it is in the power-etched relationships within (dis)order that the nature of social problems in the city is best understood. And, it is in the accommodation of the contestations and resistances necessary to those relationships, Sennett's 'equilibrium of disorder' (Sennett, 1996: 191), that the possibilities for their amelioration may be identified. The resistance of marginalised groups to the imposition of order by urban regimes is best viewed through a set of relationships between the identity (-ies) of a city, the notion of urban citizenship and the nature of urban democracy.

Order and disorder

It is something of a paradox that both chaos and patterning appear to be characteristic of the nature of cities. Approaching this paradox requires the careful reading of the intricate spatial text comprised of the intense differentiation of urban space. Thus, the qualities of disorder and order, and their complex interrelationships, are best understood in the context of the inherent openness, diversity and intensity that defines cities (Mooney, Pile & Brook, 1999). Pile *et al.* put it as follows:

> Cities are ... not entirely random assemblages of things and people ... Instead, we argue that the almost unimaginable intricacy of cities arises from both the specific ways in which they bring things and people together (i.e. the mixings and meetings of cities), and also from the ways in which cities are built to sort, sift and segregate things and people (i.e. the patternings and orderings of cities).
>
> (Pile, Brook & Mooney, 1999: 1)

Thereby, cities are defined by a chaotic patterning, a complex set of 'jumbled orderings' (Mooney, Pile & Brook, 1999: 348). Interwoven in these jumbled orderings are power and its uneven and unequal impacts. In this context, it becomes clear that notions of order and disorder are not absolute and objective categories but rather they are value-laden terms, defined by relationships to power, and inherent to the range of processes that result in spatial differentiation in cities is a sense of ambiguity with regard to a simplistic dichotomy of order and disorder.

It is necessary, therefore, to problematise order and disorder – (dis)order. We can turn to the work of Howard, on the one hand, and Le Corbusier, on the other, as a starting point for unpacking (dis)order. Their work has in common the assumption that urban planning on a grand, strategic scale can solve the social problems in the city. Their shared vision of cities as planned utopias has been very influential on the various professionals – architects, planners, developers, politicians – engaged with urban development. Differences may be noted between the two. For example, Howard's particular vision was of 'networks of relatively small garden cities linked into a social city' (Cochrane, 1999: 310), a low-density social and physical infrastructure intended to erode the intensity of urban life. In contrast, Le Corbusier considered this intensity to be very important to city life but thought that it required to be managed. Like Howard, he believed that open, green spaces in the urban landscape were central to positively ordering city life. However, Le Corbusier sought to create this space by constructing high-rise buildings and elevated roadways, whereas Howard inserted green space in wedges within and on the same level as the physical form of the city. Despite these differences, what Howard and Le Corbusier share is a view that urban social problems can be solved through the hierarchical imposition of particular physical forms. Harvey puts it as follows:

> [T]he proper design of things would solve all the problems in the social process. It was assumed that if you could just build your urban village, like Ebenezer Howard, or your Radiant City, like Le Corbusier, then the thing would have the power to keep the process forever in harmonious state.
>
> (Harvey quoted in Cochrane, 1999: 311)

While the visions of Howard (in the late 19th century and the early part of the 20th century) and Le Corbusier (in the early and mid-20th century) were never put into practice on a grand scale, the impact of their ideas can be seen in many cities. For example, after the Second World War the city of Glasgow in the UK was substantially redeveloped with a view to solving some of the problems associated with its extensive slum areas – chronic overcrowding, poverty, ill health, crime and pollution (Mooney, 1999: 76). The city authorities proposed to radically reshape the city through the implementation of a grand strategic vision – The Clyde Valley Region Plan (1946). As a result of this plan hundreds of thousands of people were to be moved out of the centre of Glasgow to a series of New Towns to be built in central Scotland as well as to four extensive housing developments on the margins of the city – Drumchapel, Easterhouse, Pollok and Castlemilk – and new dual carriageways and motorways cut through the urban landscape, enabling the further dispersal of the population. Despite the original intentions, as Mooney points out, the practical application of the plan had unintended consequences:

> The absence of 'community', and feelings of isolation and anonymity which was characteristic of many of these new estates, was compounded in many cases by their relative geographic isolation from the main centres of employment and entertainment, a problem further magnified by poor public transport provision.
>
> (Mooney, 1999: 77)

This was because the plan was predicated on the continuity of the nuclear family, a gendered division of labour and modern, industrial forms and patterns in employment. All of these were undermined, not just in Glasgow but throughout the UK, during the second half of the 20th century. It is, perhaps, ironic to note that as Glasgow embarked upon a new period of reshaping during the last quarter of the 20th century these areas were identified as severe obstacles to the successful reworking of the social and physical fabric of the city (Mooney, 1999: 77). More generally, this phenomenon has also been noted elsewhere in Europe by other commentators. Like Easterhouse, the *banlieue* (suburbs/outskirts) of urban France have come to be associated with the very poverty, polarisation and social dysfunction that they were designed to overcome (e.g. McDowell, 1999: 116–24). Similarly, the process of the 'modernisation' of Istanbul by the city authorities and associated elite interest groups has had impacts that have served to make life in the city less rather than more tolerable for many of its inhabitants. Drawing upon the work of Aksoy and Robins, Mooney (1999: 66–70) describes how the construction of new motorways has increased levels of pollution, how the high-rise office blocks impose themselves incongruously upon the low-level skyline that is the Islamic architecture of the city and how the residential housing is increasingly polarised both spatially and socially. The middle class and the business elite pursue increasingly 'westernised' lifestyles in exclusive housing developments while others – many of whom are recent migrants from rural Turkey, of diverse ethnic and culture backgrounds and of conservative Islamic persuasion – settle the *gecekondus* on the edges of the city. The result is the emergence of a new order but an order that is increasingly disorderly (Mooney, 1999: 69). In this way, the hierarchical imposition of order upon Istanbul has created its own disorder.

Other hierarchical approaches, with lesser claim to universal utopian ambition, may be noted so that we might further deconstruct (dis)order. The work of Baron Haussmann on remodelling Paris between 1850 and 1870 was, according to some (see McLaughlin & Muncie, 1999: 113), a response by the city authorities to the regular riots and the constant threat of revolution by the denizens of the working class *quartiers*. Haussmann's work can therefore be read as an attempt to resolve the 'incessant clash of alternative conceptions of social order' (McLaughlin & Muncie, 1999: 113). The result of his work was the reordering of Paris through the wholesale construction of a modern physical infrastructure, comprising wide boulevards, public parks, railway stations, zones specific to particular economic activities, semi-enclosed shopping streets, a sewerage system, public lighting, water supply and class-specific residential zones. The boulevardisation of Paris provided a template for many other cities. For example, it was applied to Rio de Janeiro in the period 1902–6. In this case, race along with socio-economic class was a very significant factor in the rationale that underlay the planning process. The inhabitants of the *corticos*, the tenement slums of Rio de Janeiro, and their associated criminality, poverty, disease and interraciality signified, for the city elite, a serious threat to social order. By 1906 the *corticos* had been demolished and their residents removed to peripheries of the city, and the downtown area became the exclusive domain of the europhile élite.

Such segregation did not, as McLaughlin and Muncie note, realise the aim of solving the social problems as perceived by the authors of the various plans. Instead, it had the effect of increasing the sense of anxiety and fear felt as physical separation, and displacement served only to reinforce the strangeness of the 'other' inhabitants of the city, or, to put it another way the social differentiation at the root of the problems was made deeper and more tangible through giving it expression in the physical form of the city. More recent ordering impulses seem to bear this out. The rigorous application of state-sanctioned segregation along the lines of race in apartheid South Africa resulted in urban space being very clearly differentiated but did not have the effect of making white South Africans feel safer or actually be safer. Also, critics of the gated communities (McLaughlin & Muncie, 1999: 117–22) that now proliferate in many urban societies argue that the aggressive territorialisation that these 'fortified enclaves' represent rationalises fear of the urban stranger, engenders extreme conceptions of the 'other' and sanctions discourses that stigmatise outsiders. Caldiera explains it as follows:

> [W]hile heterogeneous contacts diminish, social differences are more rigidly perceived and proximity with people from different groups considered as dangerous, thus emphasizing inequality and distance.
> (Caldiera quoted in McLaughlin & Muncie, 1999: 121)

The complex 'nexus of powers and exclusions' (Watson, 1999: 211) that is inherent to hierarchical impulses towards ordering can take forms other than physical. For example, Robinson (1999: 163–8) shows how the multiple, largely unco-ordinated, but still deliberated, actions of bankers, estate agents, planners and residents in many cities in the USA have contributed to a racial segregation of space that, contrary to popular misconceptions, is not contoured by relative levels of poverty. Equally, contemporary forms of Bentham's panopticon – that is, the incessant possibility of inspection, observation and surveillance by authority so as to maintain order through instilling in the individual a conscious sense of their permanent visibility to those in authority – contribute to ordering regimes in many cities. The contemporary panopticon, characterised as intensified circuits of policing and surveillance (McLaughlin & Muncie, 1999: 126–34), includes the assertive beat policing (popularly termed as 'zero-tolerance' policing) as initiated in 1990s New York and also the electronic monitoring of largely mundane activities conducted through CCTV, Internet websites, the telephone, cashpoint and credit cards, market research companies and others. Whether this panoptic gaze is benign or sinister depends upon the manner in which power relationships are configured in this medium. It may be used to impose new, electronic walls for the purposes of separation, partition and exclusion, to reinforce difference and inequality. Thus, whole communities may be confined or imprisoned, in a virtual sense, via their thoroughgoing subjection to modern surveillance methods and technologies (Davis, 1994). That said, the capacity for technology to be resisted, adapted or reapplied, according to social context, is stressed by many observers of the virtual society (Woolgar, 2001). Technology also underscores the paradox of ordering and its creation disorder.

As disorder is internal to order, so ordering impulses can also be perceived within patterns of disorder. In this sense, ordering is not simply owned by empowered socio-economic elites. Ordering impulses have alternative sources. Empowerment configurates (dis)order. And if power is best viewed in terms of its circulation, constant negotiation and contestation (following Foucault) rather than as a capacity or resource that is in the exclusive possession of a hierarchical elite, then it becomes possible to more firmly trace the ordering impulses inherent to disorder. For example, in their work on the notion of the urban 'underclass' in North American cities, Wacquant and Bourgois illustrate how the external image of the ghetto diverges from the internal experience of it. The ghetto has its own patterning, its own sense of order, for example:

> Yet intensive, ground-level scrutiny based on direct observation – as opposed to measurements effected from a distance by survey bureaucracies utterly unfit to probe and scrutinize the life of marginalized populations – immediately reveals that, far from being disorganized, the ghetto is organized according to different principles, in response to a unique set of structural and strategic constraints that bear on the racialized enclaves of the city as no other segment of America's territory.
>
> (Wacquant quoted in Mooney, 1999: 83)

More specifically, Bourgois show how the informal economy of drug-dealing imitates more formal economic forms, codes and practices.

Moreover, inherent to it is a sense that it provides an aesthetically superior and more meaningful means of living in the city:

> Most of the people I have met are proud that they are not being exploited by 'the White Man'. All of them have, at one time or another, held the jobs – delivery boys, supermarket baggers, hospital orderlies – that are objectively recognized as among the least desirable in American society. They see the illegal, underground economy as not only offering superior wages, but also a more dignified workplace.
>
> (Bourgois quoted in Mooney, 1999: 84)

Similarly, within the *gecekondus* of Istanbul a strong sense of communal identity, partly based upon a common religious identity in Islam but also upon a shared sense of rural values brought by them from the Turkish countryside, is articulated through complex networks of social relations, duties and codes (Mooney, 1999: 69). Much of this ordering is very mundane. For example, Naga's work in Dar es Salaam provides an insight into this (Naga, 1997). Naga's cognitive mappings crossed all parts of the city and included individuals with diverse backgrounds according to race, class, gender and education. The results of the fieldwork suggested that individual experiences of space are shaped by the immediate social and spatial structures and that '[d]espite the multiplicity of interpretations ... the common thread tying all the maps together is the rootedness of people's identities and sense of place in their communal places and neighbourhoods' (Naga, 1997: 10–11). Likewise, in the *favelas* of Rio de Janeiro (Mooney, 1999: 84–7), the *banlieue* of Paris (McDowell, 1999: 116–24) or any other such slum or shanty-town in any city in any part of the world, the survival strategies of the inhabitants impel their own banal orderings.

Under some circumstances the alternative orderings of such city worlds can 'spill over' into other parts of the city. In this way the disorder of marginal city worlds can dislodge or even impose themselves upon dominant orderings. For example, Mooney (drawing upon Perlman) argues that the *favelas* of Rio de Janeiro have, in large part, defined the international image of the city as the home of carnival as well as the cultural identity of Brazil as a whole (Mooney, 1999: 86). In a similar manner the Gay Mardi Gras of Sydney began as a local event, organised by and on behalf of a marginalised gay population, and has now become one of the defining features of the city as an open, diverse and tolerant urban polity. These cases show that the recognition of diverse sources of ordering enables the articulation of many voices, the expression of other identities, and contributes to the realisation of an inclusive urban society. In this way, disorder is not a root cause of the social problems of cities but is instead integral to their management and resolution.

Stoker's work on regime theory suggests that conceiving of (dis)order in this manner can have practical applications in real terms (Stoker, 1995 & 2000). He asserts that in recognising the reality of diversity and disorder in cities it is possible to transcend the attritional ecology of fear, exclusion and violence. This is achieved by moving away from perspectives on power that place emphasis upon its hierarchical pertrification – that is, power as a means of social control – and moving towards a view of power as a manifestation of social production. Thus, power is enabling and inclusive rather than constraining and exclusive, for example:

> Regime theory provides a new perspective on the issue of power. It directs attention away from a narrow focus on power as an issue of social control towards an understanding of power expressed through social production. In a complex, fragmented urban world the paradigmatic form of power is that which enables certain interests to blend their capacities to achieve common purposes.
>
> (Stoker, 1995: 54)

According to Stoker, urban regimes, understood as a particular way of exercising power in cities, including but going beyond agencies that have formal responsibilities, have a central role in shaping the function of power in this context. In seeking solutions to the social problems of cities, urban regimes are therefore confronted by a particular set of tensions. On one level, ordering in cities relates to the imposition of the dominant orderings of global capital, set within a neo-liberal economic discourse, in local context and in partnership with local capital and local governance (Allen, Massey & Pryke, 1999). Within the city this ordering operates through networks of influence – social, economic, cultural and political – and, in this way, a city can be successfully navigated through the ebbs and flows of the global economic system. But, on another level, such imposition of order is counter to the very nature of the city itself as an entity defined by the pronounced nature of its openness, diversity and intensity (Mooney, Pile & Brook, 1999) – disorder.

There is no clear dichotomy between order and disorder in the city. Rather, such matters turn upon questions of relative, rather than absolute, values. More than anything else, perhaps, (dis)order is a question of power, and while the particularities of the various ordering and disordering impulses may diverge, their common denominator is power and its uneven impact upon city life. The social tensions that result from this uneven circulation of power are manifest in complex relationships of inequality and their intimate juxtaposing across urban space. Solutions to the social problems of cities, relating to the intense diversity that defines urban life and expressed in the myriad contestations of the purpose and meaning of city spaces, are best approached from this perspective. Effectively addressing this unevenness and inequality requires the adoption of instruments for the negotiation of difference through the positive engagement of the manifold worlds that comprise the city. And, it is in such processes of the negotiation of difference that the particular nature of urban spatiality is constantly 'produced, maintained, challenged and transformed' (Mooney, Pile & Brook, 1999: 346). That is to say, it is through the accommodation and re-accommodation of (dis)order – understood as inclusive democracy, robust contestation and the diverse animation of power – that conceptions, as well as resolutions, of urban social problems are to be arrived at.

Conclusions

The key aspects of the city, defined in relational terms by its openness, intensity and diversity, are as follows:

- Connection and internal differentiation
- The 'stranger' and difference
- Rhythms
- Social and spatial division
- Marginalised groups and resistance
- Order and disorder.

These important features of the city will inform the discussion of the relationship between language and the city and are at the heart of the second part of this text in particular, with the aim of better understanding the critical nature of the various relationships between linguistic diversity, multiculturalism, citizenship and governance in the city. At this point, however, in order to set the stage for that discussion, it is necessary to note and reflect upon some of the key works in the area of sociolinguistics that use the city as the immediate context for the collection of the raw material of the discipline. These works, in many ways, have come to define the scope of sociolinguistics but, as we shall see, the very nature of this body of work has given rise to a number of critical limitations which inhibit our understanding of language in the city.

3
Sociolinguistics

Introduction

As sociolinguistics came into its own during the 1960s and 1970s the city was discovered as a key site for fieldwork (Gasquet-Cyrus, 2003). The reason for this is quite straightforward. Sociolinguists saw that the city was, in linguistic terms, much more complex than any other geographical context:

> Cites are much more difficult to characterize linguistically than are rural hamlets; variation in language and patterns of change are much more obvious in cities, e.g., in family structures, employment, and opportunities for social advancement or decline. Migration, both in and out of cities, is also usually a potent linguistic factor. Cities also spread their influence far beyond their limits and their importance should never be underestimated in considering such matters as the standardization and diffusion of languages.
>
> (Wardhaugh, 1998: 46–7)

Studies of linguistic variation in the urban context, first of all by Labov, and then by others such as Trudgill (1974), Cheshire (1978 & 1982) and Milroy (1987 & 1992), defined, to a great extent, the scope and nature of the discipline, *ergo* language variation in cities is 'at the heart of work in sociolinguistics' (Wardhaugh, 1998: 47). During the 1980s, however, it became increasingly clear to a number of other sociolinguists, for example Cameron (1990), Romaine (1984) and G. Williams (1992), that the approach of Labov *et al.* to the relationship between language and society suffered from some severe limitations. In particular, it adopted an uncritical position on social structure, hence severely curtailing the explanatory capacity of the discipline. Thus, sociolinguistics in that form was a useful means of describing a range of linguistic features, including variation, dialectology, style, interaction and attitude, as they relate to society, and also of describing how certain social themes, especially gender, race and socio-economic class pertain to language. But it lacked conceptual depth in societal or sociological terms. Such work assumes that the city, as a social entity, is not significantly different to society in the nation-state as a whole: it takes the city as an unproblematic microcosm of society. The implication is that the city has no particular impact on language, although this is neither made explicit nor is it tested in nay of the literature. This chapter reviews the development of sociolinguistics in the city, while returning to the roots of social views of language in order to re-approach the social from a critical perspective, and also so as to begin to problematise the city in sociolinguistics.

Sociolinguistics in the city

To begin with, let us reprise some of the key studies in the emergence and development of urban sociolinguistics and the important themes identified as a result, especially for readers from other disciplines who may not be familiar with sociolinguistic material. Labov's work in New York is regarded as the seminal study of linguistic variation (Wardhaugh, 1998: 160). He identified a range of issues, and the means of examining them, that remain central to the discipline to this day: a socially stratified community; a socially sensitive feature of pronounciation; a pattern of variation in the use of the feature and a community where the speech norms are undergoing change (Coupland & Jaworski, 1997: 163). An early and very significant work was a study of the social stratification of 'r' in three New York City department stores (Labov, 1966 & 1972). Labov set out to test the following hypothesis: 'If any two subgroups of New York City speakers are ranked in a scale of social stratification, then they will be ranked in the same order by their differential use of [r]'. By social stratification Labov meant 'that the normal workings of society have produced systematic differences between certain institutions or people, and that these differentiated forms have been ranked in status or prestige by general agreement' (Labov, 1972: 43–4). He selected three department stores in which to test the hypothesis, based upon the assumption that the stores could be reasonably ranked in socio-economic terms in a number of ways. One of these was location. Saks was located near the centre of the high-fashion shopping district along with other high-prestige stores and thereby confirmed as the highest-ranking of the stores. Macy's was

Table 3.1 Advertising policy, by numbers of pages of advertising on 24–27 October 1962 in the *New York Times* and the *Daily News* (adapted from Labov, 1972)

	New York Times	Daily News
Saks	2	0
Macy's	2	15
S. Klein	1/4	10

located near the garment district along with other middle-range stores in price and prestige and therefore identified as the middle-ranking store. While S. Klein was located in close proximity to Lower East Side and, as a result, understood to be the lowest ranking of the stores. Advertising policy was also used to confirm the ranking of the stores. Labov counted the numbers of pages of advertising taken by each of the stores on 24–27 October 1962 in the *New York Times* (understood to have a middle-class readership) and the *Daily News* (understood to have working-class readership). In this case the results, once again, confirmed the relative socio-economic status of the stores (Table 3.1). Pricing policy was another way in which Labov sought to confirm the ranking of the stores. As Saks did not usually list prices, it was possible, therefore, to compare only one item (women's coats) for all three stores. The result was as follows: Saks $90, Macy's $79.95, S. Klein $23, once again confirming the relative ranks of the three stores.

The method used by Labov to obtain linguistic data was simple in the extreme. The interviewer (Labov – dressed in middle-class style, wearing jacket, white shirt and tie) put a set of questions to sales assistants in each of the department stores, as if he were an ordinary customer, with the aim of eliciting the answer *'The Fourth floor'* on each occasion. The first set of questions, comprising *'Excuse me, where are the women's shoes?'* (or whichever particular department Labov knew to be on the Fourth floor in that department store) followed by *'Excuse me?'*, so as to elicit a repetition of the response with emphatic stress. Then, upon reaching the Fourth floor, the question *'Excuse me, what floor is this?'* was put. In each case the expected reply was *'The Fourth floor'* and this would be recorded, making note of the salient linguistic patterns and variation. Thus, according to Labov, the data elicited was natural and the results of the research, therefore, objective.

The results of the study revealed that 62% of Saks employees, 51% of Macy's, and 21% of S. Klein used the 'r' variable (Table 3.2). Thus, the data appears to confirm the pattern anticipated by Labov at the outset

Table 3.2 Distribution of use of 'r' by department stores (adapted from Labov, 1972)

	Saks	**Macy's**	**S. Klein**
All 'r' (%)	30	20	4
Some 'r' (%)	32	31	17
Total number	68	125	71

in that the enunciation of words such as 'fourth' and 'floor' with the 'r' pronounced is associated with the middle class and is highly valued by the working class, even though, as Wardhaugh notes (1998: 161), the middle-class speakers themselves do not conform to type under all circumstances. Indeed, he further notes that the pronunciation of 'r' was not consistently highly valued in New York in the past (Wardhaugh, 1998: 161):

> New York City was *r*-pronouncing in the eighteenth century but became *r*-less in the nineteenth, and *r*-lessness predominated until World War II. At that time *r*-pronunciation became prestigious again, possibly as a result of large population movements to the city; there was a shift in attitude toward *r*-pronunciation, from apparent indifference to a widespread desire to adopt such a pronunciation.

Trudgill's work on the English language in the city of Norwich is, as Coupland and Jaworski note (1997: 164), both a replication and an elaboration of Labov's work in New York. Trudgill obtained his data from a set of structured interviews. He ordered the interviewees into five socio-economic classes (lower working class, middle working class, upper working class, lower middle class and middle middle class). His aims were to examine the following: the nature of the relationship between certain linguistic variables and socio-economic class, social context and gender, and which variables relate specifically to variation in socio-economic class and are significant in signalling either the social context of linguistic interaction or the socio-economic class of the speaker. The interviews comprised a set of different language-based activities designed to illuminate patterns in what he describes as 'g-dropping', as with, for example, the varying pronunciation of the suffix 'ing'. The activities were ordered according to 'contextual style' and comprised word list (the most formal style), reading passage, formal speech and casual speech (the least formal style). The results revealed that the socio-economic classes were manifest linguistically and that gender

Table 3.3   Distribution of use of 'ing' by socio-economic class and gender (adapted from Trudgill, 1974)

Social class	Number	Gender	Word list	Reading passage	Formal speech	Casual speech
Middle middle	6	Male	000	000	004	031
class		Female	000	000	000	000
Lower middle	8	M	000	020	027	017
class		F	000	000	003	067
Upper working	16	M	000	018	081	095
class		F	011	013	068	077
Middle working	22	M	024	043	091	097
class		F	020	046	081	088
Lower working	8	M	066	100	100	100
class		F	017	054	097	100

was a very significant factor in determining the identified patterns in linguistic variation (Table 3.3). A score of 000 indicates consistent use of 'ŋ', as in 'singing', and a score of 100 indicates consistent use of 'n', as in 'singin'. It is worth quoting extensively from the work of Trudgill (1974: 94–5):

This link between the linguistic characteristics of working-class speakers and male speakers is a common one. … There would appear to be two interconnected explanatory factors: (1) Women in our society are more status-conscious than men, generally speaking, and are therefore more aware of the social significance of linguistic variables. There are probably two main reasons for this:
(i) The social position of women in our society is less secure than that of men, and, generally speaking, subordinate to that of men. It is therefore more necessary for women to secure and signal their social status linguistically and in other ways, and they are more aware of the importance of this type of signal.
(ii) Men in our society can be rated socially by their occupation, their earning power, and perhaps by their other abilities: in other words, by what they *do*. For the most part, however, this is not possible for women, who have generally to be rated on how they *appear*. Since they cannot be rated socially by their occupation, what other people know about what they do in life, other signals of status, including speech, are correspondingly more important. This last point is perhaps the most important. (2) The second, related, factor is that working-class speech, like many other

aspects of working-class culture, has, in our society, connotations of masculinity, since it is associated with the roughness and toughness supposedly characteristic of working-class life, which are, to a certain extent, considered to be desirable masculine attributes. They are not, on the other hand, considered to be desirable feminine characteristics. On the contrary, refinement and sophistication are much preferred. ... From the point of view of linguistic theory, this means that, as far as linguistic change 'from below' is concerned, we can expect men to be in the vanguard. Changes 'from above', on the other hand, are more likely to be led by women.

The work of Wolfram, with others (Shuy, Wolfram & Riley, 1968 and Wolfram, 1969), attempted to show how a range of items including socio-economic class, gender, age and race are factors in determining linguistic variation. He studied the following four phonological variables:

- word final consonant cluster simplification;
- medial and final 'th', e.g. as in 'no<u>th</u>ing' and in 'pa<u>th</u>';
- syllable final 'd' and
- the occurrence of 'r' after vowels.

In addition, he studied the following four grammatical variables:

- the zero copula, e.g. as in 'He tired';
- invariant 'be', e.g. as in 'He <u>be</u> tired';
- the suffix '-s', e.g. as in 'girl<u>s</u>' and
- multiple negation, e.g. as in 'I'm <u>not</u> going <u>nowhere</u>'.

The results show some correlations between certain linguistic variables and socio-economic class. For example, the differing use of the third-person singular tense-marking 'z' is sharply demarcated by class, being markedly absent among working-class speakers and consistently present among middle-class speakers. In contrast, the pattern of use of 'r', as in words such as 'farm' and 'car', is progressive in relation to socio-economic class, with no sharp break between middle-class and working-class speakers (Table 3.4). Subsequently, these contrasting patterns were described as 'sharp stratification' and 'gradient stratification' (Wolfram & Fasold, 1974). In general terms, the work in Detroit suggested that there was a very close relationship between linguistic variation and socio-economic class – the higher the social class the greater

Table 3.4 Absence of 'z' in Detroit black speech (adapted from Wolfram, 1969)

Social class	% of 'z' absence	% of 'r' absence
Upper middle	1.4	20.8
Lower middle	9.7	38.8
Upper working	56.9	61.3
Lower working	71.4	71.7

the adherence to standard forms. As the context of language use becomes more formal so the individual speaker tends to conform more closely with standard usage, the linguistic behaviour of children tend to shift away from standard forms to a greater extent than adults from the same socio-economic class, males have a greater tendency to non-standard use than females, and, reading style most closely conformed to standard forms.

Macaulay (1977) studied linguistic variation in Glasgow. The survey sample comprised 16 adults, 16 fifteen-year olds and 16 ten-year olds with equal numbers of each gender and equal numbers from each of four socio-economic classes – professional and managerial (1), white-collar (2), skilled-manual (3) and semi-skilled and unskilled manual (4). In the case of children the socio-economic class of the parents was stated; if there was a difference between the parents then the highest class was given. He studied the use of vowels in words such as 'hit', 'school', 'hat' and 'now' and the frequency of glottal stops as replacements for 't' in words such as 'better' and 'get'. The results of the research showed a correlation between socio-economic class and linguistic variation. This much could have been anticipated, given the work of Labov etc. But, Macaulay found that the relationship between class and variation was subtler than previously thought. Gender and age were also active in shaping linguistic variation. For example, there were gender differences with regard to the classes that exhibited the greatest degrees of variation. Classes 1 and 2 displayed the greatest variation among males, while among females Classes 2 and 3 were at greater degrees of variance. Also, linguistic variation increased with age, with this trend being apparent with the group of ten-year olds but becoming more fixed with the fifteen-year olds. Macaulay also found that when the data were examined in relation to individuals rather than groups, the patterns of linguistic behaviour were less rigid. That is, the linguistic behaviour of individual subjects overlapped with that which was characteristic of other groups, leading Macaulay to postulate that a continuum of linguistic behaviour exists with regard to the individual speaker and that social classes are constructs that are imposed on this continuum. Wardhaugh explains the significance of this as follows:

> [T]he linguistic behaviour of certain individuals in one class will overlap the linguistic behaviour of certain individuals in neighbouring classes. What is important in this view is that there is still a certain homogeneity of behaviour within the classes. The majority of speakers within the various classes behave like one another even though some individuals do not. This behaviour has its own distinctive quality, and its characteristics are not just the result of some individuals behaving like individuals 'above' them and other individuals behaving like individuals 'below' them in the social hierarchy. That is, the members of each social class exhibit certain ranges of behaviour on the linguistic variables and, event though the ranges overlap, each social class has a distinctive range for each variable.
>
> (Wardhaugh, 1998: 174)

Cheshire (1978 & 1982) studied linguistic variation in relation to various groups of adolescent males and females in the city of Reading with the aim of showing how the use of various non-standard morphological and syntactic features relate to the extent to which the speakers adhere to the norms of a specific vernacular culture. Specifically, she examined patterns of use of the following linguistic features:

- The use of the present tense suffix with non-third-person subjects, e.g we go<u>es</u>
- The use of 'has' with non-third-person singular subjects, e.g. we <u>has</u>
- The use of 'was' with plural subjects and the singular 'you', e.g. you <u>was</u>
- The use of multiple negation, e.g. I'm <u>not</u> going <u>nowhere</u>
- The use of the negative past tense 'never' instead of standard English 'didn't', e.g. I <u>never</u> done it
- The use of 'what' instead of standard English 'who', 'whom', 'which', and 'that', e.g. are you the boy <u>what's</u> just come
- The use of the auxiliary 'do' with third-person singular subjects, e.g. how much <u>do</u> he want
- The use of the present tense form 'come' as the past tense, e.g. I <u>come</u> down here yesterday
- The use of 'ain't' for negative present tense forms of 'be' and 'have', e.g. I <u>ain't</u> going, I <u>ain't</u> got any.

Cheshire intended to record the spontaneous, natural and informal speech of the groups. The data was collected primarily by means of long-term participant-observation in adventure playgrounds in the city of Reading She also constructed an index for each gender in order to measure the extent to which the use of non-standard features is controlled by the norms of the specific vernacular culture. The indices included indicators such as skill at fighting, the carrying of a weapon, participation in minor criminal activities, job (that is upon leaving school the type of job to which they aspired), style (dress and hairstyle), and, swearing. Linguistic variation by individual speakers was measured against their score in this index. A score of 100.00 represents consistent use of the non-standard form and a score of 0.00 represents consistent use of the standard form. The results showed that there was a direct correlation with regard to the males (Table 3.5). For example, high frequencies of the use of the present tense suffix with non-third-person subjects and the use of 'has' with non-third-person singular subjects was associated with high cores on the index. The relationship for the females was more complex, in particular the girls tended more than the boys to shift towards conformity to standard English in more formal contexts.

The work of the Milroys in Belfast more precisely identifies how social context shapes the linguistic behaviour of individual speakers (J. Milroy, 1992; L. Milroy, 1987). Using participant-observation methods, whereby Lesley Milroy was introduced into the social networks studied as a friend

Table 3.5 Correlation between adherence to specific vernacular culture and use of non-standard forms (adapted from Cheshire, 1982)

	Group 1	Group 2	Group 3
CLASS A			
Non-standard (s)	77.36	54.03	36.57
Non-standard *has*	66.67	50.00	41.65
Non-standard *was*	90.32	89.74	83.33
Negative concord	100.00	85.71	83.33
CLASS B			
Non-standard *never*	64.71	41.67	45.45
Non-standard *what*	92.31	7.69	33.33
CLASS C			
Non-standard aux. *do*	58.33	37.50	83.33
Non-standard *come*	100.00	100.00	100.00
ain't = aux. *have*	78.26	64.52	80.00
ain't = aux *be*	58.82	72.22	80.00
ain't = copule	100.00	76.19	56.62

of a friend, they set out to understand how the relative strength of social networks helps to explain levels of allegiance to particular forms of language behaviour. The hypothesis is based upon an idealisation that in 'a community bound by maximally dense and multiplex network ties linguistic change would not take place at all. No such community can actually exist, but the idealisation is important, because it also implies that to the extent that relatively weak ties exist in communities (as in fact they do), the conditions will be present for linguistic change to take place' and therefore it follows that the 'relative strength of network tie is a powerful predictor of language use' (Milroy, 1992: 176). The networks most effective at maintaining particular linguistic forms comprise dense associations and multiplexity. Dense associations are understood as the immediate interconnection of almost all of the individuals within the social network with each other. Multiplexity is understood as a pattern of connections in which individuals relate to each other via a number of different social domains such as kinship, place of residence, employment and leisure activity. The conservative nature of the linguistic behaviour of the social networks of lower socio-economic classes is explained by the attraction of 'covert prestige'. The status benefit of the language behaviour associated with higher socio-economic classes is, in this case, more apparent than real. For example, the Protestant working-class community of Ballymacarrett showed the strongest allegiance to the linguistic norm, the local vernacular as exemplified by the deletion of the fricative 'th' as in 'mo<u>th</u>er' and 'bro<u>th</u>er'. Conformity to the norm was stronger among employment age males than females. This, explained James Milroy, was because the males were more closely involved than females in the social network through their employment, their work-based socialising, other strong ties etc.

Weak network ties are sites of linguistic change. Individuals and groups are more likely to have many more weak ties than strong ties as the latter require much higher levels of investment. Strong ties, by definition, found within the group, are internal to the group. Strong ties and multiplex relationships = close-knit social network and local cohesion. Weak ties, and not strong ties, function as bridges between groups as level of contact is more ephemeral. Weak and uniplex ties are 'important channels through which innovation and influence flow from one close-knit group to another' (Milroy, 1992: 177). The presence of diversity of groups in the city helps to explain linguistic variation:

[T]his perception is potentially very illuminating in accounting for different language states at different times and places at many levels of generality, ranging from the interpersonal situations, through dialect-divergent, bilingual and code-switching communities to the very broadest of language situations, and it throws light on the question of convergence and divergence. The model of strong and weak ties ... can be thought of as an idealized representation of (for example) an urban community which consists of clumps connected by predominantly weak ties, which in turn are connected to other clumps by predominantly weak ties, but it can of course represent other kinds of language situation that we might conceive of.

(Milroy, 1992: 178–9)

Language change and variation follows the weak ties. For example, young females of Clonard area of Belfast use of /a/-backing, adopted from Protestant speech norm despite social (limited contact between Catholic and Protestant working class) physical barriers (existence of 'Peace Line' concrete and barbed-wire wall separating Catholic and Protestant localities) against this. Milroy suggests that the weak ties through which this linguistic behaviour is diffused operates through employment of these young females in city-centre store where some of their co-workers and customers are Protestant.

Limitations

It is at this point that it is necessary to explore some of the limitations of sociolinguistics as defined by the work of Labov and those who followed in his wake. To begin with, however, it is widely recognised within all shades of the discipline that Labov engineered a crucial breakthrough in the study of language in relation to society. Cameron, a key critic of Labov, summarises it most effectively in the following terms:

The doctrine Labov was most concerned to challenge was that of 'the ideal speaker-hearer in a homogeneous speech community' (I use the familiar Chomskyan formulation, but the central point that linguistics must idealize its object in order to describe it goes back through the structuralist paradigm and to Saussure). Labov debunked this as myth by showing that language is not homogeneous, either at the level of speech community or the individual grammar. Rather, it possesses 'structured variability'. 'Structured' is important here: it means the variation found in language is not a matter of 'free' or random alterations (which mainstream linguists had recognized but excluded from consideration on the grounds that they were superficial, hence uninteresting, and difficult to model elegantly) but is, on the contrary, systematic and socially conditioned. Labov's work demonstrated that variation could be modelled, and that the analysis of variation provided insight into the mechanism of language change. In other words, he argued convincingly that to accept the myth of the ideal speaker-hearer in the homogeneous speech community was not merely to screen out a few surface irregularities, but rather to miss a fundamental general property of language.

(Cameron, 1990: 80)

This break from a view of linguistics that understands language as operating within an idealised, homogeneous society, while significant, is in itself flawed. According to Cameron, for example, the principal problem with the variationist or quantitative perspective is its assumption that language reflects society:

The account which is usually given – or worse, presupposed – in the quantitative paradigm is some version of the proposition that 'language reflects society'. Thus there exist social categories, structures, divisions, attitudes and identities which are marked, encoded or expressed in language use. By correlating patterns of linguistic variation with these social or demographic features, we have given a sufficient account of them.

(Cameron, 1990: 81)

Or, as Romaine (1984) bluntly put it, the quantitative paradigm doesn't actually *explain* anything. Instead, as G. Williams notes, it merely reflects a set of assumptions about the nature of society, whether issues of gender, race or socio-economic class:

With reference to language, as Fishman's discussion of domains makes clear, the tendency is to emphasise the claim that language reflects society and that the different features of language reflect different types and scales of society thereby establishing stages which tend to relate to one another in historical sequence.

(G. Williams, 1992: 238)

Williams suggests that this position, which he terms as a consensus perspective, causes sociolinguistics to set itself at a disjuncture to its actual object of study. For example, with regard to the work of the Milroys in Belfast, he notes that the linguistic patterns, while, related to religious identity are discussed in the absence of any meaningful discussion of the socio-political context in which the research was undertaken, *viz* the ethno-political conflict that dominated all aspects of life in Northern Ireland in the period 1969–98. As a result, the insights which such a study of language could give rise to are confined to an idealised view of society and not the actual society to which the study relates:

> Thus the individual is viewed as a free, rational being whose striving for cooperation with her/his fellow being leads to a desire for social conformity and social order. Language, on the other hand, is the means by which this is achieved. It is a symbolic system which, as such, is a means of conveying social meaning. Thus the use of language becomes a matter of free choice among rational individuals seeking to convey their desire for various social identities to their fellows, these social identities being a manifestation of belonging and integration. Language is functional and is a reflection of social order.
>
> (G. Williams, 1992: 198)

It might be reasonable to suggest, therefore, that sociolinguistics, thus formulated, does not speak of society, but rather takes a view of language that is, at best, divorced from the reality of society. At worst, this approach is the implicit servant of dominant ideologies, even when it makes explicit theoretical claims to radicalism. Williams explains it thus:

> [M]uch of the work on speech variation is merely an extension of structural functionalism. The focus is on the manner in which language is an aspect of the social norm which sets constraints upon individual action. Such norms are the product of socialisation into fixed roles within the overall structure of society. Yet, even within this framework of constraints the individual is not entirely fettered since language is, simultaneously, a feature of the rational expression of the individual expressing a social identity. If language is part both of the normative structure and of individual expression then the individual must also be a willing participant in the creation of a normative order which restrains him/her. It is as if the social structure is a product of individual decisions. Even within feminist studies, an area which has been subject to considerable theoretical innovation, this perspective has been retained by many of those studying gender language as a source of variation. Despite employing concepts such as social class, ethnicity or gender, which are explicitly related to domination and subordination, as independent variables within the

empirical framework, the conflict that is implicit in such dimensions is missing as a consequence of the structural functionalist orientation. The emphasis on normative consensus as the guiding force of individual speech results in the legitimisation of standard forms and the parallel marginalisation of non-standard froms.

(G. Williams, 1992: 92–93)

One can conclude, at this point, therefore, that the work of Labov *et al.* can be accepted as being seminal in linguistic terms but are insufficiently explanatory in social terms. The appropriate response to this, of course, is to place sociolinguistics in the context of wider social theory. Cameron outlines the key concerns in the following terms:

To address such issues seriously requires us to acknowledge that languages are regulated by social institutions, and as such may have their own dynamic and become objects of social concern in their own right. ... It would deal with such matters as the production and reproduction of linguistic norms by institutions and socializing practices; how these norms are apprehended, accepted, resisted and subverted by individual actors and what their relation is to the construction of society.

(Cameron, 1990: 85)

For some, such as Dittmar, theorising sociolinguistics has followed the pathway laid out by (post) Marxist theory. But, according to Williams, this leads to the same conceptual *cul de sac* in that inherent to the Marxist perspective on language is the tendency to fall back upon the assumption that language reflects society, for example:

These various attempts to develop Marxist analyses of language in society find it difficult to avoid the problem of language as reflection since the argument relies upon a preconceived and preformed conception of society. The analysis of language is then brought together in order to justify the implications associated with that particular model of society. Language in the form of discourse becomes a reflection of social inequality in all its ramifications; it becomes an entity separate from, but reflecting society.

(G. Williams, 1992: 246–7)

Williams suggests that French discourse analysis has underscored the theoretical inadequacy of sociolinguistics in the most basic terms.

It counters the notion that language describes a reality that is external to it, proposing instead that the notion of external reality has no objective existence but is brought into meaning *via* discourse:

> In pursuing its objective [French discourse analysis] has also redressed the tendency to see language as reflecting society as the following statements by Boutet ... indicates: 'the words, the discourses, are not simply the representation of our acts and of our thoughts, they are not only there to transmit information or the ideas of the order. They are not the *reflection* of the social order, they are a participating force and they are *active* on the social, and produce specific effects which the analyst can place reference points upon ... the semiotic materiality that is language'. Language is not a representation, a simple commentary of social processes from which reality derives but an image in words and phrases of a symbolic language.
>
> (G. Williams, 1992: 255–6)

Thus, language is not reflective of society but rather is a constitutive force: '[L]anguage is not an organism or a passive reflection, but a social institution, deeply implicated in culture, in society, in political relations at every level' (Cameron, 1990: 92). Now, it is necessary to return to the roots of sociology of language to see how language is so implicated.

Linguistic relativism

Understanding sociolinguistics in the city requires us to revisit some starting points for the discipline of sociolinguistics. This is of immediate relevance to developing an understanding of language in the city as language groups often attempt to create and to maintain their own particular and discrete worlds in the city on the basis of their own identifiable language. The origins of our understanding of the precise nature of language, whether in idealised or sociologically real contexts, is therefore critical to our understanding of language in the urban context, and that is despite the complex overlapping of linguistic worlds in the city and the language, change, shift and variation that arises from the shifting mosaic of the linguistic diversity in the city. The origins of the study of language as a means of understanding society in general are to be found in the development of the discipline of anthropology in North America during the first part of the 20th century. It was a basic tenet of these early scholars of language and society that any given culture could only be studied through the language of that culture. According to Boas, the pre-eminent linguistic anthropologist of that time, it was not only a methodological matter, requiring anthropologists to acquire the language of the cultures they study, but also theoretical. This, he explained as follows:

> In all of the subjects mentioned heretofore, a knowledge of Indian languages serves as an important adjunct to a full understanding of the customs and beliefs of the people we are studying. But in all these cases the service which language lends us is first of all a practical one – a means of a clearer understanding of ethnological phenomena which in themselves have nothing to do with linguistic problems. ... It seems, however, that a theoretical study of Indian languages is not less important that a practical knowledge of them; that the purely linguistic inquiry is part and parcel of a thorough investigation of the psychology of the peoples of the world. If ethnology is understood as the science dealing with the mental phenomena of the life of the people of the world, human language, one of the most important manifestations of mental life, would seem to belong naturally to the field of work of ethnology.
>
> (Boas, 1911: 52)

The most important methodological inference drawn from this position on the relationship between culture and language was that a culture's language, or linguistic system, could be used to understand the cultural system itself as a whole. Kroeber, another significant early linguistic anthropologist, writing in 1963, put it as follows:

> In short, culture can probably function only on the basis of abstractions, and these in turn seem to be possible only through speech, or through a secondary substitute for spoken language such as writing, numeration, mathematical and chemical notation, and the like. Culture, then, began when speech was present; and from then on, the enrichment of either meant the further development of the other.
>
> (Kroeber, 1963: 102)

Boas arrived at the view that each given culture could only be understood in its own terms and, moreover, based upon his observation that the diverse languages that he examined were employed to order and to classify the world in different ways, such order and classification was arbitrary or relative. The point was made by Boas in memorable fashion with regard to terms for the concept of 'snow' in what he described as 'Eskimo' vocabulary:

> It seems important ... to emphasize the fact that the groups of ideas expressed by specific phonetic groups show very material differences in different languages, and do not conform by any means to the same principles of classification. To take again the example of English, we find that the idea of WATER is expressed in a great variety of forms: one term serves to express water as a LIQUID; another one, water in the form of a large expanse (LAKE); other, water as running in a large body or in a small body (RIVER and BROOK); still other terms express water in the form of RAIN, DEW, WAVE and FOAM. It is perfectly conceivable that this variety of ideas, each of which is expressed by a single independent term in English, might be expressed in other languages by derivation from the same term.
>
> Another example of the same kind, the words for SNOW in Eskimo, may be given. Here we find one word, *aput*, expressing SNOW ON THE GROUND; another one, *qana*, FALLING SNOW; a third one, *piqsirpoq*, DRIFTING SNOW; and a fourth one, *qimuqsug*, A SNOWDRIFT.
>
> (Boas, 1911: 19)

By implication, experience of the world, or sense of reality, is directly codified or systematised by language, an insight that was seized upon and extended further by Sapir, and subsequently Whorf. They argued that if language has such properties, then it follows that it induces the speakers of a given language to a view of the world that is particular to and is derived from that language:

> Language is a guide to "social reality" ... Human beings do not live in the objective world alone, nor alone in the world of social activity as ordinarily understood, but very much at the mercy of the particular language which has become the medium of expression for their society. It is quite an illusion to imagine that one adjusts to reality essentially without the use of language and that language is merely an incidental means of solving problems of communication or reflection. The fact of the matter is that the "real world" is to a large extent unconsciously built up on the language habits of the group. No two languages are ever sufficiently similar to be considered as representing the same social reality. The worlds in which different societies live are distinct worlds, not merely the same world with different

labels attached. ... we see and hear and otherwise experience very largely as we do because the language habits of our community predispose certain choices of interpretation.

(Whorf in Mandelbaum, 1949: 162)

This particular perspective was characterised by Whorf as the principle of linguistic relativity. According to which the logical end point of the determining properties of language was that language did more than merely predispose certain possibilities on reality for the speakers of that language but that it encompassed the *only* world view accessible to the speakers of that language. According to Whorf, the result of this was that

Users of markedly different grammars are pointed by the grammars toward different types of observations and different evaluations of extremely similar acts of observation, and hence are not equivalent as observers but must arrive at somewhat different views of the world.

(Whorf, 1956a: 221)

Whorf further drew from this insight the notion that the grammatical structures of each language contains within it a metaphysics comprising the conceptual structure of the universe, a world view particular to that language and its culture:

Thus, the Hopi language and culture conceals a metaphysics, such as our so-called naïve view of space and time does, or as the relativity theory does; yet it is a different metaphysics from either.

(Whorf, 1956b: 58)

Thus, the strongest versions of what is widely known as the Sapir–Whorf hypothesis states that a speaker of a particular language is subject to a particular world view by that language. As Fasold, however, points out (1990: 63–4), few scholars today would agree with the strong versions of the Sapir–Whorf hypothesis, although many would accept that linguistic relativism has some general validity. Others again disagree with the hypothesis entirely – 'it is wrong, all wrong' (Pinker, 1994: 57). It is in this vein that Malotki (1983) has rather successfully demolished Whorf's particular claims regarding the Hopi concept of time. The impact of semiotics and Marxism on various disciplines has been most instrumental in the retreat from the strongest versions of linguistic relativism. Briefly, semiotics, understood as the study of the meaning of language conceived of as a system of signs, offers the insight that

The views are likely to spread and be shared by ethnolinguistic groups.

language is not a simple reflection of reality; it is instead a signifier of it. Language, to borrow from Eagleton (1991: 203), carves reality into conceptual space – a multilayered, contested and mobile space; the constituent features of which are thrown into sometimes startling relief in linguistically diverse societies. This position on language problematises its relationship to social reality so as to conceive of language and society as being interlocked – language both shapes and is shaped by social reality. Or, as Dittmar (1976) puts it, language and society are conjoined in a dialectic *chez* Hegel. Thus, language is a social artefact and an artificer of social reality. In this way language is central to a sense of place in the world. Something of this function of language is at its most intense in the urban context where it is a central factor in the making and re-making of worlds in the city. DeBernardi weaves these insights together in the following manner:

> Contemporary ethnographic linguistics are driven by functional questions regarding the role of linguistic interaction in expressing social identity and shaping value. Research into the pragmatics of language use suggests that people not only speak about the world 'out there'; they also create a good deal of their social reality in the very act of speaking. Thus the acquisition of a language is not only the internalization of a linguistic code, but also entails the learning of status and role, of appropriate social effect, and (ultimately) of worldview. Language provides both the foundation of a shared cultural identity and the means for the reproduction of social difference.
>
> (DeBernardi, 1994: 861)

From such a perspective, the work of Labov *et al.* appears to be far removed from the origins of the discipline of sociolinguistics in linguistic anthropology. They appear to assume that language reflects society whether as regards socio-economic class, race, age, or gender, for example. This is in total contrast to linguistic relativism where language is understood to 'make' social reality. At this point, it is useful to accept the assertion that language is constitutive of social reality, but it is necessary to explore some ways in which this might be understood.

Habitus and discourse

The discussion may be progressed through returning to the (post) Marxist contribution to our understanding of language in society, although it is essential to consider how it is possible to move beyond

G. Williams's criticism of this perspective on language as one that assumes a normative social structure. The work of Bourdieu has been used by a number of scholars currently working in different areas of sociolinguistics (e.g. Calvet, 2002, and May, 2001). Certain concepts from his work can help to open up a means of better understanding language and society with regard to the city. To begin, two concepts are most important to understanding Bourdieu's perspective on language in society, namely 'habitus' [pl. habitūs] and 'market' (also referred to as 'field'). Bourdieu's concept of the market is conceived of as an economic marketplace that is structured by the relationship between producers and consumers. It is a site of struggle in which the competitive capacity of agents is determined by the value of the capital that each possesses. This capital can take various forms – economic , cultural and symbolic. These forms are convertible and, as such, possess differing values in each specific market and across different markets, society as a whole being comprised of a series of markets – economic, political, legal, religious, linguistic. In this context, linguistic competencies function as language capital and the market value of particular competencies and languages vary from market to market. The exact market value is ascertained by the key agents in the market, namely the producers and the consumers. As a result, language behaviour varies according to the market value of the linguistic competencies and the languages available to the market. Particular linguistic competencies and languages, thereby, have greater potential to yield advantage, or profit, than others. In short, in this linguistic market an individual will acquire, employ or adopt an attitude towards a language, languages or linguistic competencies that is most likely to accrue capital for them, whether economic, cultural or symbolic.

Bourdieu derives the term habitus from classical philosophical language by which it is defined as an acquired ideal or perfect state or condition. Bourdieu employs the term to refer to the environmental and other conditions that shape an individual in society. These conditions, or, as Bourdieu puts it, set of dispositions, predispose individuals to particular behaviours, and these behaviours are likely to be held in common with the society of which the individual is a part. These behaviours are understood by Bourdieu as subconscious patterns, taken for granted, and governed by an unarticulated sense of appropriateness, for example:

> The habitus is a set of dispositions which incline agents to act and react in certain ways. The dispositions generate practices, perceptions and attitudes which are 'regular' without being consciously

co-ordinated or governed by any 'rule'. The dispositions which constitute the habitus are inculcated, structured, durable, generative
and transposable.

(Editor's introduction in Bourdieu, 1991: 12)

A more refined examination of the concept of habitus is required so as
to understand how it is the case that it is 'inculcated, structured, durable,
generative and transposable' and how such properties of the habitus
impact upon the individual and society. According to Bourdieu, the dispositions that comprise the habitus are acquired by the individual grad-
ually from an early age and largely through the family unit, but also
via the educational system. The result of this process of acquisition is
that the individual experience of the world, of social reality, is filtered
through these dispositions, thus:

> Unlike scientific estimations, which are corrected after each experi-
> ment in accordance with rigorous rules of calculation, practical esti-
> mates give disproportionate weight to early experiences: the
> structures characteristic of a determinate type of conditions of exis-
> tence, through the economic and social necessity which they bring
> to bear on the relatively autonomous universe of family relation-
> ships, or more precisely, through the mediation of the specifically
> familial manifestations of this external necessity (sexual division of
> labour, domestic morality, cares, strife, tastes, etc.), produce the struc-
> tures of the habitus which become in turn the basis of perception
> and appreciation of all subsequent experience.
>
> (Bourdieu, 1977: 78)

This set of dispositions is structured in that it reflects the social environment or conditions in which it is acquired. And, while possibilities
for variation in behavioural practice exist, it is only in the context of
the structuring properties that constitute the habitus. Bourdieu puts it
as follows:

> The habitus, the durably instilled generative principle of regulated
> improvisations, produces practices which tend to reproduce the reg-
> ularities immanent in the objective conditions of the production of
> their generative principle, while adjusting to the demands inscribed
> as objective potentialities in the situation, as defined by the cogni-
> tive and motivating structures making up the habitus.
>
> (Bourdieu, 1977: 78)

The durability of the set of dispositions relates to it being embedded deeply in the individual beyond the point of the individual being normally conscious of it. Thus, according to Bourdieu, the set of dispositions is not readily accessible to self-aware determinations and is not easily capable of modification or change:

> The habitus is the product of the work of inculcation and appropriation necessary in order for those products of collective history, the objective structures (e.g. of language, economy etc.) to succeed in reproducing themselves more or less completely, in the form of durable dispositions, in the organisms (which one can, if one wishes, call individuals) lastingly subjected to the same conditions, and hence placed in the same material conditions of existence.
>
> (Bourdieu, 1977: 85)

The set of dispositions is generative in that it enables the performance of a wide range of behaviours or practices. And it is transposable in that the practices thereby generated can be performed in areas other than those in which they originated. But, it is a function of the habitus to homogenise such behaviours or practices in whichever field they might be enacted, despite the individual. The effect of this is to further reinforce the set of dispositions as societal norms. In this way, according to Bourdieu, the specific performances of behaviour or practices (including the linguistic) by the individual are taken for granted:

> One of the fundamental effects of the orchestration of habitus is the production of a commonsense world endowed with the objectivity secured by consensus on meaning (*sens*) of practices and the world, in other words the harmonization of agents' experiences and the continuous reinforcement that each of them receives from the expression, individual or collective (in festivals for example), improvised or programmed (commonplaces, sayings), of similar or identical experiences. The homogeneity of habitus is what – within the limits of the group of agents possessing the schemes (of production and interpretation) implied in their production – causes practices and works to be immediately intelligible and foreseeable, and hence taken for granted.
>
> (Bourdieu, 1977: 80)

Bourdieu also contends that in such a context the individual, society and social reality are the products of an unproblematised past. The past is still active in that it is embodied in behaviours and practices, internalised beyond consciousness, as if it were not history at all. In this sense habitus is predisposed to continuity – the co-presence of past, present and future. It is also through the active presence of the past that, according to Bourdieu, contemporary behaviours and practices are largely autonomous of the stimuli of the present:

> In short, the habitus, the product of history, produces individual and collective practices, and hence history, in accordance with the schemes engendered by history. The system of dispositions – a past which survives in the present and tends to perpetuate itself into the future by making itself present in practices structured according to its principles, an internal law relaying the continuous exercise of the law of external necessities (irreducible to immediate conjunctural constraints) – is the principle of the continuity and regularity which objectivism discerns in the social world without being able to give them a rational basis.
>
> (Bourdieu, 1977: 82)

> The habitus – embodied history, internalized as a second nature and so forgotten as history – is the active presence of the whole past of which it is the product. As such, it is what gives practices their relative autonomy with respect to external determinations of the immediate present.
>
> (Bourdieu, 1990: 56)

With regard to language, the set of dispositions comprising habitus predispose speakers to a range of behaviours and practices specific to language. These relate to the linguistic capacity of individual speakers, to their given social capacity in certain situations, and are shaped by the expectations and demands of the market:

> Every speech act and, more generally, every action, is a conjuncture, an encounter between independently casual series. On the one hand, there are the socially constructed dispositions of the linguistic habitus, which imply a certain propensity to speak and to say determinate things and a certain capacity to speak, which involves both the linguistic capacities to generate an infinite number of grammatically correct discourses, and the social capacity to use this competence adequately in a determinate situation. On the other hand, there are the structures of the linguistic market, which impose themselves as a system of specific sanctions and censorships.
>
> (Bourdieu, 1991: 37)

The notion of politically structured space is very important in understanding the function of language in habitus and market. And, bearing in mind Castells remark that the city is given meaning through its governance, the implications of this assertion for language in the city are potentially far-reaching. Bourdieu conceives of language as a system which is actively defined by socio-political processes and institutions. The state is certainly implicated, especially with the creation of official languages. In this context the linguistic market is entirely dominated by a single language, for example:

> The official language is bound up with the state, both in its genesis and in its social uses. It is in the process of state formation that the conditions are created for the constitution of a unified linguistic market, dominated by the official language.
>
> (Bourdieu, 1991: 45)

An implication of this is that language can be understood as a form of habitus and that the linguistic habitus conceals within it the traces of struggles, past and ongoing, for the empowerment of the other non-dominant languages by various agents:

> A language only exists as a linguistic habitus, to be understood as a recurrent and habitual system of dispositions and expectations. A language is itself a set of practices that imply not only a particular system of words and grammatical rules, but also an often forgotten or hidden struggle over the symbolic power of a particular way of communicating.
>
> (Duranti, 1997: 45)

But, as the state is implicated so is the contemporary city, as it emerges as a key site in a network of flows of people, capital and products in a globalising world and as it, along with other forms of polity, steps out from the shadow of the nation-state that, as we have already noted, is simultaneously too small and too big an entity in the current political landscape.

Ideology

Notions of contestation, resistance and conflict have already been identified as being important in this study. In the context of the intellectual challenge of postmodernity and the material challenge of globalisation, these may be regarded as imperative. For Jameson the nature of the challenge inherent to the postmodern condition is characterised as follows:

> There are, of course, ways of breaking out of this isolation, but they are not literary ways and require the complete and thoroughgoing transformation of our economic and social system, and the invention of new forms of collective living. Our task – specialists that we are in the reflections of things – is a more patient and modest, more diagnostic one. Yet even in such a task as the analysis of literature and culture will come to nothing unless we keep the knowledge of our own historical situation vividly present to us: for we are, least of all, in our position, entitled to claim that we did not understand, that we thought all those things were real, that we had no way of knowing we were living in a cave.
>
> (Jameson, 1975: 187)

Becoming aware of the cave requires us to observe that Bourdieu's position on language as a system that is actively defined by socio-political processes is not necessarily dependent upon conceptions of socio-political space as comprising a set of simple autonomous and durable units. Habitus is a 'stable, tradition-bound social order in which power is fully naturalized and unquestionable' (Eagleton, 1991: 157) but it is also dynamic, and the keys to opening up its dynamism are the related concepts of 'doxa', 'heterodoxy' and 'orthodoxy'. According to Bourdieu, the properties of continuity that characterise the habitus are a function of the dialectic of subjective aspirations and objective structures. Arising from this are the practices of subjective agency that reflect the structuring dispositions of the objective system. When the two are perceived to be in total correspondence, whereby the sense of reality or of limits precludes the potential for other social possibilities, this condition or experience is termed 'doxa'. Such a condition in which the arbitrariness of society is wholly hidden from it by an overwhelming sense of its own naturalness is extreme. Bourdieu explains this in the following terms:

> Every established order tends to produce (to very different degrees and with very different means) the naturalization of its own arbitrariness. Of all the mechanisms tending to produce this effect, the most important and best concealed is undoubtedly the dialectic of the objective chances and the agents' aspirations, out of which arises

the *sense of limits*, commonly called the *sense of reality*, i.e. the correspondence between the objective classes and the internalized classes, social structures and mental structures, which is the basis of the most ineradicable adherence to the established order. Systems of classification which reproduce, in their own specific logic, the objective classes, i.e. their divisions by sex, age, or position in the relations of production, make their specific contribution to the reproduction of the power relations of which they are a product, by securing the misrecognition, and hence the recognition, of the arbitrariness on which they are based: in the extreme case, that is to say, when there is a quasi-perfect correspondence between the objective order and the subjective principles of organization (as in ancient societies) the natural and social world appear as self-evident. This experience we shall call *doxa*, so as to distinguish it from an orthodox or heterodox belief implying awareness and recognition of the possibility of different antagonistic beliefs.

(Bourdieu, 1977: 164)

Contestation, resistance and conflict serve a crucial function in revealing the condition of doxa. This is achieved through engagement in discourse. As Bourdieu (1977: 168) states, 'the truth of doxa is only ever fully revealed when negatively constituted by the constitution of a *field of opinion*, the locus of the confrontation of competing discourses'. In this sense, discourse may be regarded as the articulation of the potential for difference, and the critical boundary between Bourdieu's respective universes of doxa and discourse is in the imaginative interface of misrecognition and consciousness:

It can be seen that the boundary between the universe of (orthodox or heterodox) discourse and the universe of doxa, in the twofold sense of what goes without saying and what cannot be said for lack of an available discourse, represents the dividing-line between the most radical form of misrecognition and the awakening of political consciousness.

(Bourdieu, 1977: 170)

This boundary is subject to the dynamics of contestation, driven by the awareness of disjointedness and the possibilities of diverse action and language is central to this. As Bourdieu notes, the relationship between language and society is at its least ambiguous when the awareness of disjointedness is at its most pointed. Under these circumstances Bourdieu forsees the emergence of an 'extraordinary discourse' whereby language is revealed as ideology:

> The relationship between language and experience never appears more clearly than in crisis situations in which the everyday order (*Alltäglichkeit*) is challenged, and with it the language of order, situations which call for an extraordinary discourse (the *Ausseralltäglichkeit* which Weber presents as the decisive characteristic of charisma) capable of giving systematic expression to the gamut of extra-ordinary experiences that this, so to speak, objective *epoche* has provoked or made possible.
>
> (Bourdieu, 1977: 170)

Characterising language as ideology is an important feature of post-modernity. For some protagonists of postmodernism the notion of consciousness, as awakened political awareness, helps to explain the fragmentary nature of contemporary society and the resultant sense of isolation. According to Jameson (1991) the condition is defined by the linguistic fragmentation of social life to the point where the norm is eclipsed. This disintegration of dominant norms accounts for the social fragmentation which is inherent in the contemporary world, according to Jameson, and this crisis of language has a range of implications:

> The stupendous proliferation of social codes today into professional and disciplinary jargons, but also into the badges of affirmation of ethnic, gender, race, religious, and class-fraction adhesion, is also a political phenomenon, the problem of micropolitics, sufficiently demonstrates. If the ideas of a ruling class were once the dominant (or hegemonic) ideology of bourgeois society, the advanced capitalist countries today are now a field of stylistic and discursive heterogeneity without a norm. Faceless masters continue to inflect the economic strategies which constrain our existences, but no longer need to impose their speech (or are henceforth unable to); and the postliteracy of the late capital world reflects, not only the absence of any great collective project, but also the unavailability of the older national language itself.
>
> (Jameson, 1991: 201)

This can be couched in terms familiar to Bourdieu in that the erosion of the hegemony of a dominant group and the resultant contraction of the universe of doxa exposes the arbitrariness of society. In this new context power can no longer be legitimised and imposed through unspoken rules and symbolic violence. Instead, power is shown to be a construct that requires active as opposed to tacit endorsement. The contemporary contestation of hegemony that is a feature of postmodern societies and the resulting redefinition of the social specifics of cultural and symbolic capital will, of necessity, determine afresh the capital value of each language of the linguistically diverse city.

Eagleton suggests that postmodernism eschews claims to hegemonic values or to authoritative forms of discourse, those 'single frameworks, grand narratives or ultimate grounds of explanation'. However, it is important not to overstate the extent to which the postmodern condition gestures towards anarchy. Jameson, for example, offers an escape from total subjectivity through conceiving of postmodernism as culturally dominant. This perspective on the discourse of postmodernism argues for the necessity for a 'systematic cultural norm' while at the same time making accommodation for diversity. Thereby, postmodernity may be regarded as a prism for the rigorous contemplation of emergent 'radical cultural politics' and the contemporary socio-political trajectory in general:

> I have felt, however, that it was only in the light of some conception of a dominant cultural logic or hegemonic norm that genuine difference could be measured and assessed. I am very far from feeling that all cultural production today is 'postmodern' in the broad sense I will be conferring on this term. The postmodern however is the force field in which very different kinds of cultural impulses – what Raymond Williams has usefully termed 'residual' and 'emergent' forms of cultural reproduction – must make their way. If we do not achieve some general sense of a cultural dominant, then we all fall back into a view of present history as sheer heterogeneity, random difference, a coexistence of a host of forces whose effectivity is undecidable. This has been at any rate the political spirit in which the following analysis was devised: to project some conception of a new systemic cultural norm and its reproduction, in order to reflect more adequately on the most effective forms of any radical cultural politics today.
>
> (Jameson, 1991: 193)

In this way the postmodern condition is situated in the universe of discourse and heterodoxy. Its key features, comprising the awareness of structural crisis, the conscious knowledge of the manipulation of ritual and the realisation of the possibilities for the transgression of anachronistic norms are notions that are familiar to the work of Bourdieu. In this context, the potential for the radical transformation habitus, of the individual and the collective, may be regarded as being at its greatest. In periods of rupture, such as at present, the structural continuity of habitus is under challenge. With its erosion, or fracturing even, there exists the potential for the emergence of diverse structural dispositions and some of these will be contradictory. Under such material conditions, in which agency is differentially oriented in relation to the diversity of structural dispositions of a radical and contested present, it is transformation rather than continuity that is foregrounded. The implication for language is the reshaping of its relationship to the individual and society. This may mean that language contributes to the socio-political disorientation that is characteristic of this age – 'an exhilarated vision of ceaseless difference, mobility, disruption' (Eagleton, 1996: 3–4). Equally, it is in such contexts that DeBernardi asserts that language actively engages not with homology and autonomy but instead with heterogeneity and overlap: 'Language is profoundly social, and language use both constitutes shared worlds and realizes social diversity in practice' (DeBernardi, 1994: 883). In the urban context, the challenge to the structural continuity of the habitus and of the market by these postmodern shifts is very substantial. The contemporary interrogation of the city as polity by the various social, economic, cultural and political processes associated with globalisation underscores both the potential for and the momentum towards profound change. This points towards the emergence of a new set of structuring dispositions and of an alternative range of capital values; that is, the forging of novel perspectives, behaviours and practices in relation to language in the city.

Conclusions

A more comprehensive view of language in society is possible through what may be termed. This is a position that is characterised by a number of key features. These are as follows:

- Language carves reality into conceptual space. That is, it is neither simply a reflection of social reality nor is it the overwhelming determinant of world view. In this way, language and society are locked into a dialectic relationship whereby language may be understood to signify reality.

- Bourdieu's concepts of habitus, market and doxa are useful conceptual devices for understanding the organisation of society and the shaping of the individual as a member of society. In this context language is understood as a form of capital, the value of which relates to particular behaviours and practices to which the individual is predisposed by the conditions of society. His model is not necessarily statist but can be applied to various forms of polity, including the city.
- Language and power are interwoven *via* the polity. The contemporary city may be taken as an important point of reference. The substantive transformation of the city under the current form of globalisation – characterised by stretched social relations, the increasing interpenetration of local and global processes, the intensification of interactions and flows, and the development of a global, transational infrastructure – implies changes for language in relation to novel forms and modalities of citizenship, capital, labour, information exchange information and governance. The impact of this is, and will continue to be, uneven and unequal. The city is a key to understanding this uneven-ness and inequality through its openness (related to the connectedness and movement of people, capital and products), diversity (the co-presence of contrasting worlds in the city and physical proximity but social distance), and felt intensity (offering the potential for various forms of emancipation but suggestive of alienation and threat).
- The study of language in the city is both interlinguistic and intralinguistic. City life impacts upon language in both of these senses. The city 'causes' variation through the intimate juxtaposition of different worlds – people, cultures and languages. In the context of the possibility for social mobility between and through these different worlds that is inherent to the urban condition – crossing issues of gender, class, ethnicity and sexuality – language is not merely defining feature of such worlds in the city, but it is also a means of transcending them.

Several language combinations of languages AND cultures constitute code-switching in Reading.

#: Polish. Are there dialects? How do these mix with English & what attitudes do they attract? What's the impact on the Polish Community if there's one?

4
Language Planning

Introduction

One may be quite safe in assuming that the notion of language planning is familiar to most sociolinguists, but it is the certainly the case that it remains rather an alien concept to city and urban planners. Here, the roots and assumptions of the theory and practice of language planning are reviewed so as to engage explicitly with those outside of this sub-discipline who may be, quite reasonably, unfamiliar with it. Beyond that, a number of important models, developed by certain key thinkers in language planning, are critically introduced. This includes an examination of the model of ethnolinguistic vitality and a critique of a number of important aspects of the emerging field of study known as ecolinguistics. Some of the better known works in ecolinguistics (e.g. Fill, 1993; Fill & Mühlhäusler, 2001; Mühlhäusler, 1996, 2000 & 2001) are not taken to offer a useful model as this work is extremely limited in its engagement with the urban context as well as notions of power. Rather, it is necessary to expose language planning to assume the nation-state as the normative polity, the only political unit that provides an adequate basis for language planning and policy activity. This compares to the conceptual disjuncture that features in sociolinguistics where there is a failure to identify the problematic nature of the city as a site for the discipline. The assumption by language planning of the primacy of the nation-state leads to complications in developing our understanding of minority language situations (e.g. Wright, 2004), but is especially problematic in the urban context given the linguistic diversity which is characteristic of so many of the world's cities. By way of progressing the conceptual reach of language planning, critical ecolinguistics is postulated as a means of addressing the language in the city as a diverse, dynamic and competitive ecology. In more general terms, the city may be conceived of as a critical feature of the global linguistic ecology and as an important site for a wide range of practices in the area of language planning.

Defining language planning

Language planning describes the activity of the purposeful intervention in the place of language in society. The practice of language planning has a long pedigree (Wright, 2004: 1). It is possible, for example, to talk of language planning in relation to the Republic of Ireland in the first half of the 20th century, or France during the modern historical period, especially post-1789, or even the city-empires of the Classical Ancient and Medieval Europe. Language planning as a discrete discipline only emerges, however, during the course of the 1960s, as exemplified by the work of Haugen on language issues in Norway. Its emergence relates to the development of a particular view of language in society as a social construct, which may be subject to the manipulation of a wide range of actors. Baker and Jones contrast this position with a view of language change as an individualistic, *ad hoc* and rather chaotic phenomenon:

> Two opposing views may be held regarding change and development in language. The first view holds that language is an organism that gradually changes over time. A language evolves gradually as its speakers make unplanned and usually unconscious innovations. ... Language change may also be caused by external influence such as language contact where one language may borrow words and phrases from another. ... A second view is that language is a social institution and that the speakers of a language may wish to control and adapt their language for a variety of non-linguistic purposes: political, literary, economic, educational, religious, nationalistic, traditional or social purposes.
>
> (Baker & Jones, 1998: 2003)

Clearly, language planning is situated within the second view.

According to Haugen, language planning is 'the activity of preparing a normative orthography, grammar, and dictionary for the guidance of writers and speakers in a non-homogeneous speech community' (Haugen, 1959: 8). This early definition of the discipline is too narrow to describe adequately the nature and scope of language planning today. The discipline has, in theory and, moreover, in practice, grown in many directions since the pioneering work of Haugen. Some important thinkers within the discipline have sought to define language planning more fully. According to Kloss (1967 & 1977), language-planning activities comprise corpus planning and status planning. Corpus planning relates to the modification of language itself. This involves specifically codification, standardisation and elaboration (Haugen, 1983). Status planning relates to the modification of the environment in which a language is used. This is the allocation, including through legislation, of certain societal functions to certain languages. Cooper (1989: 45) has added to this the activity of acquisition planning. That is the range of actions, almost wholly undertaken in the sphere of education, relating to the acquisition of a certain language. According to Cooper (1989), language planning is not merely concerned with language issues understood as problems of communication, but instead it relates to a wide range of socio-political concerns, of which communication is but one. Indeed, nor is it the case that the goals of language planning are directly linguistic:

> It is hard to think of an instance in which language planning has been carried out solely for the sake of improving communication, where problems of communication are the only problems to be solved, or when the facilitation of communication is the only interest to be promoted. Language planning is typically carried out for the attainment of non-linguistic ends, such as consumer protection, scientific exchange, national integration, political control, economic development, the creation of new elites or the maintenance of old ones, the pacification or cooption of minority groups, and mass mobilisation of national or political movements.
>
> (Cooper, 1989: 34–5)

Whatever the goals, the object of the activity of language planning, its raw material, however, is language. Such purposeful intervention in the state of language is widely understood to encompass a few different types of activities. These are intervention with regard to the status of a language in society and intervention with regard to the linguistic condition of a tongue. These two forms of language planning activity are described as *status* and *corpus* planning and are defined by Wardhaugh in the following terms:

> Language planning is an attempt to interfere deliberately with a language or one of its varieties. That attempt may focus on either its

status with regard to some other language or variety or its internal condition with a view to changing that condition, or on both of these since they are not mutually exclusive. The first focus results in *status planning*; the second results in *corpus planning*. Status planning changes the function of a language or a variety of a language and the rights of those who use it. ... Corpus planning seeks to develop a variety of a language or a language, usually to standardize it, that is, to provide it with the means for serving every possible language function in society. Consequently, corpus planning may involve such matters as the development of an orthography, new sources of vocabulary, dictionaries, and a literature, and the deliberate cultivation of new uses so that the language may extend its use into such areas as government, education, and trade.

(Wardhaugh, 1992: 347)

Language planning is intended to bring about change in society and as such it is not merely purposeful but is, as Kaplan and Baldauf put it, 'future oriented':

Language planning is a body of ideas, laws and regulations (language policy), change rules, beliefs, and practices intended to achieve a planned change (or to stop change from happening) in the language use in one or more communities. To put it differently, language planning involves *deliberate*, although not always overt, *future oriented* change in systems of language code and/or speaking in a societal context. ... In the simplest sense, language planning is an attempt by someone to modify the linguistic behaviour of some community for some reason.

(Kaplan & Baldauf, 1997: 3)

It is this sense of the ambition of language planning as a practice that is profoundly related to the destiny of society that raises it to a level beyond value-free technocratic or bureaucratic agency. Language planning is an ideological exercise. Wright, following Halliday, responds to this notion that the meaning of society is at stake in language planning, thus:

Language planning is a highly complex set of activities involving the intersection of two very different and potentially conflicting themes: one that of 'meaning' common to all our activities with language, and other semiotics as well; the other theme that of 'design'. If we start from the broad distinction between designed systems and evolved systems, then language planning means introducing design processes and design features into a system (namely language) which is naturally evolving.

(Wright, 2004: 1)

Wright concludes, therefore, that the boundaries of the discipline of language planning are difficult, if not impossible, to define (Wright, 2004: 2). Cooper too takes the view that language planning is so profoundly embedded in society that it is difficult to think of any aspect of society upon which it does not impact, for example:

[n]ot only because it is directed toward so many different status, corpus and acquisition goals, but more fundamentally because it is a tool in the service of so many different latent goals, such as economic modernisation, national integration, national liberation, imperial hegemony, racial, sexual and economic equality, the maintenance of elites and their replacement by new elites.

(Cooper, 1989: 182)

This is, of course, the condition of all ideologised activities in theory – when the fundamentals of society are at stake there are no boundaries.

When viewed as practice the limits of language planning are clearer. For example, according to Cooper, language planning comprises 'deliberate efforts to influence the behaviour of others with respect to the acquisition, structure and functional allocation of their language codes' (Cooper, 1989: 45). To this extent Cooper (1989: 31 & 98) formulated a question that is used by many when interrogating the nature and scope and any particular language planning action and still used by many working in the area: *Who* plans *what* for *whom* and *how?*' ... *What actors attempt to influence what behaviours, of which people, for what ends, under what conditions by what means, through what policy-making processes and with what effect?*

Until relatively recently the question of 'who' was invariably answered with 'the government'. Take this assertion from Weinstein, for example: 'Language planning is a government authorized, longterm, sustained, and conscious effort to alter a language's function in a society for the purpose of solving communication problems' (Weinstein, 1990: 56). Also, until recently, language planning has almost exclusively been an activity associated with the nation-state in the eyes of most sociolinguistics and language planners: 'Language planning has become part of modern nation-building because a noticeable trend in the modern world is to make language and nation synonymous' (Wardhaugh, 1992: 346). The role of other agents is increasingly being recognised in the literature, as noted by Kaplan and Baldauf, for example:

> The language planning that one hears most about is that undertaken by government and it is intended to solve complex social problems, but there is a great deal of language planning that occurs in other societal contexts at more modest levels for other purposes.
>
> (Kaplan & Baldauf, 1997: 3)

The notion of 'micro language planning', for example, is beginning to receive some attention in the literature (e.g. Mac Giolla Chríost, 2001; Liddicoat, forthcoming). Kaplan and Baldauf also bring to our attention the fact that language planning activities also occur in contexts other than the nation-state and have impacts beyond the nation-state, for example:

> Language planning must recognise ... that language modification may not be susceptible to containment within a particular nation-state or other entity that may be isolated for the purposes of discussion but which in truth always remains embedded in a larger context ... Rather, the language plan may cause a ripple effect in proximate communities, nation-states, across a region (or in other smaller or larger entities).
>
> (Kaplan & Baldauf, 1997: 269)

Indeed, it is the case that there is an emerging literature on language planning of a transnational nature, focussed on the European Union (e.g. Creech, 2005; O'Reilly, 2001; Van Els, 2006). That said, it remains the case that the basic assumption is that the principal agent in language planning is the government, in particular the central government of the nation-state. This is reflected in the range of illustrative cases of the ecosystem model of language planning offered by Kaplan and Baldauf – they are all nation-states: Australia, Malaysia, Mexico, South Africa, Sweden, United States (Kaplan & Baldauf, 1997: 313–18). The text also includes an appendix describing 'language planning in national contexts' (Kaplan & Baldauf, 1997: 324–40). Language planning has been subject to other criticisms. The principal concerns have been identified by Fishman (1994: 91). They are that language planning

- is conducted by elites that are governed by their own self-interest;
- reproduces rather than overcomes sociocultural and ecotechnical inequalities;

- inhibits or counteracts multiculturalism; and
- espouses world-wide westernisation and modernisation leading to new sociocultural, ecotechnical and conceptual colonisation.

Fishman recognises that there is a significant gap between theory and practice, accepting that some of the criticism may hold for language planning theory but not practice. Some of these deficiencies arise, in part, from a confusion in some of literature between language planning and language policy. Calvet (e.g. 2002) suggests avoiding differentiating between the two at all and advocates the use of the term 'interventions sur les situations langières' [interventions in language situations]. It is contended here, however, that it is in fact valuable to differentiate between planning and policy as, while they are related activities, they are nonetheless quite discrete areas of action, often pertaining to very different actors, and with contrasting engagement with power and ideology. Some see policy everywhere: '[N]o societies exist without a language policy, although many policies exist implicitly and in the absence of planning' (Eastman, 1983: 6). But, this position is probably better understood as comprising a set of attitudes and values or as the culture that defines the institutions of society. According to Kaplan and Baldauf, following Chaudensen, language policy:

> Specifies the overall national choice in some matter of language or of language cultivation ... Language policy defines general long-term objectives (i.e. educational levels, formations, uses, functions, and language statutes) and which are based on as precise and complete an analysis of the initial problem as possible.
>
> (Kaplan & Baldauf, 1997: 206–7)

While reasonable in theory, this appears to be rather optimistic in practice as policy is often imprecise, very often not long-term, nor based upon the rational and value-free analyses of language problems. As G. Williams notes, language policy is value-laden and ideological:

> Language planning emerged side by side with the theory of modernisation which not only was closely integrated with a specific theoretical perspective – structural foundational – but also involved a specific conception of the world. This world view involved dividing states into the modern and the traditional.
>
> (G. Williams, 1992: 124)

It would appear that language policy, as opposed to language planning, is best defined in the following terms. Language policy is expressly related to the mission or vision of an organisation – it is aspirational, an aim, a statement of intent; it is determined by actors empowered at the highest levels of the organisation; it relates to the acquisition, operations and maintenance of power. The content of policy is immediately informed by the imperatives of the empowered actors, and these actors are shaped by the set of attitudes, values and culture of the organisation. Also, defining the nature of the language problem and the nature of the policy response to it is therefore as act of politics and is value-laden and ideological. The shelf life of policy is determined by the timetable of power election and re-election – therefore, in democratic societies, the lifespan of any given policy is usually around 4–5 years. Understood in these terms, language policy is, at best, a medium-term position. Language policy is defined more closely again by other commentators either according to the types of actors engaged with the policy process (Pueyo & Turull, 2003) or according to the aims of the policy or specific types of policy (Leclerc, 2001). These approaches are useful in that they allow for description of policy with regard to theory and practice while maintaining the discrete identity of the activity. The range of actors, divided between two spheres – the public and the private, is extensive (Table 4.1). Although it could be argued that it does not adequately identify community-based or voluntary organisations, including language issue ginger groups, lobby groups or protest movements.

Table 4.1 Language policy according to actors (adapted from Pueyo & Turull, 2003 and Puigdevall i Serralvo, 2006)

Sphere	Actor level	Examples
Public	1. Supra-national or inter-national level	1. EU, UN
	2. State or national level	2. Nation-state
	3. Sub-state or regional level	3. Devolved government, local government
	4. Para-public	4. Statutory publicly funded education
Private	1. Business	1. Bank, shop
	2. Associations, NGOs	2. Trades' union, chamber of commerce, consumer council

Table 4.2 Language policy according to objectives (adapted from Leclerc, 2001 and Puigdevall i Serralvo, 2006)

Type of policys	Description
Assimilation	Consists of adopting measures, often planned, in order to reduce the numbers of speakers of minority languages
Non-intervention	A 'laisser-faire' approach that favours the *status quo* and dominant languages. Legitimised in terms of individual freedom, choice and respect for diversity
Valorisation	Policy in favour of promotion of a single official language throughout society. Some limited rights may be given to minority languages or speakers of minority languages
Sectorial	Policy that adopts *ad hoc* restricted legislative measures regarding the use of sanctioned languages in certain domains
Differentiated legal statute	Comprehensive but unequal accommodation of linguistic diversity, granting full range of rights to dominant language or speakers but restricted rights to minority language or speakers
Bilingualism or trilingualism	Recognition of 2 or 3 languages on the basis of equality. Rights may be granted to languages or speakers and may also be determined according to a discrete linguistic territory defined by statute
Multilingualism	Policy that accommodates, whether *de jure* or *de facto*, a range of languages across the full range of possible language domains or sectors
Internationalism	The promotion of a language by a polity beyond its own borders
Mixed	The simultaneous practice of different types of policies

Defining language policy according to aims or specific types of policy allows one to easily conceive of individual policies in terms of particular ideological positions – whether implicit or explicit (Table 4.2).

It can be concluded, therefore, that language planning, in contrast to language policy, is the activity by which policy is implemented, or indeed resisted. But, both language planning and language policy are deeply implicated in society. To paraphrase Bourdieu (1977), language is not merely a means of communication but is an instrument of action and power and, as such, language planning and language policy are bound up in relationships that are profoundly shaped by ideological concerns with the nature of society and its organisation. At this point, a brief analysis of the main models of language in society that inform language planning and policy activities is necessary in order to identify the extent to which they can be applied effectively to the linguistic diversity in the city.

Ethnolinguistic vitality

The ethnolinguistic vitality model of language in society is probably more widely used as a point of reference in the area of language planning and policy than any other model. The brief, analytical description offered here is drawn from two sources (Mac Giolla Chríost, 2003 & 2005). According to this model, the focal point for developing an understanding of language in society is the group defined in terms of ethnicity and language together. The authors of the model (Giles, Bourhis & Taylor, 1977) are of the view that the vitality of an ethnolinguistic group is that which makes a group likely to behave as a distinctive and active collective entity in inter-group situations and that the potential for the continuity for the given language of the group is dependent upon that. A number of factors are held to determine the vitality of a given language community or ethnolinguistic group. Three broad categories of variables are identified as status, demography and institutional support and each of these comprise further subdivisions (Figure 4.1). The three broad categories can be described in the following general terms. The first broad category, status, comprises what Giles *et al.* describe as the prestige variables. The more prestige an ethnolinguistic group possesses the more vital it is as a collective entity. Status is subdivided into a number of more specific variables. They are economic status, social status, socio-historical status and language status, both within and without. Economic status is

Ethnolinguistic Vitality		
Status	**Demography**	**Institutional support**
Economic	Distribution	Formal
Social		
Socio-historical	*National territory*	*Mass media*
Language – within/without	*Concentration*	*Education*
	Proportion	*Government Services*
	Numbers	Informal
	Absolute birth-rate	*Industry*
	Mixed marriage	*Religion*
	Immigration	*Culture*
	Migration	

Figure 4.1 Model of ethnolinguistic vitality (adapted from Giles *et al.*, 1977)

the extent to which a language community has access to and control over the material resources of the given geo-political unit(s) with which they are associated. That is to say, it refers to the degree of control the group has over its own economic destiny as relates to the economics of the nation-state, region and locality. Social status refers to the value the language community gives to itself; it is the level of contemporaneous self-esteem possessed by the group. Socio-historical status is regarded as a significant variable as ethnolinguistic groups are distinguished by their different histories and their specific sense of their relationship with the past. The historical past as it is seen to relate to the group can be drawn upon in order to effect the socio-political mobilisation of the group for various strategic purposes. It is underscored that it is not the actual historical past that is crucial in this context but rather the meaning of that is ascribed to the past by the group and the animators of the desired mobilisation of the group. It may well be the case that the group regards there to be few such symbolic, historical events with the potential for their mobilisation or some events may even be considered to have the effect of de-mobilisation. Language status is the esteem specifically afforded to the given language of the group. This esteem is variously ascribed from both within and without the language group. For ethnolinguistic groups that are minorities within their given state and whose language is deemed as having less value than that of the ethnolinguistic group that constitute the societal majority will, as a result, be less vital as a group. Conversely, a minority group whose language is regarded as being more prestigious than that of a majority group is, by definition, a more vital collective entity.

The second broad category, demography, constitutes two main variables – numbers and distribution. Demographic trends are understood to contribute to the vitality of an ethnolinguistic group as a collective entity in various ways. The two main variables are each subdivided into a range of other factors. Distribution encompasses national territory, concentration and proportion. According to the model, the relationship between an ethnolinguistic group and an identified national territory is a significant factor with regard to the vitality of the group. The possession of the idea of a national territory or an ancestral homeland or, even better, the actual possession and residence in such a territory by the ethnolinguistic group is held to be a crucial element of vitality. Groups which are divided by borders or which have been dispossessed of their traditional homeland are likely, it is argued, to be less successful in maintaining their collective vitality than those groups which have retained possession of their homeland. According to the model, immigrant ethnolinguistic minority groups tend to more ready to assimilate, or to be more susceptible to assimilation, than are indigenous ethnolinguistic minority groups that continue to reside in what they regard as their ancestral homeland. Concentration is regarded as a significant factor in relation to ethnolinguistic vitality. A diffuse geographical distribution is seen to be inimical to group vitality, whereas the concentration of numbers is regarded as contributing to the vitality of the group through enabling frequent interaction between group members while, at the same time, engendering feelings of group identity. The matter of proportion is deemed important as the relative proportions of in-group and out-group speakers will effect the dynamics and the nature of inter-group relations.

The other main variable within the broad category of demography is numbers. This variable includes four specific factors, namely absolute birth rate, mixed marriage, immigration and migration. Numbers and ethnolinguistic vitality can be seen to relate in a very crude and straightforward manner. Put simply, higher absolute numbers will make an ethnolinguistic group more vital while, on the other hand, it may well be that case that there exists a minimum threshold of numbers beyond which the prospects for the survival of an ethnolinguistic group are deemed to be very bleak indeed. Birth rate is an important factor in relative terms. A higher or lower birth rate in relation to the out-group can be a factor in determining the likely trajectory of the ethnolinguistic vitality. Clearly, the higher the relative birth rate, the greater the levels of vitality of the ethnolinguistic group. Mixed marriage between in-group and out-group members is an important factor in this model as, it is argued, it often results in one of the languages being displaced from the domain of home. Generally, according to the model, the higher status language will displace the lower status language as the language of the home. Immigration is a factor which can either enhance or decrease the vitality of an ethnolinguistic group. For example, immigrants may assimilate into the ethnolinguistic group, acquire its language and use it as the means of communication between them. On the other hand, immigrants, when geographically juxtaposed with a subordinate ethnolinguistic group, could opt not to assimilate to that group and instead acquire the cultural attributes of the dominant ethnolinguistic group within that society as a whole. Under such circumstance the effect upon the vitality of the subordinate ethnolinguistic group is wholly detrimental. The fourth factor with regard to numbers is that of migration. According to the model, this is largely economic and means the departure of the younger and often more able members of the ethnolinguistic group and,

almost inevitably, their subsequent assimilation into another ethnolinguistic group, often proximate as well as dominant. This variable might
also include forced migration or depopulation or genocide.

The third broad category pertaining to the model of ethnolinguistic
vitality is that of institutional support. This relates to the representation
of the ethnolinguistic group and its values or cultural attributes in the
various institutions of the nation-state, region and locality associated
with the group. Ethnolinguistic vitality relates, in this context, to language use in the various institutional domains related to government,
organised religion, business etc. Institutional support comprises two sets
of variables that are characterised as formal and informal. Informal support is defined as the degree to which an ethnolinguistic group has
organised itself to promote its self-interest. Such organisational activity
could include lobby groups, ginger groups, pressure groups and similar
movements in support of the interests of the group. According to the
model, the greater the volume, quality and level of organisation, the
more vital the ethnolinguistic group is. Formal support is regarded as
the degree of representation a group enjoys at the decision-making levels of the various domains, social, economic and political, of the state
and its various institutional and policy apparatus. Crucial domains for
ethnolinguistic vitality include in particular the mass media, education,
government departments and services, state supported arts, the security
services and the armed forces. Other important domains are industry,
organised religion and the workplace in both the public and the private
sector. The authors offer a few significant caveats to their model. Firstly,
the potential impact of macro-level factors, such as processes of modernisation, industrialisation and economic depression, is alluded by
Giles *et al.* (1977: 316–7) but are not regarded as being wholly central to
its application. Also, they suggest that an ethnolinguistic group's subjective perception of its own vitality may well be just as important with
regard to the continuity of the group and its ethnocultural attributes as
would any objective assessment of the actual ethnolinguistic vitality of
the group as might be achieved through the scientific application of the
model (Giles *et al.*, 1977: 318).

Language in a network of ecological relations

A major critic of the model of ethnolinguistic vitality is Haarmann
(1986). As with the analytical description of the model of ethnolinguistic vitality, this concise overview is drawn from two sources (Mac Giolla

Chríost, 2003 & 2005). Haarmann's main criticism of the model of ethnolinguistic vitality is that it fails to detail specific language relations. As a result, while the model may be effective for theorising language-related factors at macro levels, Haarmann argues that it is inadequate for this purpose at micro levels. Instead, he contends that an adequate theory of language ecology must take into account the full range of possible variables, both general and specific, which either directly or indirectly affect language structure, choice and behaviour (Haarmann, 1986: 9–10). It is his view, therefore, that the range of factors affecting ethnolinguistic vitality as devised by Giles *et al.* is a partial inventory. He argues that only by adopting an ecological approach to language is a holistic view of language–society relations possible. Thus, he states that 'Language ecology should cover the whole network of social relations which control the variability of languages and their modal speakers' behaviour' (Haarmann, 1986: 3). However, while Haarmann differs from Giles *et al.* on the matter of the impact of external and environmental factors on the language community, he too asserts the centrality of ethnicity to understanding language in society. For example:

> Following the basic assumption that the interaction between ethnic groups is the result of environmental factors influencing their members, phenomena have to be analyzed in terms of ecological relations. The ethnic identity of any ethnic group comprises elements which are the reflection of a sum of experiences in the group's ecological settings.
>
> (Haarmann, 1986: 1)

The centrality to Haarmann's model of the ethnic group as a key point of reference and the definitive collectivity for understanding language in society as a network of ecological relations system is reinforced elsewhere (Haarmann, 1986: 25–31). It is to Haarmann the 'central point' and the 'focus' of his model. Unfortunately, however, he does not engage in defining the term 'ethnicity' for the benefit of better understanding its operation in the model. Rather, the term ethnic group appears to be taken as a discrete and unproblematic concept as appears to be the case also with Giles *et al.* in relation to their model. None the less, Haarmann continues to offer some important correctives to the ethnolinguistic vitality model and, using the work of Haugen (1972) as an important point of departure, he enunciates a number of valuable points of principle with regard to the further development of ecological perspectives on language.

According to Haarmann, an ecological perspective on language is achieved through the application of the principles of ecology to the study of language (Haarmann, 1986: 3). His model, termed 'language in ethnicity' – a view of basic ecological relations, is the result of this and it merits description in some detail so as to understand how the model functions. Haarmann puts forward a basic set of relations as 'the most comprehensive as a general framework for an ecological system' (Haarmann, 1986: 4–5), that is: INDIVIDUAL – GROUP – SOCIETY – STATE. According to Haarmann, this framework, which he also describes as a 'string of concepts', comprises a hierarchical structure, beginning with the most specific (individual) and culminating in the most general (state). Haarmann's definitions of society, on the one hand, and state, on the other, require closer examination in order that their respective places in this hierarchical string of concepts is clear. Society is defined by Haarmann (1986: 5) as the 'most complex organization of social groups'. He considers it to be subordinate to the state due to the 'political implications of state organization' (Haarmann, 1986: 5) whereby, he asserts, society cannot exist without the leadership of the state but that the state can exist without the support of society. The conceptual hierarchy is thereby formulated in relation to language as follows:

> Language ecology is primarily concerned with language in its fundamental forms of existence which correspond to the different levels in the above string of concepts: language behaviour of the individual speaker, the role of language in group relations, the functional range of language(s) in a given society, and language politics in a given state.
>
> (Haarmann, 1986: 6)

Thus, language for the individual relates to specific language behaviours, for the group it relates to inter-group relations, for society it relates to defined functions and for the state it relates to politics. On the basis of this framework, Haarmann proposes an inventory of variables for the analysis of language from an ecological perspective. He emphasises, however, that the focal point of the inventory is the ethnic group. To attempt to devise a model from the perspective of the individual speaker, Haarmann believes, would be enormously complex and would necessitate the construction of a model that would be bewildering in its complication (Haarmann, 1986: 6).

The inventory of basic ecological variables is extensive and comprises seven categories. These are defined by Haarmann (1986: 7–9) as follows:

- The ethnodemographic range of ecological functions is the general demographic factors that are of importance to the evolution of communities in general.
- The ethnosociological range comprises the social conditions affecting the ethnic group in contact settings.
- The ethnopolitical range of ecological functions comprises those variables that influence relations between the social structure of the ethnic group and the political structures of state.
- The ethnocultural range of ecological functions is based upon the identified cultural traditions and behavioural norms specific to and distinctive of the ethnic group.
- The ethnopsychological range of ecological functions is the set of attitudes relating to group solidarity that function as control mechanisms in relation to both intra-group and inter-group communication.
- The interactional range of ecological functions comprises the variables relating to interaction in the speech community.
- The ethnolinguistic range of ecological functions comprises the variables that are directly related to the language of the ethnic group.

The detailed inventory of the variables that constitute the different categories or ranges devised by Haarmann (1986: 11–16) offers further explanation of the implications of these various categories and their specific variables. It is presented here at some length:

I. *Ethnodemographic variables*
   (i) The size of an ethnic group (number of members in a community) (ii) The polarity between focused and dispersed population in ethnic groups concentration versus dispersion as features of a settlement. (iii) The polarity between ethnic homogeneity and heterogeneity in the area of an ethnic group's settlement (monoethnic versus polyethnic area of settlement. (iv) The polarity between urban and rural settlements within an ethnic group. (v) The polarity between static settlement and migration movement in an ethnic group.

II. *Ethnosociological variables*
   (i) The polarity between stability and dynamic change in the ethnic profile of areas of settlement. (ii) The distribution of the population in an ethnic group by sex. (iii) Age–group distinctions as an

ecological variable influencing language choice and speech behaviour. (iv) The specifics of social stratification in an ethnic group. (v) The specifics of family relations in the social structures of an ethnic group.

III. *Ethnopolitical variables*

(i) The ethnos–state relation. (ii) The speaker–language–state relation (group-and non-group related bilingualism). (iii) The institutional status of a community's language (cf., categorisations like the language of the state, official language, language for administrative usage etc.). (iv) The reproduction potential of a community's language (referring to its special status as a medium for instruction or as a subject at school). (v) The characteristics of the division of labour (hierarchical versus segmented division of labour in the relations of an ethnic group with other ethnic communities in a state).

IV. *Ethnocultural variables*

(i) Ancestry (descent) as a criterion of group solidarity. (ii) The polarity between ethnocultural patterns and social distance in interethnic relations. (iii) The relevance of cultural and/or political organisations for the promotion of a community's interests. (iv) The relevance of the language's *ausbau* status. (v) The specifics of the language's sociocultural potential.

V. *Ethnopyschological variables*

(i) The relevance of enculturation for ethnic identification. (ii) The relevance of self-categorisation (self-identification) among the members of a community. (iii) The relevance of and ways of categorising other ethnic groups among the members of a community. (iv) Language maintenance as a measure of ethnic identity. (v) The attitude of the members in a community towards interaction with members of contacting ethnic groups (inclination towards interethnic communication versus rejection of contact).

VI. *Interactional variables*

(i) The relevance of communicational mobility in a language community (low-level mobility of monolingual speakers versus high-level mobility of multi-lingual speakers in a community). (ii) Interactional determination in the use of communicational means (cf., language varieties in diglossic and polyglossic settings). (iii) The relevance of intra- and interethnic role relations for interaction. (iv) The degree of routine interaction with members of other ethnic groups (degree of familiarity with interethnic communication among members of a community). (v) The degree of publicity

(publicness) of speech settings. (vi) The relevance of topic for intra-
and inter-group interaction (with topics ranging from general
political to special private subjects).
VII. Ethnolinguistic variables
  (i) The relevance of linguistic distance between contact languages
  (problem of contacting languages with different degrees of linguistic distance/*abstand*). (ii) The relevance of ethnically specific
  pragmatic strategies of verbal interaction. (iii) The role of grammatical determinism within the framework of deictic categories
  (specifics in the system of deictic categories and their usage in
  contacting languages). (iv) The characteristics of language contacts with respect to the sociocultural status of the contacting
  languages (sociocultural categorisation of language contacts).

The various ecological functions are understood by Haarmann to be
interdependent and in this regard the ethnopyschological variables play
a crucial role in inter-group relations in the operation of the model.
These variables act as a set of filters that shape the nature of interaction
between groups. Also, these filters relate to the ways in which the group
views not only its own ethnicity but, in addition, the ethnic identity of
contact groups. Haarmann considers (1986: 26) that it is only possible
to perceive these factors and their influence indirectly. According to
Haarmann (1986: 28), the interactional variables also possess filter type
properties but, in this case, they relate in a more general fashion to a
number of the categories of ecological functions other than the interactional range. They are the ethnodemographic, ethnosociological, ethnocultural and ethnolinguistic categories (enumerated above as I, II, IV
and VII). While one notes that Haarmann asserts that 'there is a close
interdependence between all ecological ranges and that no range dom-
inates the others (1986: 9), it appears that the ethnopolitical range does
possess a certain overarching quality. The necessary qualification is
made by Haarmann by way of explanation of the role of ethnopolitical
factors in the model:

> The functional range of ethnopolitical factors is best understood as
> an embracing category comprising all other functional ranges. This
> indication of an outer framework of ecological relations implies that
> political factors influencing the behaviour of ethnic groups form a
> general background for all other societal and intergroup relations ...
> As all social conditions of ethnic groups are bound to the political
> organization of the society in a given state, the components of

the political systems must be indicated separately. It is assumed that the effect of ethnodemographic, ethnocultural or other factors on the behaviour of reference and contact groups can only be represented in an overall ecological system when these have been integrated into the general framework of a society's political foundation (or organization).

(Haarmann, 1986: 28)

This, therefore, is the model that for Haarmann (1986: 29) is unique in integrating the shaping of communicational systems and the verbal interaction of ethnic groups asserts and in allowing for the comprehensive viewing of language in social context, incorporating micro- and macro-level factors as well as accounting for language specific relations.

Linguistic ecosystem

Another influential model broadly situated within ecolinguistics is that proposed by Kaplan and Baldauf (1997). The basic assumptions behind this model, according to Kaplan and Baldauf (1997: 269–95), are intended to challenge the dominant position within language planning that is concerned with the modification of one language. They reject the formula one nation = one state = one language and instead argue that the total ecology of the linguistic environment means that 'planning activity can not be limited to one language; it will affect all the languages in the environment. Each language has its own ecology of support and relationships to other languages' (Kaplan & Baldauf, 1997: 271). They use the case of Québec as an exemplar and offer the idealised schematic below (Figure 4.2). Each circle represents a different language, and the size of the circle represents the relative size of the population of speakers of that language. The arrowed circles on the model are indicative of the direction of change in relation to the dominant language. The polity illustrated comprises a single national and official language, a language other than the national and official one that is dominant in the field of religion, and eight minority languages – one of which may be a non-standard or dialect form of the national and official language. The schematic also includes a proximate language belonging to a neighbouring polity but having an impact on the polity. The language planning arrow to the right of the model shows how 'everything in the environment will be affected by some degree by the language planning effort' (Kaplan & Baldauf, 1997: 271).

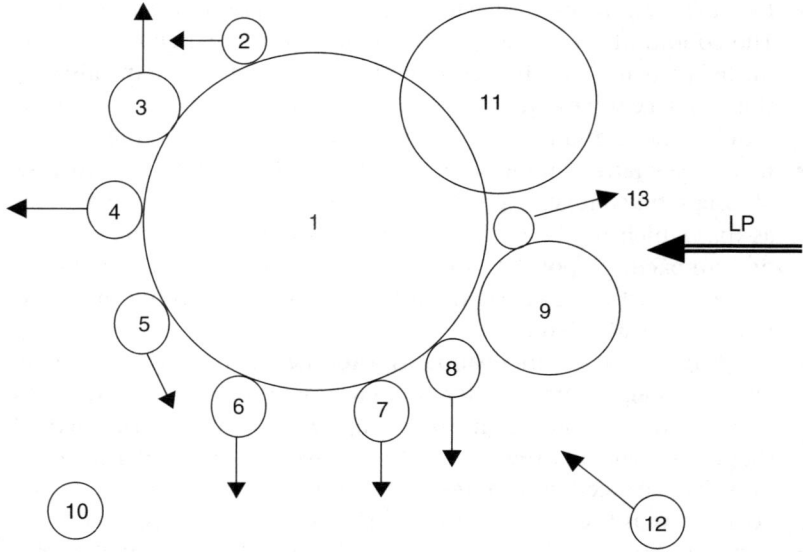

1. National / official language
2. Minority language
3. Minority language
4. Minority language
5. Minority language
6. Minority language
7. Minority language
8. Minority language
9. Neighbouring language (another policy)
10. Classical / historial languages
11. Religious language
12. Language revival in progress
13. Minority language

Language planning
effort

Figure 4.2 A schematic view of a national language planning situation (reproduced from Kaplan & Baldauf, 1997)

They identify a number of language variables as follows (Kaplan & Baldauf, 1997: 271–89):

• Language death – understood as occurring when a language has no viable function. This can result from the introduction of another language whether subtly or through force, or the actual disappearance of the population that speak a particular language.

- Language survival – understood as the opposite of language death. The conditions of language survival are that the language be transmitted by parents to their children (inter-generational transmission), the language serves important communicative functions in the community, the community of speakers is vibrant, stable or increasing.
- Language change – understood as either codified, linguistic processes of long-term change, or change as the result of language contact such as that which results from the introduction of new technology not only impacting upon lexicon but, because of new other values and societal structures associated with new technology, other more profound linguistic changes.
- Language revival – understood as a reversal of processes associated with language death. Relates to educational, economic and ethnic revival. Notes problematic that language revival is 'past-oriented' (Kaplan & Baldauf, 1997: 282), thus is likely to be undermined by unrealistic expectations of restoring a mythical *status quo* unless it is accepted that the revived language is substantially transformed.
- Language shift and language spread – informed by Fishman's (1991) seminal text on reversing language shift, wherein it is defined as 'speech communities whose native languages are threatened because their inter-generational continuity is progressing negatively, with fewer and fewer users (speakers, readers, writers and even understanders) or users every generation' (Fishman, 1991: 1). But Kaplan and Baldauf note that the shift is not necessarily threatening to language. Shift from one language to another occurs as result of development of more favourable attitude to other language, coincided with shift in political and social environments. Shift may also be driven from 'underground', that is from the margins of society. Language spread is understood as a more active notion of language shift. Informed by Cooper who defines it as 'an increase over time, in the proportions of a communicative network that adopts a given language or language variety for a given communicative function' (Cooper, 1982: 6).
- Language amalgamation – understood as 'the folding together of two independent language systems' (Kaplan & Baldauf, 1997: 285). This usually occurs over very long timescale and gives rise to a completely new language.
- Language contact and pidgin and creole development – a pidgin is understood as a reduced form of language, occurring when two mutually unintelligible languages come into sustained contact. When a pidgin begins to develop it may give rise to a creole. A creole ultimately tends towards the dominant language.

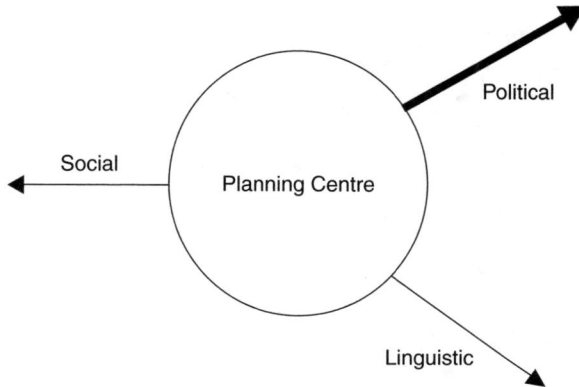

Figure 4.3 The pull of political, linguistic and social forces on language planning (reproduced from Kaplan & Baldauf, 1997)

- Literacy development – understood as a form of language modification that, in contrast to the above which are largely concerned with oral forms of language (Kaplan & Baldauf, 1997: 288), relates to the written form of language in all its guises.

They illustrate in their model the impact of a variety of forces upon language, language planning and language policy (Kaplan & Baldauf, 1997: 296–323 & 311–23). This includes recognition of the fact that the language planning process may be subject to conflicting interests, pulling in different directions (Figure 4.3). It is the function of language planning to bring a degree of coherence and co-ordination to this condition, involving negotiation, consensus building and compromise. They also recognise that a range of forces operate upon language planning activity. The model (Figure 4.4) shows these at work. In the figure the largest circle represents the linguistic ecosystem of the polity in which the language planning activity is taking place. Within this circle is a number of other circles, each representing different languages, including the national and official language. Circle 6 represents a minority language that is at a grave risk of disappearing. The items listed along the left-hand axis are the various forces that impact upon the ecosystem while the items listed along the bottom axis are the groups or actors that may play a role in language planning activity. The degree of influence exercised by any of these groups or actors varies from situation to situation, suffice to say that they are cross-cut by unequal and uneven relationships of power. This also varies with time, a point they illustrate in relation to the city-state of Singapore (Figure 4.5). In this case, the circle representing English

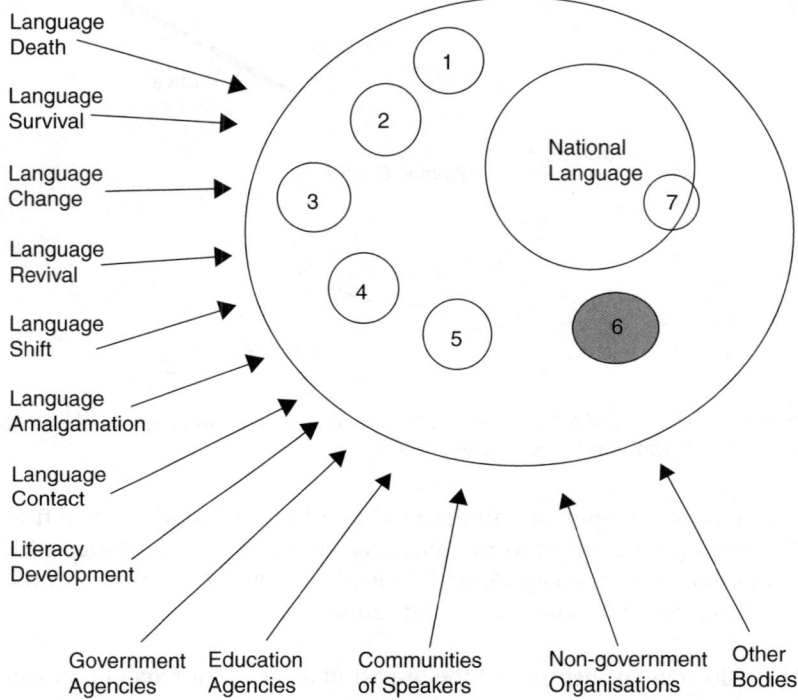

Figure 4.4 Forces at work in a linguistic ecosystem (reproduced from Kaplan & Baldauf, 1997)

increases throughout the period from 1960 to 1990, while Mandarin jumps exponentially around 1980, subsequent to the 'Speak Mandarin' campaign. The circles representing the other, local and indigenous, languages – including Malay, Hakka and Cantonese – show progressive contraction in this period. Kaplan and Baldauf note (1997: 312) that these 'forces at work' in the linguistic ecosystem are related to the ecolinguistic variables identified by Haarmann (1986), as discussed above.

They note a further, final complexity. Linguistic ecosystems are not wholly discrete, but rather proximate linguistic ecosystems will impact upon one another. Language planning activity must account for this impact (Kaplan & Baldauf, 1997: 319–20). According to their model, political boundaries do not necessarily coincide with those of linguistic ecosystems and, moreover, the same languages will often be present in proximate ecologies but take a very different shape. For example, in the illustration (Figure 4.6), two languages are represented as minority

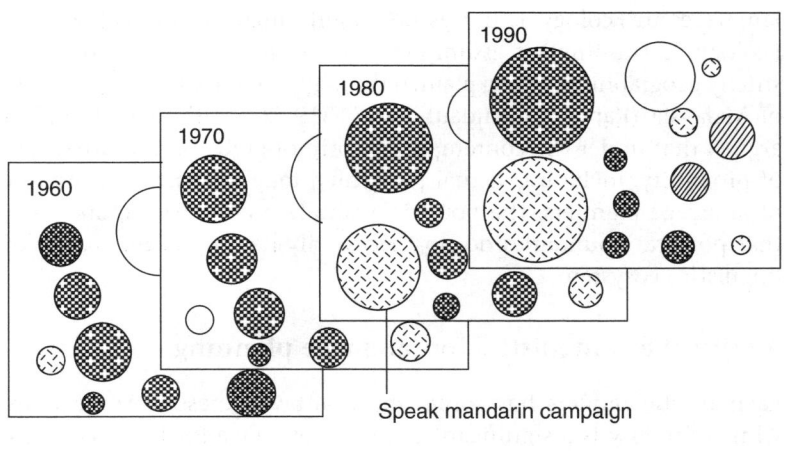

Figure 4.5 Effect of time on a linguistic ecosystem (reproduced from Kaplan & Baldauf, 1997)

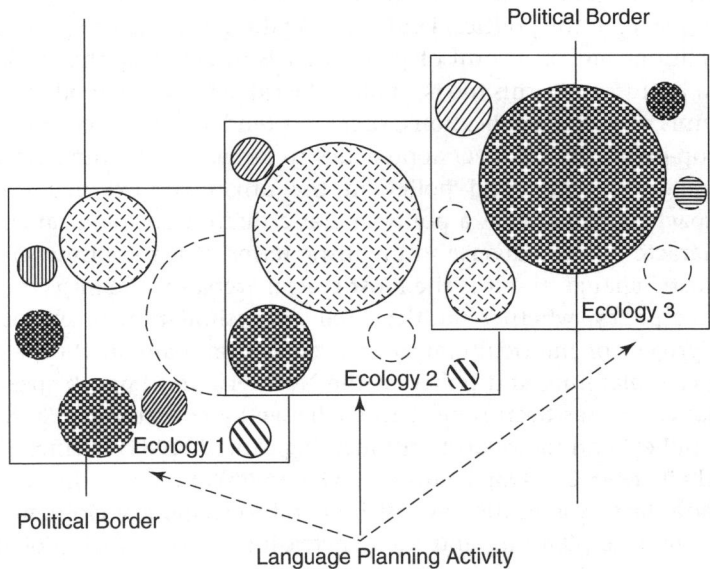

Figure 4.6 Effect of an ecological perspective on a language planning activity (reproduced from Kaplan & Baldauf, 1997)

languages in Ecology 1, but as dominant languages in Ecology 2 and Ecology 3. The implicit assumption in the model is that proximity is strictly geographical. It is explained through reference to the nation-state of Malaysia (Kaplan & Baldauf, 1997: 319–20). Although it could be argued that under the contemporary form of globalisation other forms of proximity, including virtual proximity, may be worth the attention of language planners, the point is a simple one, however, and that is that political boundaries do not necessarily determine the extent of a linguistic ecosystem.

A critical ecolinguistics for language planning

Each of the models has some important weaknesses. For example, while ethnicity is a significant point of reference for Haarmann, as it is with Giles *et al.*, the term is not subjected to critical examination. Indeed, implicit to the models is an essentialist and deterministic position on the cultural attributes of ethnicity and on the collective organisational form of ethnic identity. Considering the position adopted in this study on the matter of ethnicity and the functioning of language in society, this must be regarded as a limitation of substance. The models also presume the exclusive hegemony of the nation-state in the political landscape. Again, given the perspective on the nation-state as a form of polity that is under siege that is delineated in this study, this too is a point of weakness for the models. Also, in terms of policy applications, there is a tendency to place emphasis on top-down, macro-level approaches to language planning activity. Language planning and policy in the urban context defies such approaches. The city, as a polity and as a discrete sociological entity, is characteristically diverse in linguistic terms, it is the prime site for linguistic change and it is the most crucial arena for the implementation of policy, whether multiculturalism, assimilation or exclusion. The project of multiculturalism, currently dominant in the field of language planning and policy in the Northern and English-speaking global cities, has been subject to challenge by conservative, left, liberal, radical and nationalist critiques (e.g. Anctil, 1984; Levine, 1990; Mitchell, 1996 & 1993; Vertovec & Cohen, 2002). Set in the context of those factors identified as instrumental to shaping sociolinguistics and language planning and their increasing concern with globalisation, the new linguistic world order and linguistic human rights (e.g. Blommaert, 2003; Coupland, 2003; Phillipson, 1992; Ricento, 2000), it may be timely to begin to consider a post-multicultural trajectory for language planning and policy in the city. Also, the models proposed by Haarmann and Kaplan and Baldauf are, to varying degrees, rather innocent of questions of power and contestation. This is characteristic of much of the work on the ecology of language as reflected, for example, by Mühlhäusler:

> Functioning ecologies are characterised by predominantly mutually beneficial links and only to a small degree by competitive relationships.
>
> (Mühlhäusler, 2001: 1)

This merely reinforces G. Williams's criticism of sociolinguistics in general that it assumes consensual and normative perspectives on society. Therefore, it is necessary give consideration to a number of methodological and theoretical points at this juncture. The dynamics of the relations between language, power and contestation in ecological context must be located. The collapse of conceptual form and clarity that constitutes the notion of the ethnolinguistic group and its unproblematised centrality to language–society models must be addressed. While building upon these models, a resolution of these tensions is sought here through the further examination of language in ecological context and within a wider sociological framework.

The devising of an alternative approach to the ecology of language which embraces questions of power and contestation and accounts for the impact of processes such as globalisation requires that the notion of the ecology be revisited so as to achieve a realistic understanding of the term, as opposed to simply conceiving of the ecology as an ideal or as a mere metaphor. This realist approach to an ecological perspective on language may be termed critical ecolinguistics (Mac Giolla Chríost, 2005). In order to achieve this it is necessary to refer to how the ecology is conceived as the discrete subject of specialist scholarly and professional activity. Most of those who are engaged in the study of the ecology, termed ecologists, would agree with Odum in defining ecology as '[t]he totality or pattern of relations between organisms and environment' (Odum, 1975: 1, 4). In their study of organisms in their environment, ecologists identify two distinct components to the environment. The physical component is one. This comprises the climate, water, temperature, radiation and nutrients. The other is the biotic component, comprising the organisms that coexist in the environment. Understanding the complexity of relations between organisms and their environment is a central concern for ecologists. This is undertaken at a number of levels, namely individual, population, community, ecosystem and biosphere. Other than the term individual, which is self-explanatory, these terms merit definition. A population is understood as a group of organisms of the same species in a given area. A community is the sum, or assemblage, of species populations found in a given area. An ecosystem is the complexity of relationships between a biotic [organic or living] community and the physical environment and the biosphere is understood to constitute the global sum of ecosystems.

Central to ecological thought is the notion of finitude. As Odum puts it: 'the living space functions of one's environment are interrelated, mutually restrictive, and not unlimited in capacity' (Odum, 1975: 204). Given the restrictive nature of the environment, its limited capacity, and the interrelations between and across the biotic community and the physical environment, the various organisms impact upon each other at the level of individual, community and population. This can cause adaptation on the part of organisms or competition between or among them over the resources necessary to their continuity. The resultant competition can take various forms, including unreconstructed violence. Ecologists understand competition to relate to access to and the use of the resources of the environment that are variously necessary to the survival of the different organisms that comprise the biotic community. Competition can take place between different species as well as among different individual members of the same single species. The specific nature of the competition is determined by what ecologists understand as the niche. A niche is the place that is occupied by a given species in the environment. This comprises both the conditions within which the species exists and also the resources that it utilises. The maximum potential niche that could, in theory, be occupied by a given species in the absence of competition is described by ecologists as the 'fundamental niche'. In reality, species occupy reduced niches due to competition. The actual niche thus occupied is termed the 'realized niche'. In this way, competition in ecological context may be viewed as a mechanism for gaining access to resources and of denying that access to others. The securing of a niche and its effective, exclusive protection from potential competitors is vital. Competition is widely understood by ecologists as an important 'clue to community organisation' (McIntosh, 1985: 93). Competition relates to community organisation in that under circumstances in which competition is intense one of the competitors might suffer ejection from the niche or be destroyed.

Alternatively, the competitors could achieve means of sharing the niche through adaptation. Odum puts it as follows:

> Where there are two or more closely related species adapted to the same or a similar niche, interspecific competition becomes important. If the competition is severe, one of the species may be eliminated completely, or forced into another niche or another geographical location; or the species involved may be able to live together at reduced density by sharing resources in some sort of equilibrium.
>
> (Odum, 1975: 130)

Thus, competition in ecological context is considered to be a mechanism for bringing about the displacement or exclusion of rivals from the environment. This behaviour is often termed 'competitive exclusion' by ecologists and, as asserted by McIntosh the 'idea of competitive exclusion ... [is] a cornerstone of population and community ecology' (1985: 183–4). Adaptation is an alternative to exclusion and it can take different forms. It can give rise to behavioural and physiological changes in a species. This is described as 'character displacement' by ecologists. Species can seek to avoid having to compete with each other through undertaking contrasting adaptations to the environment, especially with regard to the manner in which they utilise resources (Owen, 1980: 179). The implication of this is that competition causes selection for difference. Thus, it is a central tenet of ecology 'that no two species found together are ecologically identical and that the differences between them result from and are maintained by competition' (Owen, 1980: 98).

Competition in ecological context works in two main ways. These are termed exploitation or resource competition and interference competition. Exploitation competition is understood to operate under circumstances in which organisms together deplete a finite resource thereby competing with each other indirectly. The result of such resource depletion is the reduced fitness of the organisms, understood as the ability of the organisms to secure their reproduction. Interference competition is when individuals compete directly, largely through violent confrontation. Under these circumstances, reduced fitness results from injury and death in addition to that which results from the depletion of resources. It is also the case that the specific impact of competition, of both types, upon the various competitors differs. The cost of competition is not borne equally. Responses to competition include 'territoriality' – that is, the active interference of individuals or groups to maintain territory boundaries, thereby securing exclusive space for the species to the extent that is possible. Another response is known as 'dispersal'. This entails the actual movement of organisms away from locations of high population density. This is a common strategy for younger members of a given species in particular. A third response to competition is known as 'resource partitioning'. This is the only option that does not directly result in either the physical displacement or the expiration of organisms. This response allows for the coexistence of species: 'The competitive exclusion principle states that coexistence can only occur in a stable, homogenous environment if the species niches are differentiated, because if two species had identical requirements one would dominate and outcompete the other' (Mackenzie, Ball & Kirdee, 1998: 103). In practice, ecologists are of the view that, under most circumstances, coexistence is likely to include an element of competition. Non-competitive coexistence is only likely to occur under special conditions. According to ecologists, the extent of niche differentiation is the most important factor in enabling non-competitive coexistence (Mackenzie *et al.*, 1998: 103). This relates to two variables, namely the range and the volume of resources utilised by a species. In theory, this condition relates to attaining a balance between the narrowness of range – thereby reducing the likelihood of interspecies competition and the flatness of volume – thereby reducing the likelihood of intraspecies competition. In reality, few such ecological scenarios have been reliably identified. In those cases where competition is not apparent, ecologists assert that the observed patterns derive from historical competition rather than niche differentiation. For example: 'Evolution may act to reduce the degree of competition of species – thus current patterns of resource utilization are a result of competition over time, even though little or no competitive interactions are currently observed. This phenomenon is known as 'the ghost of competition' (Mackenzie *et al.*, 1998: 103). In general terms, ecosystems are not stable or homogeneous entities, but are dynamic and diverse. The main implication of the spatial and temporal heterogeneity of the ecology is that the properties of the physical environment and the various resources necessary to the continuity of given organisms are subjected to change. Change has many intended, and unintended, consequences and will variously impact upon the totality of the ecology. The effect of this ecological heterogeneity is to continually modify the relations between the principal components of the ecology, the biotic community and the physical environment and their specific constituent parts. Therefore, there is no permanently fixed and unchallengably durable disposition in any ecosystem that works inevitably in the favour of certain given species over others. In this way, heterogeneity and diversity are inherent to understanding the ecological context.

This brief reflection upon the nature of ecology can be grounded in sociological terms. This shift from biology to sociology can be engineered *via* the field of study known as human ecology. A number of commentators indicate a number of points of engagement (Steiner & Nauser, 1993). They consider that Giddens reworking of the conceptions of social reproduction and of social transformation in structuration theory is a significant means of making the joins. The introduction of the concept of the duality of structure by Giddens is intended as a means of transcending the subject–object dichotomy that confounds the social sciences. By this, action and structure are regarded as a dialectical process in which the rules and resources of society are recursively involved in social reproduction (Giddens, 1986: 25). In this context, structure refers to the systemic ordering of societal rules and resources, and some points of engagement between ecology and structuration are identified by Werlen (1993) as follows:

- Systems of semantic rules – structures of *Weltanschauungen*
- Systems of resources – structures of domination
- Systems of moral rules – structures of legitimation.

These structures, Giddens argues, only become real or meaningful through action. Structuration comprises 'the dynamic process whereby structures come into being' (Giddens, 1976: 121). The idea of structuration, therefore, implies the structuring of social relations as a result of the duality of structure and, in this sense, structure is both constraining and enabling (Giddens, 1986: 376). As it is only through action that the social world is constituted, it follows that the concept of interaction is critical in understanding social reproduction and transformation. In is in this context that contestation arises. This will be in either of two forms, according to Giddens, namely 'conflict' and 'contradiction'. The former may be described as a type of competition in which the interacting agents operate according to the same structuring principles. This type of competition is most likely to arise in relation to contestation over resources. The latter form of contestation, contradiction, may be regarded as the more profound form as it relates to actual structural oppositions in which the complete system of order is under challenge.

According to structuration theory, this spatial contextuality is constitutive of action. In this sense, the environment, or ecology, is manipulated by agents so as to enable or to constrain social reproduction and transformation:

> The communication of meaning, as with all aspects of the contextuality of action, does not have to be seen merely as happening 'in' time-space. Agents routinely incorporate temporal and spatial features of encounters in processes of meaning constitution.
>
> (Giddens, 1986: 29)

It would appear that Giddens adopts a conservative view of society through viewing institutionalised societal practices in terms of the reiterative and routine quality of group and individual interaction with institutions. This he terms purposive behaviour. The possibility of change, however, is inherent to the notion of purposive behaviour. For example, purposive behaviour has outcomes that are not predicted by the agents of reiterative and routine interaction with institutions. Such outcomes are described by Giddens as the 'unintended consequences of intentional conduct' (Giddens, 1986: 12). In this way, both routine and change are properties of purposive behaviour. A similar duality is discerned in relation to power in that it can be both enabling and constraining:

> [P]ower is the capacity to achieve outcomes; whether or not these are connected to purely sectional interests is not germane to its definition. Power is not, as such, an obstacle to freedom or emancipation but is their very medium – although it would be foolish, of course, to ignore its constraining properties ... Power is generated in and through the reproduction of structures of domination.
>
> (Giddens, 1986: 157–8)

Contestation, in the context of power, is management and resolved through an understood set of regulatory mechanisms based upon 'tacit knowledge', that is a set of rules that, in practice, are explicit, absolute, fixed and prescribed. Their most common form is that of the written constitution. These regulatory mechanisms are, in themselves, a significant resource. Under the circumstances of contestation they may become the focal point of competition and the key point of access to domination. It is a function of the ecology that issues of power and competition bear a strong relationship to the gaining of accessibility to and the exercise of control over resources. Two types of resource are identified by Giddens, namely allocative and authoritative. They are defined as follows:'Allocative resources refer to capabilities – or, more accurately, to forms of transformative capacity – generating command over objects, goods or material phenomena. Authoritative resources refer to types of transformative capacity generating command over persons or actions' (Giddens, 1984: 33). Hence, while the specific nature of the resources may vary between the natural and social ecology, their function remains consistent. Resources are integral to the competitive fitness of agents. Thus, drawing from structuration theory, one can assert that in an ecological perspective on language, spatial contextuality is constitutive of action, that is to say that the environment is manipulated by actors or agents with a self-interest in enabling their own social reproduction and transformation and to constrain that of others. Given the nature of the linguistic diversity that characterises the urban space, language planning and policy is an essential arm of urban regimes in the management of that space in the broader interests of the city as a socially integrated whole.

Conclusions

Language planning and policy in general and in the city, in particular, benefits from a view of language in society which may be termed critical ecolinguistics. This is a position that is characterised by a number of key features which relate to the concerns of this study of language in the city in the following terms. Language and power are interwoven *via* the polity. The city in a globalising world is understood to be an increasingly important point of reference. In this context, the key properties pertaining to the city are in relation to novel forms and modalities of citizenship, capital, labour, information exchange information and governance. The impact of this upon the languages in society is uneven and unequal. An ecological perspective on language aims at accounting for the totality or pattern of relations between language and agency in the social world, it is more substantial than an idealist or biological metaphor. The contribution of a critical ecolinguistics to this perspective on language is to show how questions of competition and contestation operate in relation to language in ecological context. As we have seen, the city is a competitive, dynamic and diverse ecology and approaching language planning and policy must account for how such competition and contestation will manifest itself in the relationships between society and language in the urban context.

Part II Towards a New Conceptual Terrain

5
Place

Introduction

Language is profoundly implicated in the social constitution of space. If it is in a constant 'state of becoming', as Thrift (1983) claims, then space, in relation to language, is in a similar such state:

> [L]anguage is ... primarily a practical tool that gains its meaning from doing as doing gains its meaning from language. Language is therefore always in a state of becoming ... It is a semantic field that shifts as the practices and projects of the material world alter, setting new limits as old ones are overtaken, inventing new meanings for old words, or bringing new words and meanings into existence.
>
> Thrift (1983: 46)

It is with the resulting negotiation between language and space that we are primarily concerned here. Language does not merely give meaning to words, but it also gives meaning to worlds. It is fundamental to the sense of place that defines worlds in the city and city worlds. Equally, the city is implicated in linguistic diversity, as Dorier-Apprill and Van Den Avenne argue:

> La ville en effet, lieu de l'hétérogène et de la mise en présence de langues différentes, est le terrain privilégié pour observer des pratiques langagières plurilingues quotidiennes, notamment à travers l'observation de pratiques sociales et de pratiques de l'espace, qui impliquent rencontres, traversées, passages d'un quartier à l'autre. [The city in fact, a place of heterogeneity and of the presence of different languages, is the privileged arena for the observation of daily multilingual

111

language practices, notably through the observation of social practices and the practices of space, which is implicated in meetings, crossings, passings from one quarter to another.]

(Dorier-Apprill & Van Den Avenne, 2002: 151)

These practices of the social and of space are manifest in language behaviours in various ways: in the official names of places and mundane resistances to them, in the making of state-sanctioned spaces for languages and the popular remaking or appropriation of space for language. The particular cases that comprise this chapter relate to the nature of the diversity of worlds in the city and the function of language in their construction, and to the use of language in making sense of space through place names, in particular. Both of these functions of language are features of language planning and policy (formal and informal). Moreover, these language behaviours and practices are not neutral but are ideologically embedded and help to understand the mechanisms and patterns of domination and resistance that define the urban condition.

Worlds in the city

Language is a fundamental feature of the urban locale, understood to mean space constituted by social relations, as proposed by Giddens (e.g. 1984). Some new work on the sociology of language is beginning to show appreciation to this. Block (2006), for example, notes the importance of the environment as asserted by Giddens:

[I]ndividuals do not develop their sense of self working exclusively from the inside out or from the outside in; rather, their environments provide conditions and impose constraints whilst they act on that same environment, continuously altering and recreating it.

(Block, 2006: 29)

He also rightly draws attention to the distinctiveness of the city apart from the nation-state, and both the nation and state, that is:

I must say that walking the streets of London, I often get the impression that the city has seceded from the nation state called Britain. And I begin to ask myself if London is perhaps no longer a city, but a kind of reinvention of the city state, such as those which arose in Italy during the European renaissance.

(Block, 2006: 212)

But, despite this sensitivity, Block misses the idea of 'citiness', the urban condition, and its specific relationship to and its impact upon language. The function of language in social reproduction and transformation in the city is profound. Pred's (1990) study of language in 19th-century Stockholm is an outstanding example of how the mundane and profane use of the language of the street and the use or mis (re?)use of the names of the street makes and remakes the city and its worlds. Yet, his study remains virtually unread in sociolinguistics and in language planning. He rightly points out that a wealth of linguistic material can be mined from historical and archival sources from which an insight into the meaning of city life can be delineated, for example:

> [T]he volume of linguistic evidence contained in these sources is so great as to permit extensive observations regarding lost worlds of everyday life in late nineteenth-century Stockholm; lost worlds in which the language of production, distribution, and consumption practices subsumed a language of discipline-avoidance and survival tactics; lost worlds in which the 'folk geography', or language used for negotiating the city streets and getting from here to there, subsumed a language of ideological resistance; lost worlds in which much of the language of social reference and address, the tagging of nicknames on groups and individuals, subsumed a language of boundary drawing, social orientation, and boundary transgressions; lost worlds in which all of these languages were cross-cut and peppered by folk-humor, by the mustering of malicious metaphors, by a vocabulary of comic irony and irreverence, or mocking and reducing social inversion, of laughing lewdness and licentiousness.
>
> (Pred, 1990: 26)

The world of 19th-century Stockholm which Pred explores is shaped by a number of ideological concerns. It is, in the first place, a world that was formed by unequal relationships of gender and of socio-economic class. For example, the public space is, in many ways, shaped by the male perspective:

> The syntax of any western language of urban spatial orientation builds in large measure upon a juxtapositioning of variously scaled and areal designations, precise reference points, and streets or other linear route indicators. As the folk geography of late nineteenth-century Stockholm, revealed in available sources, was an overwhelmingly male language, and as public bars and cafés, where drinking and eating

could be combined, were the primary *loci* of male working-class sociability, such establishments were the most frequently occurring points of locational reference.

(Pred, 1990: 112)

As the most significant male working-class social loci, the public bars of the city are the most important sites in which 'the city's folk geography was constituted and reproduced, casually invented and passed on' (Pred, 1990: 114). They contributed to the linguistic segregation of the city in terms of socio-economic class through the physical separation of the classes within the public space of the bar. Hence, not only would different classes occupy separate rooms but they would also enter and depart the premises via different doors, thus:

> Numerous public bars simultaneously facilitated the reinforcement of heteroglossia and the construction and diffusion of a popular geography because they kept the classes beyond voice reach of one another, because they were subdivided into two spaces, providing separate sections with dissimilar furnishings, even different entrances.
>
> (Pred, 1990: 115)

According to Pred, the public bar as a specific social space served to contribute to the linguistic segregation of the city in another sense. Public houses tended to recruit their customers from within particular sections or occupational groups within the classes, in particular the working class. As a result, the linguistic worlds of what was a very diverse working class did not easily interact in this space:

> Split-space drinking establishments and other public bars further contributed to the preservation of particular tongues, to the deepening of Stockholm's heteroglossia, by drawing customers from a limited number of laboring groups rather than attracting a highly heterogeneous working-class clientele.
>
> (Pred, 1990: 116)

From this, in part, arose a sophisticated popular geography that included the non-use of official street names along with the creation and use of unofficial names. This, and the rapid growth of the city during the course of the 19th century, the result of which was a rapidly changing physical and social environment – a highly disorientating environment, created the need for an 'elaborate language of spatial orientation' (Pred, 1990: 122). The rural background of the migrant population of city was a factor in shaping the precise nature of this language, drawn as they were from an environment with which they were to become most intimate. That intimacy, described by A. D. Smith in another context as a 'ceaseless encounter' (1986: 183), was and still is mediated by language:

> The rural backgrounds of many reinforced the need for a language of spatial orientation engendered by these transformations, reinforced the need for a language of orientation stemming from the recurrent disorientation, bewilderment, and confusion produced by these fleeting spaces of modernity. The cultural baggage of most people arriving from the countryside, including those who had been landless or had operated small subsistence-production farms, contained a well-developed ability to negotiate one's local environs with the help of a fine-grained vocabulary of landscape details, with the help of words for specific meadows, cultivated fields, groves, dells, marshes, lake points, islands, houses, cottages, huts, and entire holdings … Cast adrift in an environment with no physical resemblance to the one they had departed, thrown into an environment where so much was unfixed, and finding themselves, like Baudelaire's 'archetypal modern man', frequently jolted by the 'moving chaos' of city traffic … such people, if not desperate for a popular language of spatial orientation, presumably found it imperative either to latch onto such a vocabulary and syntax, or to contribute to its continual invention and renewal.
>
> (Pred, 1990: 123)

Place names are, according to many commentators (e.g. Robinson, 1996; Monmonier, 1991), the most immediate link between people and place, although this has not often been well understood in the urban context. Pred, however, recognises their value most clearly. His detailed study of the use, misuse, reuse and non-use of street names reveals patterns of oppression and resistance, for example:

> To argue that frantically paced creative destruction, the fluidity of circumstances, and biographical background helped shape the need for a comprehensive and nuanced popular language of spatial orientation is not to account for the relative paucity of official street names and other proper locational signifiers in that language, or for the pervasiveness of its unrestrained, unself-censored humor.

Although not definitely demonstrable, these latter puzzling attributes of Stockholm's folk-geographic discourse were almost certainly in some measure a form of conscious and sub-conscious resistance to the attempt at ideological domination embedded in the street-name revision of 1885 and the street-naming policy of subsequent years.

(Pred, 1990: 126)

The new names chosen by the city council of 19th-century Stockholm were 'ideologically pregnant', arising from the interests of the politically empowered middle class and hence reflected in their disposition for, for example, patriotic and historical names, names derived from Nordic mythology, names associated with famous places near the city, the names of famous Swedish authors as well as the names of prominent men within technology and engineering (Pred, 1990: 128–9). Moreover, the act of naming was very much implicated in a wider set of power relations:

This ideological stratagem, this impression of ideological expressions upon the expanding street network, was not an isolated phenomenon, but part of a larger interwoven context, part of a set of variously scaled, ongoing structuring processes in which concretely situated practices, power relations, and individual and collective forms of consciousness were dialectically intertwined with one another.

(Pred, 1990: 129)

The Stockholm of Pred is not, of course, unique in this respect. For example, Mac Giolla Chríost (1996) remarks upon the ideological implications to be read in the act of the renaming of the main streets and the principal features of the city walls of the city of Londonderry at the outset of the modern period (Table 5.1). The imposing city walls were first constructed following the sacking of the city in 1608 by the rebellious Irish chieftain Cahir O'Doherty. The city was further subjected to siege-like conditions in 1641 and again in 1649. The final siege occurred in 1689 and it was an event that was of significance to the course of Irish, British and European history – according to the Whig version of history in any case. Very briefly, as a result of the crisis of the Williamite succession, the Catholic King James II travelled to Ireland to reassert his claim to the English throne. The Protestants of the city of Londonderry closed the city gates on the Catholic king who subsequently failed to capture the city and went on to lose his crown. The renaming of parts of the city following this turn of events is indicative of the new meaning of the city. The name changes are the product of the 'commodification' of the city as the 'Maiden City' – untaken in

Table 5.1 Historical changes of gate names in city walls of Londonderry (adapted from Mac Giolla Chríost, 1996)

Name of gate prior to 1689 siege	New name of gate post 1689 siege
Prince Charles's	Double
Lord Docwra's	Royal
King James's	Church
Mayor of London Derrie's	Gunner's
Lord Chichester	Coward's
Governor of the Plantation's	Water
London	Newgate
Lord Deputie's	Ferry
Unnamed	Hangman's

siege. Also, they actively enable the 'consumption' of the city as a monument of particular historical and political values:

> It signifies an attempt to re-identify the physical landscape within a revised concept of the cultural landscape as a whole. The new names of the bulwarks provide clues as to the details of the re-identification. King James is obviously rejected, but perhaps more surprisingly, so are other previously well-regarded individuals of the pre-siege plantation establishment: Lord Docwra, Lord Chichester, the governor of the plantation, the mayor of the plantation town, the 'Lord Deputie' and Prince Charles. A revolution of thought seems to have occurred in the minds of the besieged Protestants.
>
> (Mac Giolla Chríost, 1996: 131–2)

The walls of the city were carefully maintained in the centuries after siege, while other city walls in Ireland and Britain were falling into disrepair. Also, the gates were subject to monumental refurbishment during the 18th and 19th centuries. The ritual 're-enactment' of key events of the final siege has been developed during this period and are practised to this day, though not without some controversy and resistance on the part of the, largely Catholic, Irish nationalists and republicans of the city. The majority of the resident population of the city today is Catholic.

Returning to Pred, such an ideological stratagem drives the popular geography of the folk memory underground through 'the displacement of old signifiers'. Pred elaborates upon this point at some length:

> As a stratagem to help bring order, control and discipline to the city's streets, the imprinting of dominant ideology upon the topography of Stockholm through street-name revision cut two ways. As an

on-the-ground effort to impose ideology, as an attempt at making cultural hegemony concrete, street-name revision involved both the emplacement of new signifiers and the displacement of old signifiers. Many preexisting street names were deeply sedimented usages, once spontaneous on-the-spot popular creations resulting from events, persons, physical features, or economic activities associated with the street in question or its immediate vicinity. The erasure of former names, in other words, often involved the censuring of an intergenerationally transmitted folk geography that dated back decades or centuries that had begun to obtain legitimacy in 1763 when a royal proclamation went into effect requiring the placement of name signs at the corners of important streets.

(Pred, 1990: 135)

One response to this erasure or displacement is resistance. In the case of 19th-century Stockholm, this took the form of the non-use of official street names and the use instead of alternative names, resulting in a bawdy geography of ideological resistance:

Given the context of street-discipline and population-control strategies, given the resistance simultaneously expressed in the multitude of discipline-avoidance and retaliatory tactics employed on the job by industrial laborers, dockers and construction workers, given the localization of the most thorough revision of thoroughfare names to a portion of eastern *Södermalm* containing an extremely high working-class population density, given the unmistakable thrust of street-naming policies and their resultant expunging of long-standing folk usages, it is difficult not to connect the apparent reluctance to utter official street names and the heavy reliance upon an extensive, humor-filled geography with ideological resistance, difficult not to see the lost worlds of footing about Stockholm, the lost worlds of spatial orientation and popular geography, as in some measure subsuming a lost world and language of resistance to ideological domination.

(Pred, 1990: 136)

Similarly, alternative urban toponyms mark the cityscapes of Londonderry and Belfast in Northern Ireland. Here, the adoption and erection of Irish language street names, banned as a result of legislation during the 1940s, emerged during the 1980s, in particular, as a means of reclaiming the city by Irish nationalists (e.g. De Baroid, 1990; Maguire, 1991; O'Reilly, 1999; Mac Giolla Chríost, 2005). Subsequent to the political agreement of 1998, the use of Irish language street names came to be tolerated by the city authorities. It is also the case that the very act of the naming of the city of Londonderry resurfaced as a matter of controversy during the 'troubles' or 'long war' in Northern Ireland between 1969 and 1998 (Whyte, 1990; Mac Giolla Chríost, 2005). It is commonly known that the official name of the city, 'Londonderry', relates to the British historical tradition in Ireland, while the name 'Derry' is associated with the Irish historical tradition. That said, it is the case that prior to the 'troubles', most locals of the city would have used the name 'Derry' rather than 'Londonderry'; indeed, a wide range of local 'British' organisations make use of the name 'Derry' in their historical titles. Similar such controversy regarding tension between officially sanctioned street names and the names of streets given by the residents may be noted in many cities. For example, the use of street names in the Chinese (sic) language only in the Monterey district of Los Angeles was recently a matter of considerable tension between local residents and the city government (Ed Soja, pers. comm., 2005). Also of note is the fact that the government of the Basque Autonomous Community in Spain completed a comprehensive survey of place names during the 1990s in order to establish official and authoritative versions in the Basque language. During the course of the project it became clear that its application to the urban domain was much more complex than originally envisaged and, as a result, the final survey largely excludes the urban Basque Country (Mac Giolla Chríost, 2001: 121–7).

The resistance that is realised through alternative street names is described by Pred as 'oral recalcitrance' (Pred, 1990: 138). As a form of resistance it is characterised by the persistence of 'deeply sedimented terms' and the 'use of naming to recover memory and meaning' (Pred, 1990: 138). More specifically, for example, despite official changes of the street name *Trebackarlånggatan* to *Tegnératan*, the subsequent use of *Trebackarlång* illustrates the persistence of the use of the popular name for the public bar on that street (Table 5.2). The relationship between the street names *Holländaregatan*, *Ölandsgatan* and *Holländaren* is most similar. Also indicative of the same such resistance is the use of the term *Besvärsbacken* by the working class to describe a section of the street officially known as *Brännkyrkagatan*, in honour of a noteworthy place near to the city, and a replacement for the previous name of the street, namely *Besvärsgatan* (Troublesome Street). In some cases there was explicit and politicised resistance to such changes. For example, the residents of *Parisgränden* (Paris Lane – after a 17th-century resident of the area) unsuccessfully petitioned the city council not to change the

Table 5.2 Terms of spatial orientation belonging to the 'folk geography' or 'popular geography' of the working class (adapted from Pred, 1990)

Word or expression	Definition or usage (literal translation)
Babelstorn	(The Tower of Babel); building and surrounding play area on *Vita berget* (The White Mountain, eastern *Södermalm*)
Fyllbacken	(The Booze Hill); hill on *Kungsholmen* leading up to Bolinder's Engineering Works
Träsktorget	(The Marsh Market-Place); market-place then officially called *Roslagstorg*
Barnkrubben	(The Children's Manger, or Crib); separate workshop building at Wester and Norgrens Mechanical Stone-Woks where most of the employees were young boys
Snobbfabriken	(The Snob Factory); L.M. Ericsson Factory
Korvkasern	(The Sausage Barracks); building housing the second regiment, or *Göta Garde*, *Södermalm*; name carry-over from an earlier period when the building was occupied by the predecessors of the city's police force, who were popularly called sausages, or *korvar*
Kungens tandpetare	(The King's Toothpick); obelisk, The Old City
Sirapskyrkan	(The Syrupy Church); Moravian Brethren Church
Skojartian	(Cheaters', or Con-Men's, Number Ten); residential building, popularly named after horse traders who lived there
Besvärsbacken	(The Trouble's, or Troublesome, Hill); steep hill portion of *Brännkyrkagatan* (after a church south of Stockholm) which until 1885 had been known as *Besvärsgatan* (Trouble's, or Troublesome, Street)
Hällbacker	(Bedrock, or Pouring, Hills); a portion of *Biblioteksgatan* (Library Street), near the end of the so-called *Snobbrännan*, where middle-class women sat to view the elegantly dressed who poured by
Horstret	(Whore Street [from English]; or Fornicatio Street [in standard Swedish hor = fornication or, in a more strict legal sense, adultery]); *Birger Jarlsgatan* (Birger Jarl was a 13th-century Swedish ruler)
Löjtnantskuporna	(The Lieutenant's Hives); portion of *Lutternsgatan* (after 1911, the eastern portion of *Kungsgatan*, or King Street), located near the eastern termination of the street at *Birger Jarlsgatan*, this was an area where the more expensive prostitutes kept their quarters
Pelarbacken	(The Colonnade Hill); *Kapellgränd* (Chapel Lane); popular name dating back to the 17th century based on raised stones placed along the alley (which led to the Holy Cross Chapel), in order to symbolise the stations of the cross
Rännan and Snobbrännan	(The Gutter and The Snob Gutter); street-wide eastern promenade of *Kungsträdgården* (The Royal Gardens); plus, in the latter case, the route leading to *Stureplan* (Sture Square) via *Hamngatan* (Harbour Street), *Norrmalmstorg* (Norrmalm's Market-Place) and *Biblioteksgatan* (Library Street)

street name to *Observatoriegatan* (Observatory Street). The city council claimed that the change was necessary as the street, located in the area of *Norrmalm*, had an identically named counterpart in the district of *Södermalm*. Though Pred suggests (1990: 139) that this argument conceals an ideological reason for the change in that the name 'paris' is also a lower *Stockholmska* pejorative term for policemen patrolling the city in pairs. Instructively, the name of the other street in *Södermalm* was also changed at this time. Perhaps the most striking example, and certainly the basest, relates to the street *Arsenalsgatan*. During the late 19th century, this street name began to be used by the male working class of the city as the term to describe, as Pred puts it, 'the "space" running from a woman's asshole – "anus" to her cunt – "pudenda"' (Pred, 1990: 140). According to Pred, the particular physical and social geography of this street gives rise to the practice:

> At its western end *Arsenalsgatan* merged into a large opening, *Gustaf Adolfs torg*, a square adorned at is midpoint with an equestrian statue of ... King Gustav II Adolf ... Flanking the three built sides of this opening in the central body of Stockholm were the Royal Opera House ... the Hereditary Prince's Palace which housed the Foreign Ministry, and the Hotel Rydberg, one of the city's two most fashionable hotels ... It would have been from these edifices that the wastefully dressed and the filthy rich, or those shitty with money exited, from these edifices that the posh and powerful ... poured out into the city via the anal terminus of *Arsenalsgatan*.
>
> (Pred, 1990: 140)

At the other end of the street was the *Kungsträdsgårdsgatan* (Royal Gardens Street), known by the working class as *Snobbrännan* (The Snob Gutter) and according to Pred this place was

> [A] dirty groove, a flowing channel, a rut for the morning-time display of feminine elegance, a vegetation-bordered furrow belonging to the city's finest, most splendidly dressed women, this, in the eyes of working-class males, would have been the "cunt" to which Arsenalsgatan ran.
>
> (Pred, 1990: 141)

Thus, the novel use of the street name turns the socio-economic hierarchy of late 19th-century Stockholm upside down.

For some other commentators, within the discipline of sociolinguistics, the street name is rich with linguistic meaning in a number of ways, including in a descriptive sense. For example, Dorier-Apprill and Van Den Avenne understand the street name as a place at which linguistics, geography and history – language, space and the past – are brought together, thus on toponym:

> L'étude de la toponymie permet également de rendre compte des dif-férentes langues en présence dans une ville, à la fois d'un point de vue synchronique et diachronique. La toponymie depuis son origine est le point de rencontre entre la linguistique, la géographie et l'his-toire (parce que les noms de lieu décrivent des espaces tels qu'ils sont ou tels qu'ils étaient, parce qu'ils témoignent de différentes activités humaines présentes ou passées, parce qu'ils inscrivent dans la nomi-nation les différentes langues et donc les différents peuplements), elle est par ailleurs instrumentalisée par la cartographie. [The study of the toponym permits the accounting of the different languages that are present in a city, from a synchronic and a diachronic point of view at the same time. Given its origination the toponym is the meeting point between linguistics, geography and history (because the place names describe such spaces as they are or as they were, because they witness different human activities past and present, because they inscribe in naming different languages and therefore different peoples), it is moreover instrumentalised by cartography.]
>
> (Dorier-Apprill & Van Den Avenne 2003: 151)

The fact that the toponym is 'instrumentalisée par la cartographie' means, according to Dorier-Apprill and Van Den Avenne, that it is implicated in acts of appropriation, ownership and control:

> Travailler cependant sur des toponymes oraux contemporains, actu-alisés en discours, permet de rendre compte des liens constants qui se tissent entre pratique de l'espace et pratique langagière, et de la question de l'appropriation. L'appropriation d'un espace se fait 'par le corps', dans l'usage, les pratiques quotidiennes, mais également par langage, la mise en mot de cet espace. La denomination d'un espace atteste de son appropriation….mais pas seulement, elle est prenante de cette appropriation: toute pratique sociale est tissée de langage, ponctuée de langage, pourrait-on dire. [However, to work on the contemporary oral toponyms, realised in discourse, allows one to account for the continuous connections weave between the practice of space and the practice of language, and the question of appropriation. The appropriation of a space is made 'by the body', in

use, the daily practices, but equally by language, the placing of word in that space. The naming of a space affirms its appropriation ... but not only that, it is absorbed in that appropriation: all social practice is woven in language, punctuated by language, one could say.]

(Dorier-Apprill & Van Den Avenne, 2003: 151)

This sense of appropriation is, in part, a reflection of history: 'Les langues qui fournissent la toponymie à Mopti donnent donc à voir les différentes strates de l'histoire linguistique de la ville'. [The languages that comprise the toponymy of Mopti provide an insight into the different strata of the linguistic history of the city.] (Dorier-Apprill & Van Den Avenne, 2003: 153). And, it is a problematic past in which local non-official languages and the language of authority and officialdom are in conflict, for example:

Si Komoguel est le toponyme officiel, connu de tous, il est supplanté dans l'usage quotidien par le toponyme *Wayenkore*, nom dérivé peul sur une base songhaï *waye* (boucher) suffixé en *koore*. Il désigne donc le quartier des bouchers. Ce toponyme désignant une zone de Komoguel s'est mis à designer par extension, selon un procédé métonymique, le quartier tout entire. Il semblerait que cette appellation non officialisée soit d'usage plus frequent. Les plus jeunes et les nouveaux arrivés en ville ont créé, en calquant le peul, un toponyme bambara *wayenkin*, composé à partir du nom *kin* (quartier). Comme en peul, le mot bambara désignant le boucher est un emprunt au songhaï (les bouchers sont originaires de cette ethnie). De même, dans les usages contemporains, le toponyme bambara Mossinkin tend à supplanter le toponyme peul Mossinkoré. [If Komoguel is the official toponym, recognised by all, it is displaced in daily use by the toponym *Wayenkore*, a name derived partly from a songhaï base *waye* (butcher) with the suffix *koore*. Thus, it identifies the butchers quarter. This toponym identifies a zone within Komoguel that identifies by extension, according to a metonymic process, the entire quarter. It appears that this unofficial appellation is in very frequent use. The youngest and the newest arrivals to the city create, almost exactly, a bambara toponym *wayenkin*, composed partly from the word *kin* (quarter). The bambara word that identifies the butcher is a borrowing from songhaï (the butchers are originally of this ethnicity). Similarly, in contemporary usage, the Mosssinkin bambara replace the toponym with Mossinkoré.]

(Dorier-Apprill & Van Den Avenne, 2003: 154)

They argue that their particular case study of street names and the names of places in the city of Mopti in Mali demonstrates that a gulf exists between the official and symbolic name, on the one hand, and the popular and daily name, on the other. The official toponym in French certainly exists and has a public presence on postcards and other written material, but it is not a feature of common oral use (Dorier-Apprill & Van Den Avenne, 2003: 156). Instead, the street name, properly understood, is the product of a consensus born from daily practice. And, it is understood in the mouth or on the ear, not on a name plaque mounted on a wall:

> L'attribution d'un nom à un lieu procède de deux pratiques: l'une populaire, des usagers, l'autre administrative, qui, soit entérine un usage populaire, soit au contraire impose un nom symbolique ... Les noms des lieux, sauf très rare exception, ne sont pas inscrits sur les murs, ils font l'objet d'un consensus né d'une pratique quotidienne, et non d'une imposition officielle. Il s'agit d'*appellations de bouche à oreille*, comme les appelle l'un de nos informateurs, ou, en argot bambara-français, de *togo-façon*. [The attributing of a name to a place arises from two practices: one popular, of users, the other administrative, that is, one confirming popular use, the other in contrast imposing a symbolic name ... The names of places, with a few rare exceptions, are not registrations inscribed on walls. The place name is the object of a consensus born of daily practice, and not as a result of official imposition. They may be *appellations of the mouth and the ear*, as they are described by one or our informants, or, in bambara-French argot, *togo-façon*.]
>
> (Dorier-Apprill & Van Den Avenne, 2003: 155)

It is because of this property of the street name as the subject of a consensus negotiated on the street that its examination opens up city life. The complex and ever-changing geography of the city is bound up in the street name and in this way the toponym is a signifier of not only the reconstruction of space but also it contains within it the memory of practices in urban space and the languages of those practices:

> La toponymie à Mopti ... est fluctuante, cette fluctuation étant liée à des facteurs géographiques: développement du site, usages des lieux (stables ou évolutifs), mais également à des facteurs linguistiques ou sociolinguistiques: changement de langue véhiculaire, étymologie populaire ... La toponymie urbaine, au-delà de son aspect fonctionnel (établir des cartes), donne donc à voir la ville comme lieu de

recomposition permanente, géographique et linguistique. Par ailleurs, elle garde en mémoire des usages anciens de l'espace urbain, et des langues qui ne sont plus pratiquées dans la ville. [The toponymy of Mopti fluctuates. This fluctuation is bound up in geographical factors: the development of the site, usages of place (stable or evolutionary), but equally so in linguistic or sociolinguistic factors: the change of the vehicular language, popular etymology ... The urban toponymy, beyond its functional aspect (the drawing up of maps), provides an insight into the city as a place of continuous geographic and linguistic reconstruction. Moreover, it protects the memory of former uses of urban space, and languages that are no longer practiced in the city.]

(Dorier-Apprill & Van Den Avenne, 2003: 157)

For Dorier-Apprill and Van Den Avenne, the street name is an especially valuable means of opening up the social landscape of the city in another sense. They noted that during the course of their fieldwork in Mopti the city residents were much more willing to talk at length about the names of streets and places in the city than a great many other topics. The reason for this, they adduce, is because the names of things are not perceived by the city residents as a matter of political or financial sensitivity. As such, their discussions flowed freely, touching upon many concerns and revealing much of interest:

On peut noter d'ailleurs que, dans une ville comme Mopti où se cristallisent des enjeux développementaux autour des questions d'assainissement, faire une enquête toponymique reçoit un accueil bienveillant: elle est perçue comme un intérêt pour l'histoire locale, les petites choses du quotidien, une recherché sans enjeu politique ou financier. Dès lors, les citadins racontent volontiers, et parfois de tout autres choses. La toponymie urbaine partaît dès lors comme une manière 'd'ouvrir' un terrain (d'autant plus qu'elle permet de s'approprier l'espace urbain). [One might further note that, in a city like Mopti where matters of development are crystallized in relation to questions of purification, conducting a toponymic enquiry receives a watchful reception: it is perceived as an interest in local history, the small every-day things, research without a political or financial stake. Consequently, the city-dwellers discuss freely, and sometimes on all sorts of things. As a result, the urban toponymy becomes a means of 'opening' a landscape (more so than it permits the appropriation of urban space).]

(Dorier-Apprill & Van Den Avenne, 2003: 157)

According to standard texts in sociolinguistics and language planning, the full range of publicly visible signage taken together, described as 'linguistic landscaping', is defined by Landry and Bourhis as 'the visibility and salience of languages on public and commercial signs in a given territory or region' (Landry & Bourhis, 1997: 23), and also in the following terms: 'The language of public road signs, advertising bill boards, street names, place names, commercial shop signs, and public signs on government buildings combines to form the linguistic landscape of a given territory, region or urban agglomeration' (Landry & Bourhis, 1997: 25). Much of this literature, however, remains rather innocent of the engagement with ideology that is so explicit in the work of others from outside of these disciplines, in particular Pred. A recent paper by Backhaus (2005) is, in many ways, quite typical. Here, the capacity of the street name to embody the memory of urban space is conceived of by Backhaus (2005) as 'layering', comprising the coexistence of signs from various historical periods and in various languages or combinations of languages in the streets of the city. These layers can be peeled back, or excavated, so as to allow the city to be read in some sense: '[L]ayering lays bare the different linguistic states in the recent history of the city. One my consider this to be a sort of urban archaeology' (Backhaus, 2005: 107). He notes in the case of Tokyo that there is a recent historical shift from monolingual Japanese (both Kanji and Kana) only to the increasing presence of other languages, especially English, but also Romanised Japanese, Korean and Chinese. This, he traces in street block signs, signs in railway stations, on fire extinguishers, information points regarding rubbish collection and postal services (Backhaus, 2005: 111). Backhaus, however, is not sensitive to notions of ideology and resistance, especially with regard to oral, folk or popular use, claiming that 'signs are unlikely to change any of their "speech habits" once they have been produced' (Backhaus, 2005: 107). Spolsky and Cooper (1991), while engaging more directly in ideological concerns in their study of street names in Jerusalem during 1980s, are shy of exposing the material to a more robust critique. Briefly, they identified a clear historical pattern in the evolution of street names in the city. They recorded three different types of trilingual street signs. The oldest type was from the period 1922–48, that is the period of the British Mandate, and this is reflected in the ordering of the languages from top to bottom thus – English, Arabic and Hebrew. The second type of sign, with Hebrew and Arabic-English in separate panels, relates to the period 1948–67 when the city was under Jordanian rule. That is to say that the sign was probably bilingual Arabic-English with Hebrew subsequently inset above both the Arabic and the English after capture of the city by Israel following the 1967 war. The third type of sign carried all three languages enclosed in a single panel with Hebrew on top, Arabic in the middle and English at the bottom. The historicity of the pattern is inferred, however, rather than attested through archival research – in total contrast to Pred. The history, as a result, is descriptive rather than analytical and the social world of the city thereby remains concealed from the view of the sociolinguist by dominant and unproblematised ideologies. Thus, we are returned to one of the central issues for language in the city in general. These various cases on urban place names show that the toponym is a mundane site of language practices and behaviours but that it deeply imbued with ideological concerns. If read appropriately, the place name is very revealing of the function of language with regard to the specific, and often conflictual and multiple, meaning(s) of urban space. Such acts of reading rightly address the toponym as a feature of official language policy, but they must also be sensitive to and make accessible the naming of place from below.

Ghettoes, enclaves and networks

Language is also implicated in the constitution of urban space in a social, rather than linguistic, sense. It forms an important part of the social fabric of ordinary city life in the making and remaking of sense of place undertaken by the multitude of strangers that comprise urban society. Culture in general and language more specifically are crucial to understanding this facet of the urban social condition. García and Fishman (2002), for example, in a study of linguistic and cultural diversity in New York, asserts this claim in the following manner:

[I]t is [erroneous] to equate urbanization and the breakdown of culture, if not all of human society, as even such giants as Robert Redfield ... and Louis Wirth ... unfortunately assumed in their classic studies of immigrants and rural migrants. Rather, a mix of continuity, adaptation and adoption seem to characterize the lion's share of the urban experience. ... The stress on urban dislocation posits an underlying romantic or pastoral view of a perfect past and a demonization of the present. Neither of these perspectives comes close at all to the reality of New York City life ... New York City ... is not a welter of forlorn slums and battling ghettos but, rather, congeries of urban villages that have retained a substantial amount of traditional culture and have integrated it with an equal or even grater dose of *in situ* innovation and culture contact. ... the ethnic revival was an urban phenomenon ... traditionalization ... and the reinvention of *Gemeinschaft* are urban phenomena, but neither of them are true returns to the past but, rather, byproducts or interactions of both continuity and culture change.

(García & Fishman, 2002: 346–7)

The city, therefore, is not necessarily inimical to sustainable linguistic diversity and those who argue otherwise are guilty of an idealising rural society as bounded, homogeneous and never-changing. Such a monolithic and essentialist perspective on society is not rooted in the reality of language and its function in society, but is instead driven by ideological concerns. The specific cases here – urban Wales, USA and South Africa – extend the point elaborated in relation to the urban place name, which is to challenge the notion that language planning activity from above on its own, i.e. by central nation-state government, can bring about substantial change for language in society. Instead, these cases show, through the study of the making of discrete spaces in the city via language, that it is only in very oppressive regimes, or in situations where there exists very extensive popular will, that the impact of any such activity will be far-reaching. Even then, certain functions of language will intervene. For example, the sheer size of the Spanish-speaking Hispanic community of Los Angeles frustrates their desire to acquire English. Indeed, the phenomenon Spanglish is a product of this. Language may intervene in other ways too, in some cases deeply embedded historical rhythms continue to shape language behaviours and attitudes, as is the case with the specific language spaces of post-apartheid South Africa.

The case of the Welsh language is quite instructive in this context. It is understood by geographers of that language that it is, and has been for some time, an urban language:

Welsh is now, and has been from the last century, a predominantly urban language. It is difficult to specify the level of urbanization precisely, but the general proposition is surely undeniable. For the language this urban condition poses a problem, for all towns are, by their nature, meeting points ... Towns are cosmopolitan places where Welsh is inevitably brought face to face with English. It follows that it is much more difficult to live a life wholly in Welsh in an urban area, and the larger the town the more difficult it is, regardless of the number of Welsh-speakers.

(Aitchison & Carter, 1994: 112–13)

The difficulties posed by this 'urban condition' are not merely a question of communication, or living a life in the Welsh language, but they pertain more profoundly to a sense of values. It is implicitly understood by Welsh language activists, and those with a sympathy for the language in this sense, that the language is bound up in a sense of place that is defined by a certain set of values – 'ffordd Gymreig o fyw' a Welsh way of life that is inherently rural, peculiar to 'cefn gwlad' (literally 'back country'), and popularly known as 'Y Fro Gymraeg'. The urban condition of the language is regarded as largely irrelevant to the general condition of the language and the prospects for its survival or even revival, as exemplified in the original manifesto of 'Cymdeithas yr Iaith Gymraeg' [The Welsh Language Society] (Dafis, 1975). The emergence of a new Welsh language pressure group 'Cymuned' [Community] during the late 1990s further reinforces this point. The *raison d'être* of 'Cymuned' is the defence of 'Y Fro Gymraeg'. While recognising the fact of the growth of the Welsh language in urban Wales, they contend that the loss of the language in its rural 'heartland' would mean the death of the language itself (http://www.cymuned.net). But, as Aitchison and Carter argue, 'Y Fro Gymraeg' does not at present exist as a discrete linguistic space:

> [I]f Welsh looks to the marcher and urban areas where it can be thought of as resurgent, it looks to places where it can never be considered truly and properly dominant, that is where it is the mother tongue of a significant majority. Unfortunately, the same can be increasingly said of the traditional heartland which has been showing signs of serious attenuation. If only just over a half of the population speak Welsh then the basis for a true Welsh-language community in any meaningful sense is hardly present. It is of course true that there are areas where percentages are much higher and where Welsh-speaking communities can be found. But they are now scattered and isolated; there is no longer a Bro Gymraeg in the sense in which it was originally conceived.
>
> (Aitchison & Carter, 1994: 112–13)

It is with a certain sense of irony that one notes that the 'quiet revolution' (Aitchison & Carter, 1987) of the language in urban Wales is in itself a part of a wider process by which local worlds are being upturned. This is, perhaps, most marked in the dramatic regeneration project that is focussed upon Cardiff Bay (Thomas, 2004; Thomas & Cowell, 2002) in the city of Cardiff, the capital of Wales, but is also clear in other parts of the city (Aitchison & Carter, 1987). Here, the growth of the Welsh language is driven by both migrants from other Welsh-speaking parts of Wales and by the attractiveness of Welsh as a language of social and economical mobility – an essential language in the public sector labour market and of a burgeoning Welsh-language broadcast media industry. Each of these areas merits further serious investigation. Some research is ongoing in relation to the place of the Welsh language within the broadcast media and new technologies sector of economic activity. Early indications are that the economic activity in this sector is largely located in urban and, historically, English-speaking Wales and that Welsh occupies a variegated set of niches in the social practices of organisations in the field (Caroline Walters, pers. comm. 1 October 2006). The relationship between the languages of migrants from outside of the UK and the Welsh language has been a matter of some discussion within the policy circles in Wales. The urban context appears to be the key site for understanding this specific relationship and it is subject to other ongoing research. Similar tensions have surfaced with regard to the Irish language and migrants to Ireland. For example, the language lobby group *iMeasc* has been vocal in asserting contesting the view articulated in authoritative proclamations, as featured in the Editorial of the *Irish Times* (20 June 2005) that the English language is the sole language of choice for immigrants, to the exclusion of the Irish language (Ó Gairbhí, 2006). In urban Wales, the tension apparently relates much more closely to the matter of the provision of public services. The Welsh language is, by statute, a language in which public bodies are obliged to make their services available. The fact of the presence of other non-autochthonous languages in urban Wales has caused some to express concern at the lack of status of these other languages in the public sector domain and the lack of understanding and, perhaps, sympathy for this among some who campaign for the Welsh language. For example, such concerns were summarised in a letter penned by a director of the Commission for Racial Equality. The letter was published in response to an article in the Welsh language journal *Golwg*, based upon an interview with the self same director:

> Fe'i gwnes yn glir fod y materion treftadaeth ddiwylliannol ar gyfer y Gymraeg a'r Gaeleg yn holl bwysig a gwahanol, ac nad yw'r agenda cydraddoldeb hiliol ehangach yn tanseilio'r safbwynt hwn. Cyfeirias at sut a pham bod angen gwahanu'r anghenion hyn – ond eto'n pwysleisio'r angen i grwpiau lobïo iaith gydnabod bod cadw iaith a sicrhau ei hiroedledd yn rhan o'r sbectrwm cydraddoldeb yn y bôn ... Ni ddylai darpariaeth gwasanaeth ac anghenion y rheiny sy'n

arbennig o fregus o fewn ein cymdeithas, megis y rhai hynny na all siarad unrhyw iaith sy'n gyffredin i'r ynysoedd hyn, gael eu diraddio'n ddibwys. Mae gennym ddiddordeb yn hawliau pob dinesydd [I made it clear that the cultural heritage issues for the Welsh language and for Scottish Gaelic are extremely important and different, and that the racial equality agenda does not undermine this position. I referred to how and why it is necessary to differentiate these needs – and yet emphasising the need for language lobby groups to recognise that the conservation of a language and the securing of its longevity is basically a part of the equalities spectrum ... The provision of services and the needs of those who are especially vulnerable within our society, such as those who are not able to speak any of the languages common to these islands, ought not to be degraded so as to be unimportant. We have an interest in the rights of every citizen.]

(Kanani, 2003: 26)

A migrant, and yet local, language is remaking space in the urban USA. Los Angeles, for example, is home to more than 3 million foreign-born residents. According to the census of 2000, the exact figure is 3,449,444 individuals out of a total population of 9,519,338 (36.2% of the total resident population) (Benton-Short, Price & Friedman, 2004). The overwhelming majority of these are from two countries – Mexico and El Salvador (Table 5.3) and this remarkable growth of the Hispanic or Latino population in Los Angeles was at its most dramatic in the period between 1980 and 2000, growing at a rate of 105% (Suro & Singer, 2002). One can assume, therefore, that overwhelming majority of the foreign-born population of the city speaks Spanish as first language.

Table 5.3 Foreign-born population of Los Angeles (adapted from Benton-Short, Price & Friedman, 2004)

Country	As proportion of total foreign-born population (%)
Mexico	44
El Salvador	7
Philippines	6
Guatemala	4
Korea	4
China	3
Vietnam	3
Iran	3
All other	26

But, coincident with this is the emergence of 'Spanglish' as an urban linguistic phenomenon:

> ¿Como empezó everything? How did I stumble upon it? Walking the
> streets of El Barrio in New York City, at least initially. Wandering
> around, as the Mexican expression puts it, con la oreja al vuelo, with
> ears wide open. Later on, of course, my appreciation for Spanglish
> evolved dramatically as I travelled around los Unaited Esteits.
>
> (Stavans, 2003: 1)

Both of these phenomena merit some interrogation.

The growth of the immigrant Spanish-speaking population is apparent in all of the major urban centres of the USA (Tables 5.4 & 5.5). The
principal sites are the cities of Chicago, Los Angeles, Miami and New
York. A total of 9 million (over quarter of all Hispanics in the USA) reside
in these cities and Hispanics are now the largest ethnic minority group
in the USA at 12.5%. The next largest is African Americans (12.3%). This
growth is not confined to these four large cities, but is also significant
in other urban centres of varying sizes (Table 5.6). Cities with historical
Hispanic or Latino population, such as Houston, have experienced even
greater growth in this period. The fastest growth, however, is recorded
in 'new Latino destinations' such as the cities of Atlanta, Las Vegas,
Orlando or Washington, DC (Tables 5.7 & 5.8). These places experienced
a relative growth of 3003% in the Hispanic or Latino population in the
period between 1980 and 2000. But, when set in the context of overall

Table 5.4 Foreign-born population of New York (adapted
from Benton-Short, Price & Friedman, 2004)

Country	As proportion of total foreign-born population (%)
Dominican Republic	12
China	7
Jamaica	6
Mexico	5
Guyana	4
Ecuador	4
Haiti	3
Colombia	3
Trinidad & Tobago	3
Italy	3
All Others	50

Table 5.5 Foreign-born population of Miami (adapted from Benton-Short, Price & Friedman, 2004)

Country	As proportion of total foreign-born population (%)
Cuba	47
Nicaragua	8
Colombia	7
Haiti	6
Dominican Republic	3
Honduras	3
Jamaica	3
Peru	2
Venezuela	2
Mexico	2
Argentina	1
Ecuador	1
Brazil	1
Guatemala	1
All Other	13

Table 5.6 Urban centres with the largest Hispanic or Latino populations, 2000 (adapted from Suro & Singer, 2002)

Urban centre	Numbers of Hispanics or Latinos	As percentage of total resident population	Relative growth of Hispanic or Latino population (%) 1980–2000
Los Angeles	4,242,213	45	105
New York	2,339,836	25	60
Chicago	1,416,584	17	143
Miami	1,291,737	57	123
Houston	1,248,586	30	211
Riverside-San Bernardino	1,228,962	38	324
Orange County	875,579	31	206
Phoenix	817,012	25	261
San Antonio	816,037	51	67
Dallas	810,499	23	324

growth of population, the impact is greatest in the established metros such as Los Angeles, where they comprised 79% of the total population growth of the city. Indeed, it is noted that some of these urban centres would actually have experience a net loss of population were it not for the Hispanic or Latino newcomers (Suro & Singer, 2002).

Table 5.7   Hispanic or Latino population growth in 'new destinations', 1980–2000 (adapted from Suro & Singer, 2002)

City	Number of Hispanics or Latinos, 2000	As proportion of total population, 2000 (%)	Relative growth, 1980–2000 (%)
Atlanta	268,851	7	995
Orlando	271,627	17	859
Las Vegas	322,038	21	753
Washington, DC	432,003	9	346

Table 5.8   Hispanic or Latino population growth in three metropolitan area types, 1980–2000 (adapted from Suro & Singer, 2002)

	Relative change in Hispanic or Latino population, 1980 (%)	Relative change in Hispanic or Latino population, 1980 (%)	Relative change in Hispanic or Latino population, 1980 (%)
Established metros	43	37	97
New destinations	78	126	303
Fast-growing hubs	87	79	235

There are also a number of cities where there had been no historical base to the Hispanic or Latino population but in which the Hispanic or Latino population has emerged and grown rapidly between 1980 and 2000. All of the cities in this category are, with the exception of Phoenix, located in either California or Texas. This includes cities such as Sacramento, Orange County and Vallejo. According to Suro and Singer (2002: 6), the functions of these cities for the immigrants changed during this period from secondary destinations to initial gateways. This suggests that the older initial gateways, such as Los Angeles, are 'approaching a saturation point' (Suro & Singer, 2002: 7) with regard to job opportunities, housing and access to education. This they regard as a new dynamic:

> [I]n the past, a handful of central cities were the usual destination of immigrant newcomers from Latin America. The classic process entailed "trailblazers" leaving the ports of entry to seek opportunities in these "frontier" cities ... Family, friend, and fellow countrymen followed initial migrants and complete immigrant communities subsequently developed over time ... However, a somewhat different

process is now ... Those coming from abroad are now skirting traditional areas and settling directly in new places ... In this fashion, the
new frontier zone that has developed in the past 20 years now
encompasses many metro areas of the southeast ... And much of
Latino population growth is occurring outside of central cities
directly in the suburbs.

(Suro & Singer, 2002: 10)

It follows that this dynamic has various public-policy implications in
relation to housing, education and public transport, and language is, of
course, the key to access to public resources.

This growth has a particular geography within the city, and the
Spanish language is implicated in it. An analysis of settlement and
movement of Hispanics reveals a tension between concentration and
dispersal (Suro & Tafoya, 2004). Ethnic enclaves exist – 43% of Hispanics
live in neighbourhoods where majority of population is Hispanic – but
57% live in neighbourhoods in which Hispanics make up less than half
of the resident population (7% on average). This is a change in the pattern of the previous decade, between 1990 and 2000, during which the
increase in the Hispanic population was shared evenly between the two
types of neighbourhoods. Also, it is noted elsewhere (Suro & Singer,
2002) that the majority (54%) of Hispanics now live in the suburbs and
that this suburban population grew at a rate of 71% during the 1990s.
By 2000 the suburban Hispanic population was greater than that of the
city-centre population by 18%. In 1990, 8.7 million Hispanic individuals lived in the suburbs and 8.6 million lived in city-centre. During the
1990s there were 6.2 million newcomers to the suburban population,
bringing it to a total of 15 million, while there were 4 million newcomers to the city-centre population, bringing it to total of 12.6 million.
This characteristic is especially evident in the largest cities; for example,
the 63% rate of growth in suburbs of Chicago and 96% in the case of
Miami. Also, there is evidence that these large cities form the core of
regional clusters:

> The Latino populations of Bergen-Passaic, NJ and Nassau-Suffolk,
> NY, which adjoin New York to the east and west, together added
> some 218,000 Latinos between 1990 and 2000. Along the coast north
> of Miami, the population of the Fort Lauderdale and West Palm
> Beach metropolitan areas together increased by 242,000 Latinos. In
> each case the outlying metros of the cluster grew faster than did the
> core metro, though not in absolute terms. In Southern California,

meanwhile, the peripheral growth actually outpaced more central growth by all measures. There, the Orange County, Venture, and Riverside-San Bernardino metropolitan areas added 950,000 Latinos, which exceeded the growth in the Los Angeles-Long Beach metro both in absolute numbers and the pace of growth.

(Suro & Singer, 2002: 8)

Thus, there is an increasingly dense concentration of the Hispanic population in the established Latino locations and in the big cities, but there is also very considerable expansion into new neighbourhoods. When mapped, the spread of the Hispanic population within cities such as Chicago, Los Angeles and New York (Figures 5.1, 5.2 & 5.3) is strongly suggestive of emergence of the Spanish language as a significant feature of the social fabric of extensive parts of these cities.

The language of the spaces identified in these cities can be explored in a number of ways. The straightforward sociological studies of the Pew Hispanic Centre show that the Spanish language is a very important factor in this geography (Tables 5.9 & 5.10), for example:

Over three-quarters of Latinos who speak only English lived in minority-Latino neighbourhoods. Spanish-monolingual Latinos were more evenly divided between neighbourhoods where Latinos predominate and those where they do not. Spanish is spoken by some degree by most Hispanics living in neighborhoods where Latinos are the majority population, but English is also a strong presence. In 2000 more than half (58%) of the Latino residents of these neighborhoods were bilingual in English and Spanish and another sizeable share (14%) spoke only English. Individuals who spoke only Spanish constituted a little more than a quarter (28%) of the population in census tracts where more than half of the residents were Hispanics.

(Suro & Tafoya, 2004: 2)

Thus, while there is evidence of direct migration to suburbs by Spanish-speaking migrants, the acquisition of the English language is related to the move to the suburbs. Others, perhaps more subjective sources, state that Standard English is the lingua franca of the emerging Hispanic middle and upper-middle class (Stavans, 2003: 4). The condition of being between Spanish and English is a barrier to be overcome as quickly as possible of the migrants. Spanglish, while of interest to linguists, is regarded by many Hispanics as something which frustrates integration and socio-economic progression: 'Spanglish is often described as the

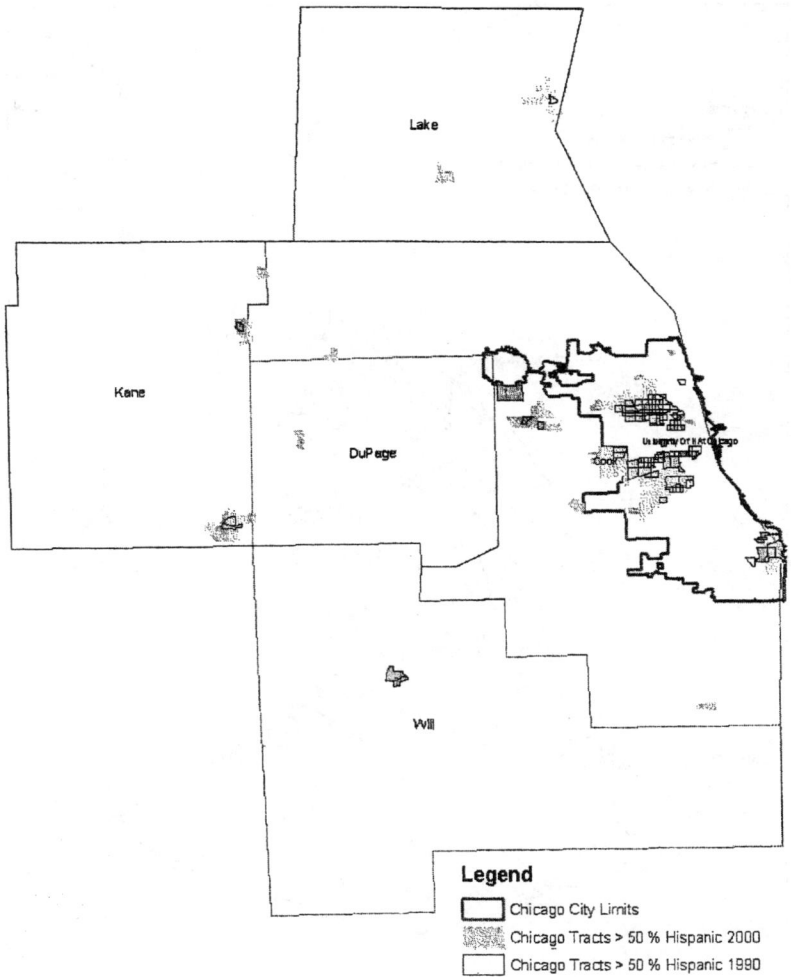

Figure 5.1 Chicago Hispanic tracts 1990–2000 (reproduced from Suro & Tafoya, 2004)

trap, la trampa Hispanics fall into on the road to assimilation – el obstáculo en el camino. Alas, the growing lower class uses it, thus procrastinating the possibility of un futuro major, a better future' (Stavans, 2003: 3). Moreover, the overwhelming majority of English monolinguals (75%) reside in minority-Latino neighbourhoods (Table 5.10). This evidence suggests that the socio-economic separation between the White and the Hispanic population of the big cities of the USA is being eroded

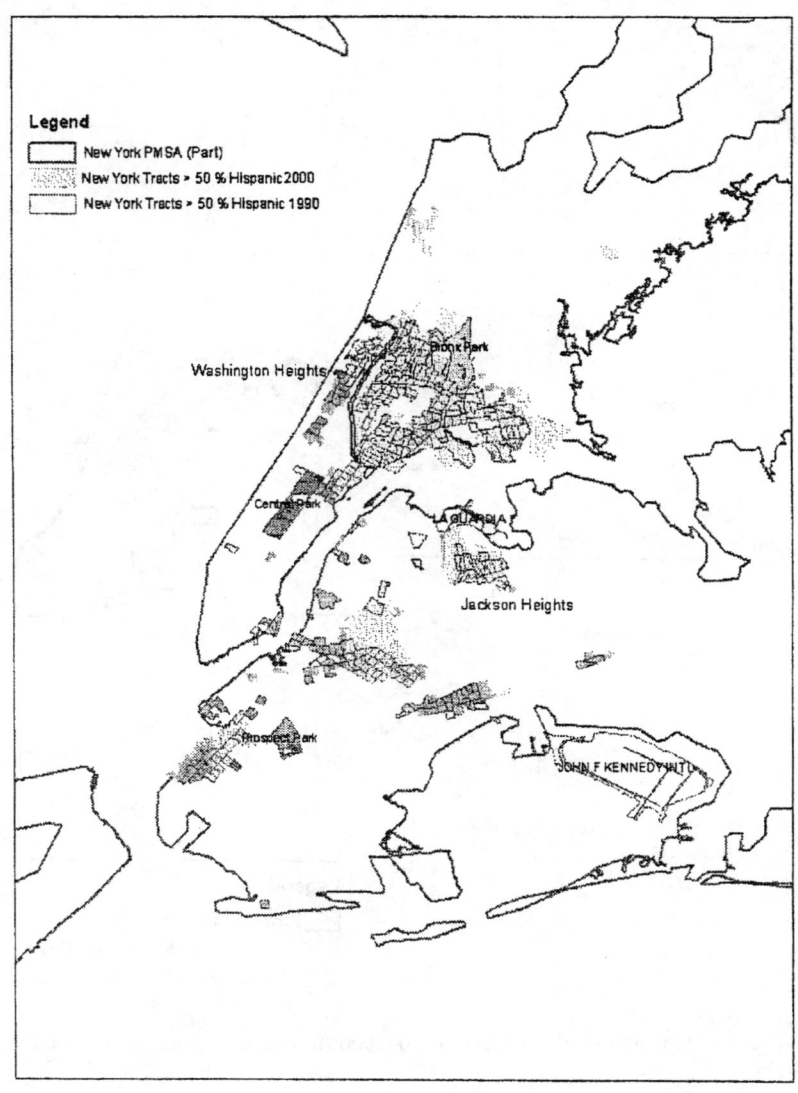

Figure 5.2 New York Hispanic tracts 1990–2000 (reproduced from Suro & Tafoya, 2004)

and that integration is being realised through the adoption of the English language, contrary to claims of commentators such as Allen (2002) and Huntingdon (2004).

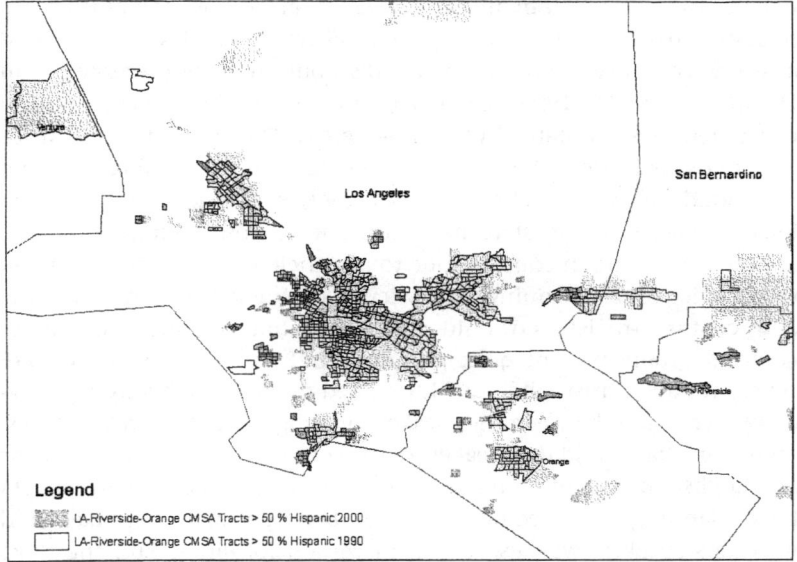

Figure 5.3 Los Angeles – Riverside – Orange County CMSA Hispanic tracts 1990–2000 (reproduced from Suro & Tafoya, 2004)

Table 5.9 Linguistic characteristics of majority-Latino neighbourhoods (adapted from Suro & Tafoya, 2004)

Spanish monolingual	28%
English monolingual	14%
Bilingual	58%

Table 5.10 Distribution of type of linguistic competence by type of Latino neighbourhoods (adapted from Suro & Tafoya, 2004)

	Majority-Latino neighbourhood	Minority-Latino neighbourhood
Spanish monolingual	53%	47%
English monolingual	25%	75%
Bilingual	55%	45%

While Spanish–English language shift in cities such as Los Angeles indicates the pathway to assimilation and is characterised by a particular geography, in the cities of South Africa the analysis of the spatial distribution reveals the persistence of the segregation associated with the practice of apartheid. Linguistic segregation arose from the pursuit of a policy of apartheid aimed at keeping racial groups apart. Often, this had a very direct impact upon the spatial distribution of languages (e.g. Van Der Merwe, 1993 & 1995) as language was frequently used as a political instrument, most notably in the urban areas. The cities of South Africa are of colonial origin, but due to heavy and constant migration from rural South Africa throughout the 20th century, the speakers of the various languages of the state have come into close contact with one another in the urban context. Due to apartheid era town planning and the practice of racial zoning, in particular during the second half of the 20th century, the levels of residential segregation between some of the language groups became quite pronounced. In an analysis of the 1996 census results, Christopher (2004) revealed that the uniformly high levels of segregation between the speakers of indigenous African languages, on the one hand, and the speakers of the colonial languages of Afrikaans and English, on the other hand, are the direct outcome of apartheid era town planning. A degree of segregation between English speakers and Afrikaans speakers was also noted in certain localities. But, the most instructive insight was that while South Africa, subsequent to the collapse of the system of apartheid by the close of the 20th century, has come to recognise itself as a multi-lingual country with 11 official languages, language contact remains at its most 'intense' in South African cities and apartheid-style patterns of segregation persist: 'Few immediate significant changes are anticipated in the present patterns of linguistic segregation, as the inherited apartheid city structure is proving remarkably resistant to transformation' (Christopher, 2004: 145). This phenomenon merits closer examination.

The colonial languages of English and Afrikaans (derived from Dutch) are the most highly urbanised of all of the languages of contemporary South Africa, and English is almost wholly so (Table 5.11). This is largely a reflection of the nature of the colonisation of South Africa and also of the particular function of English as the language of power and status. The rate of migration of other language groups to urban South Africa has accelerated post-apartheid (e.g. Western, 2002), reinforcing a process already begun during apartheid. For example, Christopher (2004) notes that in 1970 30.9% of IsiZulu speakers were urban-dwelling. By 1996 this figure rose to 44.8%, and IsiZulu speakers increased as a proportion of the total urban population of South Africa in the same period from 12.1% to 18.9%. Christopher uses an index of dissimilarity in order to measure the level of segregation in relation to indigenous and colonial languages in urban South Africa, where 0 = identical distribution and

Table 5.11 Linguistic diversity of urban South Africa (adapted from Christopher, 2004)

Language	Numbers of speakers of language in urban centres	Proportion of language community that is urbanised (%)
English	3,329,501	96.2
Afrikaans	4,880,923	84.0
Sesotho	2,152,854	65.2
Setswana	1,508,360	45.7
isiZulu	4,125,981	44.8
isiXhosa	3,210,998	44.5
isiNdebele	215,964	36.8
Xilsonga	527,878	30.1
siSwati	283,172	27.9
Sepedi	1,007,444	27.3
Tshivenda	159,427	18.2

100 = completely segregated. He found that in the period from 1951 to 1991, during the course of official apartheid, the level increased from 78 to 95. He regards a level of over 90 as 'hyper-segregation'. The results indicate a very high level of dissimilarity in general, with a national median index of 91 and with 75% of all results falling within the range 65–97. This indicates that despite post-apartheid language planning and policy changes there has been little change to the apartheid structure of urban South Africa with regard to language.

With regard to the relationship between the colonial languages of English and Afrikaans, it is the case that there never was any official segregation of speakers of English and Afrikaans. As a result, the levels of spatial segregation between these languages are lower and this is reflected in Christopher's dissimilarity index with a national median index value between English and Afrikaans of 51. There is, however, a significant variation. In 24 particular urban areas, the median index value was below 30 but in case of 19 others, the value was above 70. This is explained by the relative coincidence of race and language which Christopher describes as below:

In these cases the continuing effects of the previously legally enforced segregation between the Coloured, Indian and White populations was in evidence, where the dominant languages within these groups were different. For example, in the Albany district (Eastern Cape) the disparity between the two groups was particularly marked and may be ascribed to the different language profiles of the three population groups. Thus although 98% of non-indigenous language speakers in the former Coloured group areas spoke Afrikaans, only 23% of non-indigenous language speakers in the former White and Indian group areas did so. The result was a high degree of segregation between the two language groups as a direct result of the coincidence of race and language within a system of racially based segregation.

(Christopher, 2004: 149–50)

The persistence of the legacy of apartheid is most apparent in the city of Port Elizabeth, according to Christopher (2004). In this case, the pattern of distribution in 1996 conforms to that of apartheid era with a dissimilarity index of 96 between the largely isiXhosa-speaking population and rest of urban population. It may be provocative to suggest at this point that the persistence of linguisitic segregation can be noted elsewhere. In Montréal, for example, Elke (2002) refers to a 'conspiracy' on part of both Francophones and Anglophones to maintain the 'linguistic equilibrium' as pertained to the city during 20th century despite legislation of 1980s and 1990s (Elke, 2002: 147). This linguistic segregation is based upon many factors:

Les deux populations fondatrices et les autres communautés culturelles se partagent le territoire montréalais. Le rythme historique de leur immigration, l'affiliation ethnique ou religieuse avec les populations pré-existantes, les possibilities d'embauche et de logement déterminent l'endroit où les gens choisissent de s'installer. Ainsi, la segregation résidentielle de Montréal, quoique basée sur les traits linguistiques essentiellement, incorpore plusiers traits sociaux intimement lies aux langues. [The two founding populations and the other cultural communities share the territory of Montréal. The historical rhythm of their immigration, their ethnic or religious affiliation with pre-existing populations, the possibilities of employment and of housing determine the place where the peoples choose to locate. Thus, the residential segregation of Montréal, although based on essentially linguistic characteristics, incorporates many other social traits that are intimately bound to language.]

(Elke, 2002: 141)

To return to urban South Africa, however, Williams and Van Der Merwe, in their exploration of geolinguistic patterns in the city of Cape Town in the period 1980–91, confirm the spatial segregation of language despite their description of the city as 'unique' in South Africa, partly because of its 'tradition of racial tolerance', for example:

Cape Town, the oldest urban settlement in South Africa, is ranked third in the country's urban hierarchy with a total population of just over two million and presents a diversified economic and community structure. Because of the city's long history, a differentiated ethnic composition, its tradition of racial tolerance and the constrained physical layout, Cape Town may be regarded as unique among South African cities.

(Williams & Van Der Merwe, 1996: 58)

But even in such favourable circumstances the levels of linguistic segregation under apartheid were marked and have persisted into the post-apartheid era, with only very modest shifts. In 1991, the linguistic composition of the city was dominated by Afrikaans (47%), with smaller proportions of English (31%) and of Xhosa (20%). Mapping the relationship between language and surface area shows that Afrikaans occupies 48%, English 39% and Xhosa 13%. The mathematical imbalance is obvious, but a pattern of spatial segmentation also pertains to the geographical distribution of the languages. There is a concentration of Afrikaans in the northern and eastern suburbs, of English in the historical city-centre and the south-western suburbs, and of Xhosa along south-eastern parts of city (Figure 5.4).

They also traced the geography of language shift in the city under apartheid in 65 of 264 neighbourhoods of the city in the period 1980–91 (Figure 5.5). They noted a shift towards English at the expense of Afrikaans in some areas (34), and a shift in the opposite direction in a smaller number (26) of other neighbourhoods. While there is a general increase in the numbers of Xhosa speakers, the extent of language shift is very limited, with an increase of 4 neighbourhoods. This is a direct result of the enforcement of apartheid. The total surface area occupied by Xhosa speakers, however, expanded from 18 sq km (3%) to 96 sq km (13%), coincident to the growth of city more generally. In contrast, the extent of the English-speaking area remained constant, but proportion occupied by Afrikaans speakers contracted from 58% in 1980 to 48% in 1991.This leads Williams and Van Der Merwe to conclude that

The spatial patterns illustrated suggest underlying processes of legal separation, selected interaction, social ecology, assimilation and

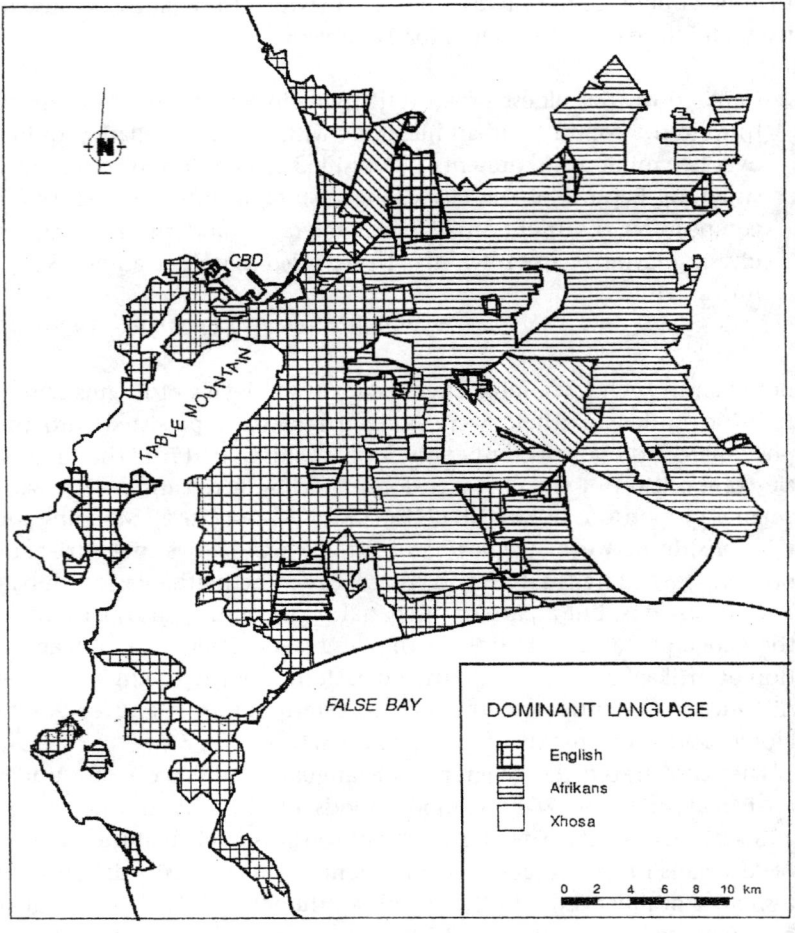

Figure 5.4 Dominant language in Cape Town 1991 (reproduced from Williams & Van Der Merwe, 1996)

language segregation. The tendency of people to settle amongst others of similar ethnic values and cultural status either willingly or by law may be statistically measured with the aid of the segregation index. Afrikaans and English do not reflect an even distribution in relation to each other in the metropolitan area of Cape Town. The relatively high index values of 57% and 60% respectively confirm

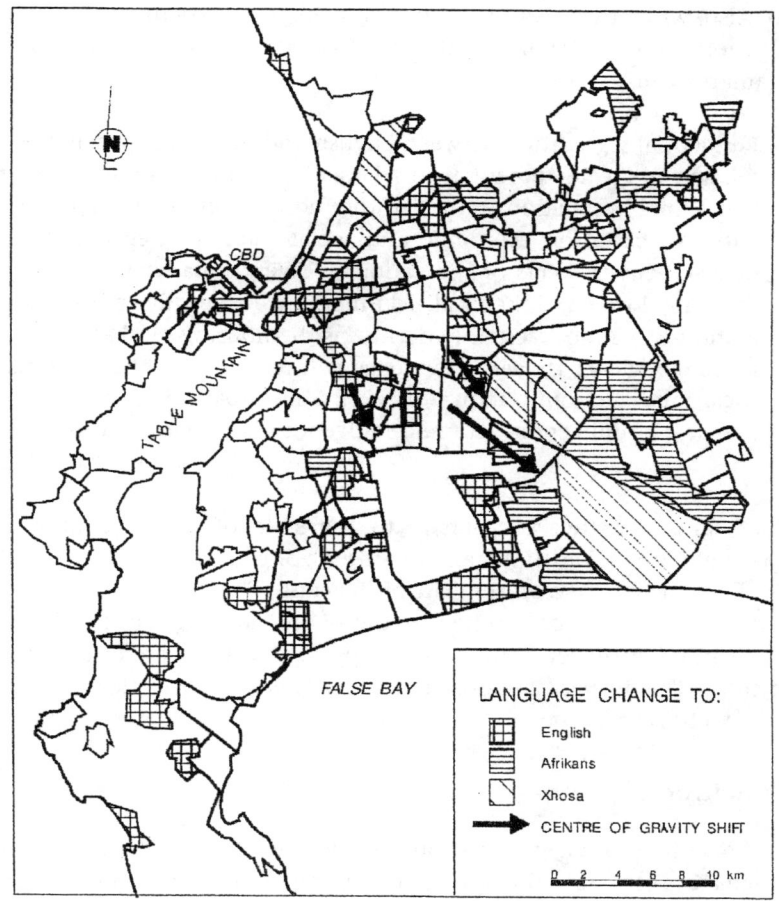

Figure 5.5 Language shift in Cape Town 1980–1991 (reproduced from Williams & Van Der Merwe, 1996)

the segregated map patterns. The comparable segregation index for Xhosa is 96%. The latter is a clear manifestation of the colonial city structure in South Africa during the apartheid era.

(Williams & Van Der Merwe, 1996: 59)

It can be concluded that, therefore, African–non-African linguistic segregation in urban South Africa is very marked and is likely to remain

so. Also, while there is the potential for the reduction of levels of segregation between English and Afrikaans, this is unlikely to be very
dramatic, thus:

> Residential segregation between English and Afrikaans speaking peo-
> ple shows greater potential for reduction as the Coloured, Indian
> and White populations return to the more integrated pre-apartheid
> patterns, based on economic and social status. Segregation levels
> between the speakers of the various indigenous languages are sub-
> stantially lower and the localised inheritance of legally enforced sep-
> aration will almost certainly decline as the housing market becomes
> more flexible ... However, language will remain a significant racial,
> social and economic indicator, when the broad division between
> speakers of indigenous and non-indigenous languages is considered.
> (Christopher, 2004: 152)

That said, a further complexity to the state of language in post-
apartheid urban South Africa is an attitude of general hostility towards
the English language on the part of the state. This may be a contribu-
tory factor in the very limited nature of the language shift at macro
levels in urban society, but it would appear that there are other resistances to this in very personal domains. This will be explored in the
next section of the book.

Conclusions

The various language situations explored in this chapter show how
language is central to the sense of place, the rhythms, the mobility, the
fixity, the connection and disconnection that variously define social
life in the city. The case of the Welsh language in Cardiff, the capital
city of Wales, and that of Spanish in the urban USA along with that of
urban linguistic diversity in post-apartheid South Africa illustrate how
language is directly implicated in the construction of social and spatial
division, manifest in language ghettoes, enclaves and networks. As a
function of the negotiation and management of difference and its
peculiar intensity in the urban context, language may serve the interests of empowered élites but it is also a useful tool in the mundane,
everyday practices and behaviours associated with the resistance of
marginal groups. The salience of mundane, yet powerful, language
behaviours and practices to the making of sense of place in the city is
clear in our study of urban place names in cities far-removed in both

time and space, from early modern Londonderry to late 20th-century Belfast, from 19th-century Stockholm to post-colonial urban Africa. Language is fundamental to the appropriation of space and the significance of place in the urban context and this fact has far-reaching implications for both the city and language. The management of language in this context is not merely a practical matter of communication but rather it relates to the very meaning of society in the city, the meaning of the idea of the city itself.

6
Identity

Introduction

The idea of the 'stranger', or 'otherness', and its relation to language is central to understanding urban life. And it is through the idea of ethnicity that community and the individual in the city are problematised. The characteristic features of the open intensity which define the city as a site of proximity and co-presence, as a multiplicity of space-times and as a meeting place, are shown to have significant implications for language. This includes, for the migrant for example, the development of hybridity that is often expressed in complex linguistic identities. It also includes the effects upon language of the increasing interpenetration of the global and the local which is a feature of the contemporary form of globalisation. Due to the nature of city life, tensions between social constructivist and primordial perspectives on ethnicity are at their most exposed and explicit in the urban context. For example, the city is the site of the re-invention or of the nostalgic authentification and commodification of ethnicity for its consumption by tourists or for political ends. In this sense, it can be argued that ideas such as nationalism are made in the city. However, in this work, ethnicity is contrasted with the nation and with national identity, which are constructs associated with a particular political project – the nation-state. Ethnicity, whatever the overarching polity, is central to identities in the city, and especially so in relation to linguistic and cultural diversity. And the notion of ethnicity in this context is best approached through the idea of the urban 'stranger'. Thus, the function of language in the city, understood as a site of multilayered and complex relational webs, is defined in part by the bonds between the known self, the alien other and the relative intimacy of the 'stranger'. Also, ways in which the inherent instability and insecurity of urban identities erode the ethnolinguistic vitality of languages are identified. The implications of these insights for language planning and policy, in relation to notions of citizenship and the nature of the spatial expression of heterogeneity *via* public places and civic values, are stated.

Ethnic identity and the urban stranger

The matter of ethnicity has been alluded to several times already in this study. The notion is crucial to the main models which variously inform language planning. In disciplines concerned with urban planning and the city there is a new emphasis on ethnic identity. Almost all parts of the globe are being shaped by unprecedented movements of peoples which are often both sudden and dramatic. The impact of this traffic is felt first and most profoundly on the city and it is a recurring theme. Issues regarding identity and ethnicity are in various ways, therefore, of significance to the sociology of language and of scholarly considerations of the nature of linguistic diversity in the city. As noted elsewhere (Mac Giolla Chríost, 2001 & 2003), the term ethnicity appears to have only entered the academic vocabulary as recently as the 1970s. According to Glazer and Moynihan, it first appeared in the *Oxford English Dictionary* as recently as 1972 as a new conceptual term (1975: 1). The relative novelty of the term may explain some of the difficulties which persist in reaching a definitive understanding of the term. Connor, for example, summarises the challenge of defining ethnicity and differentiating it from other related concepts thus:

> With nationalism pre-empted, authorities have had difficulty agreeing on a term to describe the loyalty of segments of a state's population to their particular nation. Ethnicity, primordialism, pluralism, tribalism, regionalism, communalism, and parochialism are among the most commonly encountered. This varied vocabulary further impedes an understanding of nationalism by creating the impression that each is describing a separate phenomenon.
>
> (Connor, 1978: 386)

Some other commentators of that period record that the term 'ethnicity' is used in the academic literature by many scholars without giving due consideration to the actual meaning, or possible meanings, of the term (e.g. Isajiw, 1980). May (2001) has shown, more recently, that certain presumptions with regard to the meaning of ethnicity were widely held at that time. In short, ethnicity was quite unproblematised as a concept. He puts it as follows: 'If a particular view of ethnicity was assumed in these studies it tended to accord de facto with the "cultural stuff" of ethnicity – ancestry, culture and language' (May, 2001: 26). During the last quarter of the 20th century the volume of writing in the area of ethnicity expanded substantially. As a consequence our understanding of the term has deepened, based upon various different insights into the nature of ethnicity drawn from a range of disciplines. It is not possible to present an exhaustive analysis of the historical development of the idea of ethnicity here; however, it is necessary that the term be as closely defined as is possible, given the limitations of space in this text.

It can be said that much of the work on developing an understanding of ethnicity has turned upon two distinct and wholly incompatible positions on ethnicity. These positions are termed 'primordial', on the one hand, and 'instrumental' or 'social constructivist', on other hand. In brief, it is the primordial view that ethnicity constitutes a fundamental feature of society that is both natural and unalienable. That is to say that all individuals possess and, indeed, are defined by a certain fixed sense of ethnicity from birth and that same singular sense of ethnic identity is carried by each and everyone until death. The primordialist position, therefore, is that ethnicity is defined by fixed cultural and biological heritages and that it is territorially rooted. In historical terms, this perspective on the nature of ethnic identity is most closely associated with the Romantic nationalism of Humboldt, Herder and Fichte, whereby the German *Volk* was defined by 'language, blood and soil'. The more recent development of the primordial position on ethnicity, following Geertz, moves away from the view that these attachments in language, blood and soil are primordial in any *real* sense. It is argued instead that such attachments are *perceived* to be primordial by the ethnic group. In this way, therefore, the actions of individual members of ethnic groups are rooted in their earliest socialisation as ethnic group members and arise from specific and exclusive primordial ties:

> By a primordial attachment is meant one that stems from the 'givens'
> of existence, or more precisely … the assumed givens of social exis-
> tence: immediate contiguity and live connection mainly, but beyond
> them the giveness that stems from being born into a particular …
> community, speaking a particular language … and following partic-
> ular social practices. These congruities of blood, speech, custom
> and so on, are seen to have an ineffable, and at times overpowering,

coerciveness in and of themselves. One is bound to one's kinsman, one's neighbour ... as the result not merely of personal affection, tactical necessity, common interest or incurred moral obligation, but at least in great part by virtue of some unaccountable absolute import attributed to the very tie itself.

(Geertz, 1973: 259)

The social constructivist critique of the primordial position characterises it as a form of cultural determinism. It is argued, in this context, that the primordial approach does not adequately explain the evolution over time of the sense of ethnicity held by groups. According to the social constructivist position, it is clear, in a historical sense, that ethnic groups place emphasis upon some certain ethnic attributes at some times while, at certain other times, they place emphasis on other very different attributes of ethnicity. In short, they argue that the primordial position fails to account for the variations, complexities and multiplicities of identity pertaining to the individual as well as the collective across time and place. The social constructivist position is in sharp contrast to the primordial view in which ethnicity is very much determined by fixed, objective, social constraints. Change and agency, and not fixity, are central to the social constructivist position on ethnicity. Thus, it is through subjective, social action that ethnic identity is constructed and this may take various forms. Barth (1969), for example, argues that ethnic groups are not defined by certain fixed attributes, be they grounded in culture, biology or place, but are instead made through their relationships to other groups:

[E]thnic categories provide an organisational vessel that may be given varying amounts and forms of content in different sociocultural systems ... The critical focus of investigation from this point of view becomes the ethnic boundary that defines the group, not the cultural stuff that it encloses.

(Barth, 1969: 14–15)

That is to say that while certain specific attributes become significant markers of ethnicity it is not as a result of their intrinsic quality but rather is because of their relevance in signalling difference to other ethnic groups. It is the function, therefore, of certain specific attributes to define and to maintain senses of difference between ethnic groups. Ethnic groups are, in this way, the products of the boundaries that result from the identification of difference. The cultural content, as it were, of an ethnic group is explained as a construct of the collective members of the group and is a function of the relationship between them and other groups. In this sense ethnicity is a social resource that is subject to the manipulation of the ethnic group and its individual members. Worsley (1984) puts it as follows: 'Cultural traits are not absolutes or simply intellectual categories, but are invoked to provide identities which legitimise claims to rights. They are strategies or weapons in competitions over scarce social goods' (Worsley, 1984: 249).

Perceiving ethnicity as a construct and the ethnic group as a collective of mutual self-interest can explain both the continuity and the change that can be ascribed to ethnic group identity. The social constructivist position also explains why ethnicity has been such a durable mechanism for socio-political mobilisation. The competitive efficacy of strategies and tools with regard to the acquisition of resources is critical to the material well-being of the collective. The effectiveness of such strategies and tools depend upon the capacity for the group to mobilise its members. In this context, the various attributes of ethnicity must be capable of being manipulated so as to adapt the group's strategies or tools to the particular discourse that is shaping competition for resources. In short, it is necessary to be able to mobilise the group on the basis of any ethnic attribute that is of instrumental value according to the given socio-political circumstances.

The strongest versions of the social constructivist position contend that ethnicity is based upon claims to cultural and other attributes that are of spurious authenticity. Proponents of this position argue that ethnic identity is, in the literal sense, an invented tradition (e.g. Hobsbawm & Ranger, 1983). It is argued that in order to acquire resources an individual or group will behave in the manner most likely to maximise the amount of resources that could be available to them. They will be sensitive to the market value and advantages ascribed to specific ethnic attributes and will seek to deploy or to cast aside certain attributes in accordance with their obtaining optimal profit in the market. Hence, ethnicity is nothing other than a device or commodity to be exchanged in the pursuit of self-interest. Ethnic identity is thereby taken into possession from within a hierarchy of ethnic and other attributes, any of which may be forefronted according to the demands of circumstance. This instrumental and situational contingency of ethnicity is described by Nagel thus: '[the] chosen ethnic identity is determined by the individual's perception of its meaning to different audiences, its salience in different social contexts, and its utility in different settings' (Nagel, 1994: 155). At their extremes these two perspectives on ethnicity comprise a sharply opposed dichotomy, across which there is no common ground. The result is a conceptual poverty that is described by A. D. Smith as follows:

> By fixing attention mainly on the great dimensions and 'fault lines' of religion, customs, language and institutions, we run the risk of treating ethnicity as something primordial and fixed. By concentrating solely on the attitudes and sentiments and political movements of specific *ethnie* or ethnic fragments, we risk being so caught up in the day-to-day ebb and flow of ethnic phenomena that we see them as wholly dependant 'tools' or 'boundary markers' of other social and economic forces.
>
> (A. D. Smith, 1986: 211)

In seeking a resolution of the acute subjectivity of the instrumentalist position and the rigid objectivity of the primordialist position on ethnicity, A. D. Smith argues that through adopting a 'symbolic' position on ethnicity the primordialist and instrumentalist dichotomy on ethnicity may be transcended. This is achieved by

> [A]ttending to the complex of myths, symbols, memories and values that are handed down the generations of collectivities and which define them to themselves and those outside, we can treat *ethnie* as both mutable and durable at the same time, and ethnicity as both fluctuating and recurrent in history. Ethnicity and *ethnie* are no longer purely static attributes of humanity; but neither are they the instruments of other forces or boundary mechanisms of otherwise fluid cultures.
>
> (A. D. Smith, 1986: 211)

The ethnic community, or *'ethnie'* [pl. *ethnies*], is defined both by its historical continuity and its capacity for transformation. Its key features are the ascription of a collective proper name for the group, a myth of common ancestry, shared historical memories, various peculiar elements of a common culture, an association with a homeland and a sense of solidarity. A. D. Smith conceives of ethnicity as incorporating both the 'cultural stuff' of ethnic identity and the function of agency upon it, thus:

> [Ethnicity] relates mainly to a sense of communality based on history and culture, rather than to any collectivity or to the concept of

ideology. In this, I follow the emendation proposed by Epstein to the literature of 'situational' ethnicity in which the growth of a sense of the collective self is treated as an important part of a group (especially ethnic) identity and solidarity. Only here, the sense of self is viewed through the prism of symbols and mythologies of the community's heritage ... the core of ethnicity, as it has been transmitted in the historical record and as it shapes individual experience, resides in this quartet of 'myths, memories, values and symbols' and in the characteristic forms and styles and genres of certain historical configurations of populations.

(A. D. Smith, 1986: 14–15)

More specifically, with regard to language, important critics of language in ethnicity in the contemporary world caution against placing too much emphasis on the fragmentation of identity, its rootlessness and its contingent nature, arguing that this understates the durable appeal of ethnicity. For example, May argues robustly that the disregard for the notion of historical continuity in ethnic, cultural and linguistic terms means that the situational perspective on ethnicity is over-inflated by some proponents of postmodernism (May, 2001: 39):

The fragmented, dispersed and decentred individual of the postmodern world is supposedly able to choose from a bewildering range of identity styles and forms of political mobilisation, and ethnicity, it seems, is just one of them. ... [T]his position significantly understates the key role that ethnicity often assumes in the processes of identity formation and social and political mobilisation.

(May, 2001: 24)

This, potentially, invites one to more closely examine the function of ethnicity and language in relation to socio-political organisation and mobilisation in the city. It opens up a space for a politicised ethnicity in the urban context. May, however, is correct to remind us that the range of possibilities available to individuals in relation to ethnic identity will vary according to circumstance and that the opportunities open to some will be more limited than for others. For example, in the context of contemporary USA: 'A white American may have a wide range of ethnic options from which to choose on the basis of their ancestry. An African American, in contrast, is confronted with essentially one ethnic choice – black' (May, 2001: 40). Such limitations are situated in the

structural constraints set by others, which Nagel, for example, characterises as follows:

> [T]he extent to which ethnicity can be freely constructed by individ-
> uals or groups is quite narrow when compulsory ethnic categories are
> imposed by others. Such limits on ethnic formation can be official or
> unofficial. In either case, externally enforced ethnic boundaries can
> be powerful determinants of both the content and meaning of par-
> ticular ethnicities.
>
> (Nagel, 1994: 156)

In drawing some of our lines of argument together here, it can be concluded that ethnicity cannot be considered to be 'a completely arbitrary construct' (Roosens, 1989: 156), but it is also the case that ethnic
identity possesses a certain quality of ambiguity or elasticity. This quality, according to Eriksen (1993), is related to 'a negotiable history and
a negotiable cultural content' (Eriksen, 1993: 73). The nature of such
negotiation and, therefore, the extent of durability and contingency
that is inherent to ethnicity is a key concern at this point. Let us return
to the work of Barth (1969), who understands ethnicity as the social
organisation of cultural difference mediated by stable social interactions across group boundaries. He made it clear that the nature of the
organisation of ethnicity is historically specific:

> These modern variants for poly-ethnic organization emerge in a
> world of bureaucratic administration, developed communications,
> and progressive urbanization. Clearly, under radically different cir-
> cumstances, the critical factors in the definition and maintenance
> of ethnic boundaries would be different.
>
> (Barth, 1969: 35–6)

Also, he pointed out that despite the structuring properties of ethnic
boundaries in creating dichotomised ethnic neighbours, his own fieldwork revealed that many ethnic groups 'do not tend to sort themselves
out in this way' (Barth, 1969: 29). The results of his pursuit of this
apparent anomaly appear in more recent work where he argues for the
necessity of alternative perspectives upon the functioning of boundaries in relation to ethnicity (e.g. Barth, 1984). In this, and other more
recent work again, he contends that mechanisms other than simple,
exclusive boundaries are at work and that these 'should serve to empha-
size properties both of separability and interpenetration, suggested

perhaps by an imagery of streams, or currents within a river: distinctly there, powerful in transporting objects and creating whirlpools, yet only relative in their distinctiveness and ephemeral in their unity' (Barth, 1984: 80). In one of his most recent reflections the 'cultural stuff' of ethnicity is problematised as a key site for the authentic appropriation of meaning and identity, for example: '[I]n our view of history we broke loose from the idea of history as simply the objective source and cause of ethnicity and approached it as a form of synchronic rhetoric – a struggle to appropriate the past, as one might say today' (Barth, 1998: 6). Here, his language carries some echoes of social constructivism and postmodern thought in which the 'cultural stuff' of ethnicity is a resource to be drawn upon and deployed in accordance with the interests of the individual and collective under the given circumstances. Hall (1996), for example, terms it as a matter of strategy in which identities are questions of using the resources of history, language and culture in the process of 'becoming rather than being' (Hall, 1996: 4). In the context of the historical contingency of Barth's model, it is significant that he argues that institutions, and here one might include the city as a polity or the institutions of city governance, operate in such a manner as to constrain the meaningful expression of identity for minority ethnic groups. The result of this suppression or even oppression may be sentiments of frustration and even crisis within such minority collectivities (Barth, 1998). This frustration or crisis may find outlets in relationships between ethnic groups or between a given minority group and the institutions of governance. Barth (1998) justifies revisiting his original work on ethnicity due to the changed historical circumstances of postmodernity and now identifies an amorphous mechanism characterised as a stream of tradition at work upon ethnicity and causing the notion of the ethnic boundary to be refashioned:

> Whereas my effort until now has been to emphasize the search for distinctions, for the fuller delimitation of the contradictions of pluralism, any closer and fuller analysis forces us to acknowledge the relativity of these boundaries, or rather the interpenetration and constant interchange implicit in the imagery of currents.
>
> (Barth, 1984: 83)

Thus, a specific point can be drawn with regard to Barth's view on the function of boundaries in ethnicity. Equally, a more general point is implied which is that the durability of the form of ethnicity under the conditions of postmodernity is contingent upon the particular responses of individuals and collectivities to the specifics of those conditions. It is now appropriate to turn to the particular circumstances of linguistic diversity in the city so as to attempt to understand how these issues may play out in practice.

Some language practices

Set in the context of the nation-state, the city is expected to make appropriate national citizens of its various and diverse inhabitants, many of whom may well originate from someplace beyond the boundaries of the state. The very substantial migration of millions of individuals from Spanish-speaking America to the urban USA during the 1980s and 1990s has become a very real political issue during first few years of the 21st century. This is marked by a high-profile public debate regarding the place of immigrants, especially illegal immigrants, in society in that country. On the one hand, these immigrants are an integral feature of all major US cities, but on the other hand, at a national level and in the context of the nation-state, they are viewed as an alien and the threatening other. The case of the new Spanish-speaking population in the urban USA suggests that while cities are being changed, the nation-state is resisting – an experience which is shared by many cities and states in the developed North. In Los Angeles the political impact has been especially marked, to the extent that the current mayor of the city, Antonio Villaraigosa, has found it expedient to rediscover his own skills in the Spanish language – so as to maximise and mobilise the Spanish-speaking vote. More broadly speaking, this debate has been intensified recently by attempts by the Republican President Bush to introduce legislation that will, potentially, enable illegal immigrants to obtain US citizenship, while at the same time building further physical barriers along the border between the USA and Mexico, one of the principal points at which illegal migrants gain access to the USA. The public profile of the issue has been raised enormously by a series of massive public demonstrations conducted by illegal immigrants in largest cities of the USA, including Los Angeles, Chicago and New York (e.g. Burkeman, 2006). The public debate in the USA and elsewhere in the English-speaking states of the developed North continually touches upon language as an issue and, in particular, the necessity of acquisition of the English language for the appropriate citizen (Phan, 2005; Garner, 2006; Ó Colchúin, 2006). The emphasis placed on language in the case of the Hispanic migration to the urban USA relates to the fact that the first language of these migrants is invariably Spanish. Thus, the Spanish language is a very obvious feature of contemporary city life in the USA. At one of the massive street demonstrations of 2006, a crowd in excess of half a million was reported to chant bilingually 'Sí se puede. Yes we can' (Burkeman, 2006). One may note with a certain sense of irony a very prominent advertisement located at Los Angeles International Airport for a mobile phone which states '¿Se puede cruzar la frontera usando el walkie-talkie? Yes you can. – Can you walkie-talkie across the border? Se puede'. (Photograph 6.1). Also, a crowd of half a million attending a similar such rally in the city of Dallas was noted to chant in both English and Spanish 'Today we march, tomorrow we vote' (Gumbel, 2006). This is suggestive of a place for the Spanish language in the socio-political mobilisation of, perhaps, the most audible (if not visible) ethnic minority group in the cities of the contemporary USA. Language, as a defining feature of the debate, gained a high-level focal point upon the occasion of the translation and release for sale of a Spanish language version of the national anthem of the USA. This

Photograph 6.1 Advertising hoarding at Los Angeles International Airport (the author, 2005)

event led to the introduction of a resolution in the senate affirming that the national anthem be recited or sung only in the English language (Alexander, 2006). The language issue also arose during the course of debates between 17th and 19th of May of that year on the Comprehensive Immigration Reform Act (CIRA) 2006. This act proposed that competence in the English language be required to be demonstrated by candidates for US citizenship: 'in order to adjust status to that of a lawful permanent resident [the applicant for citizenship] must demonstrate a knowledge of the English language or satisfactory pursuit of a course of study to acquire such a knowledge of the English language' (CIRA, Section 644[F]). In addition, an amendment was proposed, and passed, declaring that English language is the national language of the USA (Frist, 2006). While this was criticised by prominent Democrats as 'racist' and 'directed at people who speak Spanish' (BBC News, 2006), it is also the case that the Democratic Party have for many years declared English to be the 'unifying' and 'common' language of the USA (e.g. McCain, 1998).

A more scientific approach to this issue would uncover the fact that Spanish speakers are not a linguistically homogeneous group nor is their adherence to the Spanish language monolithic. Some of the more astute commentators are aware of the complexity and the contradictions (Hernandez, 2005). Their cultural complexity, for example, is given certain public and quite mundane expressions. This includes resistance to official categories of identity and the rejection, by some, of the labels 'Hispanic' and 'Latino' (Photograph 6.2). Both terms, however, are very widely used – often interchanged – by academics, opinion-formers and politicians alike. A brief examination of some survey data is instructive in this regard. According to the 2000 census, 90% of population of the USA was self-defined either as White, Black, Asian, American Indian or Pacific Islander. Federal law requires that the census enable the collection, analysis and publication of data on individuals of 'Spanish culture, origin or descent' (Tafoya, 2004: 4). Thus, the census question asks 'Is this person Spanish/ Hispanic/ Latino?' and, if the response is positive, the respondent is to state whether they are Mexican/Mexican American/Chicano, Cuban, Puerto Rican or Other. The census also asked a question regarding race 'What is this person's race?' and offers by way of range of possible responses the following categories – White, Black/African American/Negro, American Indian/Alaska Native, Asian Indian, Chinese, Filipino, Japanese, Korean, Vietnamese, Other Asian, Native Hawaiin, Guarrianian/Chamorro, Samoan, Other Pacific Islander or Some Other Race (SOR). Half of all Hispanics picked one of these

Photograph 6.2   T-shirt in Central City, Los Angeles (the author, 2005)

categories, but 15 million (42%) chose the category 'Some Other Race' (Table 6.1):

> According to federal policy and accepted social science, Hispanics do not constitute a separate race and can in fact be of any race. The 2000 Census asked respondents first to mark off whether they were 'Spanish/Hispanic/Latino' and then in a separate question to specify their race. Among those who identified themselves as Hispanics, nearly half (48 percent) were counted as white. Blacks made up two percent. The American Indian, Asian, and Pacific Islander categories each accounted for small fractions. Surprisingly, given the large

Table 6.1 Population of Hispanic origin in USA by race, 2000 (adapted from Tafoya, 2004)

Race	Number	Percent of Hispanic population
One race	*33,081,736*	*93.7*
White	16,907,852	47.9
Black or African American	710,353	2.0
American Indian and Alaska Native	407,073	1.2
Asian	119,829	0.3
Native Hawaiin and other Pacific Islander	45,326	0.1
Some other race	14,891,303	42.2
Two or more races	*2,224,082*	*6.3*
Total	*35,305,818*	

Table 6.2 Hispanic population in USA by race in select urban centres, 2000 (adapted from Logan, 2003)

	Los Angeles	New York	Chicago	Miami	Houston
White Hispanic*	44.7%	41.8%	49.3%	86.2%	53.8%
Hispanic Hispanic*	54.3%	49.0%	48.9%	10.9%	45.1%
Black Hispanic*	1.1%	9.2%	1.8%	2.9%	1.2%

*as proportion of total resident Hispanic population

number of Latinos whose parentage includes combinations of white, African and indigenous ancestries, only six percent described themselves as being of two or more races. The only racial identifier, other than white, that captured a major share of the Latino population (42 percent) was the non-identifier, 'some other race'.

(Tafoya, 2004: 1)

The extent to which Hispanics opt for the category SOR is quite provocative. Logan (2003) describes the SOR Hispanics as 'Hispanic Hispanics' (Table 6.2). He also notes that there are a quarter million Mexicans in the USA who identify themselves as Black, with a total of almost 1 million Hispanics who identify themselves as Black. Those most likely to do so are Dominicans and Puerto Ricans while Cubans almost invariably identify themselves as White. Given these simple facts, it is not surprising to learn that this racial structuring of Hispanic identity has a peculiar city geography. Miami has the greater share of White Hispanics, New York has the greater share of Black Hispanics, and metropolitan California and Texas have greater share of Hispanic Hispanics.

According to Tafoya (2004), Hispanics that describe themselves as White have higher levels of education, greater levels of disposable income and greater engagement with civil society than those that choose the category SOR. It is concluded that Hispanics see race as a measure of belonging, and whiteness as a measure of inclusion, or of perceived inclusion (Tafoya, 2004: 1):

> Using data from the 2000 Census this report details those differences, showing that SOR [Some Other Race] Hispanics are less educated, less likely to be citizens, poorer, less likely to speak English exclusively and are less often intermarried with non-Hispanic whites ... The socio-economic profiles, the attitudes, the language usage and even the reported political behaviour of SOR Hispanics consistently place them at a distance from non-Hispanic whites. In comparison, white-Hispanics consistently occupy the intermediate ground between SOR Hispanics and non-Hispanic whites.
>
> (Tafoya, 2004: 5)

This issue of racialised senses of appropriate forms of belonging are cross-cut by language. There are some significant differences in the use of the Spanish language and the English language by SOR Hispanics and White Hispanics. For example, SOR Hispanics and those that are foreign-born (that is, outside of the USA) are less likely to only speak English (Table 6.3). Note that, in this case, the survey population is aged 5 years and over.

There is also a patterning that relates to the relative linguistic diversity of the residential neighbourhood. According to Logan (2003), White Hispanics on average live in neighbourhoods in which 47% of the

Table 6.3 Language competence among native-born (USA) and foreign-born (ex USA) SOR Hispanics and white Hispanics (adapted from Tafoya, 2004)

Identity	Spanish only	Bilingual	English only
White Hispanic, native-born	1.1	62.3	36.2
SOR Hispanic, native-born	1.2	72.6	26.0
White Hispanic, foreign-born	18.2	74.7	6.4
SOR Hispanic, foreign-born	18.6	75.5	5.6
White Hispanic, all	8.5	67.7	23.3
SOR Hispanic, all	9.7	74.0	16.1

population as a whole speak a language other than English at home. Whereas, Hispanic Hispanics live in neighbourhoods where 49.1% of the population speak at home a language other than English and Black Hispanics live in neighbourhoods where 37.7% of population speak language other than English at home. This may be compared with the Non-Hispanic Blacks population who live in neighbourhoods in which 17.2% of the resident population speak at home a language other than English. Logan's data suggest that Hispanics who identify as neither Black nor White are much more likely to speak Spanish at home, and are more likely to be the newest immigrants and foreign-born. This complexity of language, race and Hispanic identity is described by Logan as a 'cultural turn' (Logan, 2003: 11) and it is argued that this complexity is more likely to deepen than not.

Other detailed data on actual language use illuminates some aspects of this complexity with regard to language practices and behaviours, in particular information on Spanish–English code-switching and surveys on sociological significance of Spanish language news media. For example, Toribio (2002) asserts that code-switching can be viewed as fulfilling several contradictory functions as either enabling the maintenance of the Spanish language while facilitating the juxtaposing of an authentic Latino identity in North American society or, on the other hand, facilitating the decline of the Spanish language in the USA and compromising the cultural integrity of the Hispanic identity (Toribio, 2002: 89–90). Through the construction of in-depth profiles of archetypal individuals in metropolitan California on code-switching attitudes and language use, Toribio concludes that code-switching serves an important function in signalling their identity for some speakers of Spanish. For example, 'Yanira', born in the eastern part of Los Angeles of Mexican immigrant parents, speaks Spanish at home and acquired English at school. Her profile is characterised as follows:

> Yanira's language profile is commonly attested: Spanish language use is maintained with Spanish-dominant speakers, such as older adult relatives and young children; Spanish and English are both used among in-group members including siblings, and out-group members including friends and co-workers; and Spanish is displaced in favor of English in the classroom setting. Thus, for Yanira, as for many Latinos, Spanish and English together constitute her linguistic competence in a singular sense, and her linguistic performance may draw primarily upon English, primarily on Spanish, or on a combination of the two, as required by the speech situation. It is also common in

Latino communities that as speakers develop the ability to switch between their languages in accommodating the needs of their addressees, some will also extend this ability to switching within a single conversational event – that is, to code-switching.

(Toribio, 2002: 91)

Yanira code-switches between Spanish and English in a variety of forms – written and oral. She affirms, when challenged, that 'the mixture of English and Spanish reflects who I am' (Toribio, 2002: 98). For others, however, the practice of code-switching is avoided as it is regarded as being indicative of low prestige, it is a stigmatised language practice. An example of this is the subject 'Rosabla', born in Mexico and only arriving Santa Barbara in California at junior school age. She speaks Spanish with her mother but uses more English than Spanish with the rest of her family. She does not readily code-switch – 'code-switching does not encode her bicultural experience' (Toribio, 2002: 109) but exhibits a broad sympathy with the language and its associated culture: '[her] demonstrated interest in the maintenance of Spanish resonates with other US Latinos' (Toribio, 2002: 110). The subject, 'Guadalupe', born in San Gabriel of Mexican immigrant parents, is another example of the low prestige exhibited by some towards code-switching but is more ambivalent than 'Rosalba' in this respect. She uses the English language at home although her mother responds to her in Spanish. Her levels of competence in the Spanish tongue are rather limited and this, it would appear, directly informs her attitude towards code-switching: 'Given Guadalupe's highly positive feelings toward Spanish, together with her limited Spanish-language resources, it is not surprising that she is ambivalent about code-switching. To her mind, the linguistic practice is emblematic of Spanish-language loss' (Toribio, 2002: 111). She is characterised by Toribio as having a similar sense of sympathetic, rather than instrumental, attachment to Spanish: 'She attaches a high value to both of the languages of her linguistic repertoire, and since leaving home, she has made a strong effort to maintain some level of Spanish proficiency, however minimal, though more for affective than instrumental reasons' (Toribio, 2002: 110). While Toribio contends that '[m]ost bilinguals enhance their linguistic interactions by combining the strength of both languages and, in so doing, participate in the construction of a singular, unifying, powerful voice' (Toribio, 2002: 110), Stavans counters that such a novel voice is not often welcome, especially when it takes such a hybrid form, for example: 'Almost on a daily basis, we agonize over the death of another one of the thousands of languages in some region of the globe. The emergence of a new tongue, on the other hand, particularly one that is the result of mestizaje and also of American imperialism, is dressed in a shroud of controversy' (Stavans, 2003: 38). One might also understand from the work of Stavans (2003: 12 &13) that there is more than one Spanglish – Cubonics, Dominicanish, Chicano Spanish, Tex-Mex, thus Toribio may be overstating the unity and singularity of that 'voice'. Also, there is no sense among the Spanish, or Spanglish speakers, of the cities of the USA of the 'ironic detachment' that Maher perceives among ethnic minority youth of urban Japan:

> According to the traditional formula, Japan's minorities hid their roots, concealing their public identity above ground. Now social Cool reverses the practice. It is cool to display the above ground flowers ("Yeah, I'm half Ainu"), but you lack concern about the authenticity of that statement legitimising that connection to the roots ("Nah. I don't speak Ainu. No big deal").
>
> (Maher, 2005: 96)

This sense of 'ironic detachment' is conceived as a type of designer identity, or a commodification of ethnicity – styled as 'metroethnicity' and defined as below:

> It [metroethnicity] is a phenomenon apparent among Japan's minority communities. The adoption of a metroethnic standpoint challenges ethnicity or group identity as an absolute or "natural" value. Rather, metroethnicity employs (enjoys?) ethnicity as an accessory, an accentuation. Metroethnicity employs "difference" for cultural and aesthetic effect. It elevates the importance of the critique of alleged identities. In doing so, the metroethnic joins a wider "cultural flow" of mixed and shifting allegiances which aggressively intertwine borders and transcend cultures, whereby the ethnic language is an accessory which you happen to have or not have. It is there or not there. It can be viewed as an "effect".
>
> (Maher, 2005: 88)

The strategic detachment Maher notes may, however, be more closely related to official attitudes towards ethnic minorities in Japan, characterised by denial and oppression, than to the unfettered exercise of choice by individuals to opt in or out of ethnicity (Maher, 1996; Noguchi, 2005). As with much of developed North, urban Japan has seen rapid increases in levels of immigration, including many returning diaspora (Shikama, 2005). Japanese society is only just beginning to open out a debate on multiculturalism and linguistic diversity (Shikama, 2005; Katsuragi, 2005). Officially, Tokyo has the lowest recorded foreign-born population of all of the world's global cities. It has, apparently, a very homogeneous resident population, with only 2.41% of the total population recorded as foreign-born. This is in absolute contrast to the two other global cities, London (27% foreign-born) and New York (33.7% foreign-born), identified by Sassen (1991) (Benton-Short, Price & Friedman, 2004). The reality of the situation, beyond official figures, is quite different but difficult to quantify. It is dominated by migrants from South Korea and China but actual numbers are, in all probability, greatly underestimated (Table 6.4).

It is, perhaps, more useful to speak of an 'ironic attachment' for some Hispanics in the USA. For example, Stavans (2003) asserts that Spanglish is used to achieve a sense of ownership of icons of citizenship in the USA, such as the 'Pledge of Allegiance' and 'la declaración of Independence'. The bending of such documents to Spanglish, or in the case of the national anthem of the USA to Spanish, also reflects a refusal by Hispanics to accept such facets of American identity as 'foreign'. The intention is, therefore, to overcome a sense of alienation through approaching such documents through their 'own verbal prism' (Stavans, 2003: 15). Spanglish is not, of course, a unique linguistic phenomenon. It compares to other urban hybrid forms of language such as black urban English and Yiddish (Stavans, 2003: 42–7). It might equally be compared with urban Wolof. That is a variation of the language Wolof, which is a hybrid and urban form of that

Table 6.4 Foreign-born population in Tokyo (adapted from Benton-Short, Price & Friedman, 2004)

Country of origin	As proportion of total foreign-born population (%)
South Korea	41
China	29
Philippines	7
United States of America	7
Brazil	2
United Kingdom	2
Thailand	2
Peru	1
Others	9

language, resulting from sustained contact with French language in the cities of Senegal. As with Spanglish, urban Wolof (Ngom, 2004) is more than a set of linguistic differences:

> Although 'urban' Wolof differs from 'pure' Wolof in phonology and structure, the major differences between these varieties are found in lexicon (due to extensive borrowings from French in 'urban' Wolof). French lexical borrowings in Wolof are due to the fact that many lexical items were borrowed from French to express the constructs that came along with the introduction of French culture, political system, and religion in urban areas in Senegal, or for purely prestigious reasons.
>
> (Ngom, 2004: 97)

The news media – network television, local television, newspapers, radio and Internet – are regarded by some as exerting a powerful influence on cultural change within the Hispanic population through enabling both the assimilation of US values, on the one hand, and the maintenance of transnational diasporic identity, on the other (Suro, 2004). According to Stavans, such media are extremely important to Hispanic identity in USA through their extensive use of Spanglish (Stavans, 2003: 14). Other sociological research shows that half of Latinos, or Hispanics, get news from both the English language and the Spanish language media:

> Rather than two audiences sharply segmented by language, the survey shows that many more Latinos get at least some of their news in both English and Spanish than in just one language or the other ... In their choices Latinos exercise a far greater level of bilingualism than they do in reading and writing. Getting the news could be the single most extensive cross-cultural experience for the Hispanic population.
>
> (Suro, 2004: 1)

This is probably a reflection of the fact that most Hispanic households in the USA are now bilingual and include native-born English-speaking children. The different language preference groups are English language news only (31%), Spanish language news only (24%) and news in both languages (44%), and their specific characteristics vary according to whether they were foreign-born, their levels of education and income (Table 6.5).

Table 6.5 Select demographic characteristics of language preference groups (adapted from Suro, 2002)

	English only	Spanish only	Both
Proportion of which native-born (%)	78	4	31
Proportion of which foreign-born (%)	22	96	69
Proportion of which high school graduates (%)	31	21	35
Proportion of which college graduates (%)	17	2	9
Proportion of which earn less than $30k p.a. (%)	25	65	46
Proportion of which earn more than $50k p.a. (%)	44	2	17

In general terms, Hispanics tend to migrate from Spanish language media to English over time. The big switch occurs among the second generation. For example, nearly two-thirds of native-born (i.e. USA) Hispanics get all their news in English. Although there is some persistence of Spanish media in the third generation and beyond, one-fourth of these get news in both languages (Suro, 2004: 4–5). Exposure to English language news impacts significantly upon the world view of Hispanics resident in the cities of the USA (e.g. Suro, 2002; Kaplan, Goldstein & Hale, 2005). Research shows that they tend to view illegal immigrants less favourably, be less supportive of US policy in Iraq and have less trust in news organisations (Suro, 2002: 6). For example, of the survey population, 58% of those whose preferred language for news media was English gave Bush a rating of 'poor/mediocre', while 32% of those whose preference was for Spanish gave the same rating. An overwhelming majority of Hispanics (78%), regardless of the demographics, including language, assert that Spanish language media are very important to the economic and political development of the Hispanic population in the USA. Although levels of agreement were less strong among those who indicated an English language preference (61%) and were native-born (68%) than among those whose preferred language was Spanish (87%) and were foreign-born (85%) (Suro, 2002: 8). Finally, Stavans (2001) argues that the significance of the media is wider again. This significance pertains to the impact of global migration upon cultural diversity in urban space through the creation of networks of connection beyond the city:

> The value of linking immigration and world cities is that the scale of analysis can shift from local/global to local/nodal. Global cities literature emphasizes the network among global cities ... We argue that global immigrant destinations are the nodes from which complex

linkages are formed with the economic periphery. For example, the immigrant population in Amsterdam has formed transnational networks with communities in Suriname, Morocco, Turkey and the Netherland Antilles.

(Benton-Short, Price & Friedman, 2004: 14–15)

Stavans (2001) states that the Spanglish that has developed in the urban USA, and especially in New York, Los Angeles, Miami and Chicago, has begun to have a significant impact upon Latin America. Spanglish is going home, as it were, *via* programmes produced and broadcast by Spanish-language television companies and stations based in the big four gateway cities for Hispanic communities in the USA. In particular, programmes broadcast by Telemundo and Univisión are viewed quite extensively in Latin America and are changing the nature of Spanish in urban Central and South America: '[T]he Spanish spoken in this nation [USA], in a state of degeneration by its daily contact with the English language, is spreading in Latin America, thanks to cable transmissions' (Stavans, 2001: 203). In this way the city is playing a key role, not only in respect of challenging the language of citizenship in the USA but also in the transformation of the Spanish language itself throughout the continent of America.

As with dramatic, new movements in population, the collapse of extensive hegemonic political institutions and ideologies is feature of the postmodern, globalising era (Eley, 1992). The collapse of European empires in the decades after 1945 forms a part of this. The reshaping of post-colonial identities in the former colonies is a legacy of this epoch of end of empires. The tensions inherent in this process are most apparent in the cities of these former colonies. In focussing upon urban South Africa it is possible to underscore some other language practices that pertain to the nature of identity in the city. In this case the recent, dramatic collapse of the colonial regime, of which the system of apartheid was its most widely recognisable feature, has been followed by equally dramatic efforts to build a post-colonial, civic society in South Africa. New directions in language policy and planning have been associated with this from the outset. Cities are the key sites for this project as it is in the urban context that the disparate parts of South African society are brought together whereby different cultural and ethnic groups are drawn together to live their lives in close geographical proximity while all the time remaining separated by considerable social distance. Language plays a role in the persistence of this social distance despite the adoption of multicultural style language policies by state and city authorities.

Fieldwork conducted by Kamwangamalu (2001 & 2004) on language behaviours in urban post-apartheid South Africa are especially illuminating in relation to ethnicity, or race, and the notion of 'language crossing'. Language crossing is understood as form of out-group code-switching: '[C]ode alternation by people who are not accepted as members of the group associated with the second language they employ. It is concerned with switching into languages that are not generally thought to belong to you' (Rampton, 1995: 280). Kamwangamalu (2001: 76) places significance on 'unnaturalness' as a defining feature of language crossing: '[T]he difference between out-group *crossing* and in-group codeswitching ... resides in the fact that in in-group practice, both languages can be used in the unexceptional conduct of everyday life' (Kamwangamalu, 2001: 76). It can be claimed, therefore, that a disjuncture exists between the individual speaker and the language being crossed into, it is an act pregnant with self-consciousness. Also, Kamwangamalu (2001: 76) and Rampton (1995: 283–4) note that the nature of language crossing is shaped by the perceived power of certain languages and by perceptions of their wider socio-political significance. For example, in apartheid South Africa, language was implicated in the systematic discrimination practiced by Whites against other racial or ethnic groups. It is well known, of course, that the apartheid system separated peoples on the basis of racial identity, the colour of skin. Where this was insufficient, for example in discriminating among Blacks, or between Whites of British as opposed to Dutch descent, language was used as a proxy for race. Thus, Afrikaans = White Dutch, English = White British, and various indigenous African languages were used to differentiate among Blacks. According to Kamwangamalu (2001: 80), such use of language among Blacks enabled the creation of so-called ethnic homelands or 'Bantustans'. Moreover, this societal arrangement set language and ethnicity in a relationship in which boundaries between groups and languages were not readily crossed – they were fixed and discrete phenomenon – a mythical condition, as Kamwangamalu asserts:

> [T]here was, for instance, a Zulu homeland for Zulu speakers; a Ndebele homeland for Ndebele speakers; a Venda homeland for Venda speakers; a Xhosa homeland for Xhosa speakers; a Sotho homeland for Sotho speakers, to list but a few. It follows from this background that the apartheid system had a relatively static view of

the relationship between language and ethnicity, a view that per-
petuated the myth of language as a strictly bounded phenomenon
and ethnic groups as culturally homogeneous.

(Kamwangamalu, 2001: 80)

With collapse of the apartheid system one might have expected, perhaps, to have seen evidence of the breaking down of the language borders imposed by apartheid, especially since 11 languages have been
given official status through legislation, namely Zulu, Xhosa, Ndebele,
Swati, Sotho, Pedi, Tswana, Tsonga and Venda, including English and
Afrikaans. Afrikaans has lost much of its prestige as a result. It is no
longer a compulsory subject in the educational system, it is no longer
the language of the army, and it is no longer supported by the state as
it once was (e.g. Louw, 2004). In contrast, the prestige, status and power
of the English language have accelerated in this period. This process
has been intensified by the various forces of the contemporary form of
globalisation (e.g. Hibbert, 2004). At the same time, the public profile of
the official, indigenous African language has improved markedly. Thus,
one would expect language crossing to be especially prevalent in multilingual, urban South Africa where people and languages have been
brought together in various juxtapositions. The results of research in
the field by Kamwangamalu (2001), however, does not bear this out:
'[F]or the subjects surveyed. ... *crossing* does not occur at all. This suggests that, despite the demise of the apartheid system, the walls that
the system erected to separate the language communities remain as tall
as they were during the years of apartheid' (Kamwangamalu, 2001: 91).
More to the point, when language crossing does occur it is actively
resisted by many and even triggers negative comment. This is explained
by the immediate socio-political context and by the historical baggage
of the different languages, for example:

This is where the issue of language and identity and the social histories associated with language become pertinent. In South Africa the
history of English and Afrikaans is known to be one of a struggle for
power ... Because of its current status and hegemony in South Africa,
English co-exists with the other official languages (and this includes
Afrikaans) in what Sridhar ... calls a 'state of organic tension', in which
its hegemony is felt particularly by the (white) Afrikaans-speaking
[population] ... for Afrikaans has lost the prestige and political clout
it had during the apartheid era. This hegemony of English is often

resented and at times it is residents, as is evident in the interview ...
where the Building Manager rebukes the Assistant Manager for breaking 'her promise not to speak in English'.

(Kamwangamalu, 2001: 90)

The importance of the city in shaping the relationship between language and ethnicity is indicated elsewhere by Kamwangamalu (2004)
and Jones (1998). Sociolinguisitic work on varieties of English among
the Coloured communities of urban South Africa has proved to be
most revealing in this respect. The term 'coloured' in South Africa usually refers to people of mixed race, although it has been used officially
to define a person who is of a race or ethnicity other than White or
Black. For many Whites during apartheid the Coloured identity represented a type of residual group:

> Defining the 'Coloreds' as a residual group or in terms of 'otherness'
> was vividly illustrated by the late former first lady of South Africa,
> Marike de Klerk who, in opposing a marriage between her son and
> a 'Colored' girl, described the 'Coloreds' as a 'negative group', and
> 'the leftovers', and as 'people that were left after the nations were
> sorted out'.

(Kamwangamalu, 2004: 115)

Kamwangamalu's (2004) work was set in the Coloured community of
the Wentworth district of the city of Durban. It comprises a population
of some 35,000 individuals who have largely descended from one of
three routes (roots) – Mauritians descended from Mauritian settlers of
the 19th century and employed as technicians in the sugar industry;
St Helenans descended from settlers from island of St Helena during
the 19th century and employed as the domestic servants of the wealthy
citizens of Durban; and thirdly, Eur-Africans descended from relationships between local Zulu women and British settlers. Kamwangamalu
notes that English has become the prestige language following the collapse of apartheid: 'All parents in this community of Wentworth, like
the majority of parents elsewhere in the country, want their children
educated in English-medium schools: English is the language of power,
prestige, and status' (Kamwangamalu, 2004: 118–19). The attraction of
the English language derives in large part from the fact that during the
period of apartheid it was viewed by Coloured and Black community as
the language of political emancipation: 'English was perceived as the
language of liberation; while Afrikaans was associated with apartheid

oppression' (Kamwangamalu, 2004: 119). The Wentworth Coloured community partly defines itself by laying claim to a peculiar type of English, defined by a certain type of a slang. Thus, the English language of Wentworth, according to Kamwangamalu (2004: 122), is different from the English spoken by other communities elsewhere in the city of Durban. The result of research by Jones (1998) reinforces the point that such English is peculiarly urban in nature while also demonstrating, as shown in the interview transcripts, that the English associated with Coloured people varies between specific Coloured communities:

Researcher [R]: Would you be able to tell when a Coloured person was talking?
Subject [S]: Definitely ... I thought the Coloured people have a certain type of slang...
R: What if they weren't talking slang? Everybody was talking the 'Queen's English', would you still be able to tell?
S: Yes definitely. Coloureds have an accent.
R: Do all Coloureds have the same accent?
S: No. I always say the Natal guys are totally different from the Joburg guys and the Cape Town guys.
(Jones, reproduced in Kamwangamalu, 2004: 122–3)

In another interview conducted by Jones another subject stated, in response to a question as to whether it is possible to differentiate between different types of Coloured accent: 'Yes. You could even make out, if you had all Coloured people from different parts of the country, which one is from Durban, which one is from Cape Town, which one is from Johannesburg ...' (Jones, quoted in Kamwangamalu, 2004: 123).

The shift to the English language in urban South Africa can be perceived in other ways. This includes changing practices in the area of personal names. There is considerable evidence from a range of sources that adults are choosing to change their personal name or the names of their children through privileging the English language in a number of ways. This includes changing a name so as to place an English name first, the addition of an English name, the replacement of an African name with an English name, or the deletion of an African name (Table 6.6). According to de Klerk and Lagonikos (2004), urbanisation is certainly a factor in this subtle shift in language behaviour as ties to rural, traditional communities and customs are dislocated as migrants to the cities of South Africa become increasingly exposed to English as the high status language of the city and of the state (De Klerk & Lagonikos, 2004: 64).

Table 6.6   Language shift in personal names in South Africa (adapted from de Klerk & Lagonikos, 2004)

Action	Original name	New name
Place an English name first	Mogashudi Lucas Nombulelo Isabel	Lucas Mogashudi Isabel Maud Nombulelo
Add an English name	Mahlathini Tshikane	Mahlathini Eliot Tshikane Ernest
Replace an African name with an English name	Semakatso Mmabusha Nkwenkwende	Semakatso Ivy Wilson
Delete an African name	Thandiwe Mabel Bongani Robert	Mabel Robert

Changes are being made to personal names by adults so as to reflect 'a stronger personal role for names, rather than a community function' (De Klerk & Lagonikos, 2004: 77). This is despite high profile statements and gestures on the desirability of the Africanisation of personal names led by President Thabo Mbeki and echoed by many others:

> [M]any political leaders all over the country have also set the tone ... in replacing their English names with African names. Archbishop Winston Ndungane is now known as Njongonkulu. Sam Shilowa ... is now Mbhazima Shilowa; Bennie Alexander changed his name to Khoi San X; Marks Maponyane, a famous soccer player, has become Mafa Maponyana. The Minister of Defence has changed from Patrick Lekota to Mosioua Lekota.
>
> (De Klerk & Lagonikos, 2004: 79)

The adoption of English language names is a reflection of the respondents aspirations in relation to socio-economic upward mobility, the acquisition of education and engagement with a multicultural South Africa – all of which is driven by urbanisation and the city as the site of social and economic opportunity, of access to education and the meeting point of cultural, ethnic and linguistic diversity (De Klerk, 2002).

The cities of South Africa are not unique in urban Africa in experiencing such changes in language practice and behaviour. Similar such postcolonial acculturation is easily perceived, for example, in urban Senegal where the interaction of French, Classical Arabic and local languages have given rise to a rich cultural creolisation which is, apparently, held together in a peculiarly urban form of the native African language Wolof (Ngom, 2004: 98). The influence of American English and, more generally, the western youth culture associated with globalisation is a dynamic part of this potent linguistic *mélange* (Ngom, 2004: 109). Moreover, urban Wolof is not merely the product of the urban milieu but it also defines it and the people in it, challenging allegiances to traditional forms of ethnicity and asserting identification with the city instead:

> Today, 'urban' Wolof is the variety spoken by most people from interethnic marriages. As a result, the variety has become de-ethnicized as it belongs to city people, regardless of one's ethnic group. As a consequence, 'urban' Wolof has become a convergence language where people from other ethnic groups in the country converge. It is for this reason that it has become the unstated language of urban Senegal.
>
> (Ngom, 2004: 100)

Thus, mundane language behaviours and practices are fundamental to the negotiation of the intensity of difference that defines the ordinary experience of the urban citizen.

Conclusions

Language plays a central role in the social fluidity and cultural dynamism of cities and helps us to further understand the idea of the urban stranger that is so important to the city. The dichotomies of identity that are a function of urban South Africa under apartheid and post-apartheid and equally a function of the relationship between citizens and immigrants in the contemporary cities of the USA illustrate this. The defining features of city life – its open intensity, the proximity of difference, its function as a globalised meeting place, interpenetration of the global and the local – have a range of implications for language and linguistic diversity. In the urban context, language becomes a resource that can be manipulated or mobilised in the making of sense of place, in the transformations of notions of community and in the remaking of the identity of the individual. From this may arise the linguistic hybridity associated with the migrant, shifts towards global languages, or the embedding of the languages of others within the social fabric of everyday city life. In urban South Africa the post-colonial city is a meeting place of different languages and cultures, but yet 'colonial' boundaries are being maintained. The English language confounds some stereotypical expectations in this regard in that it is not simply regarded as the language of former colonial suppression rather it is, for some marginal groups, the language of resistance for very local and stigmatised identities. Elsewhere in post-colonial urban Africa the English language in hybrid form is the language of cre-ole cosmopolitanism. In the urban USA it is this hybridity which has made Spanglish, but the extent of its attractiveness is much more ambiguous. Hence, much depends on the local context. Language makes the stranger intimate but, given the ever-changing nature of language and of the complex dynamics that relate to linguistic diversity in the city, that intimacy is, of necessity, unstable and insecure. The efforts of the nation-state to fix linguistic identity are often undermined in the city. The local resistances of the 'Colored English' of Wentworth or the 'ironic' adaptations of Spanish speakers in Los Angeles are proof of this. The very nature of urban identity, in dialectical fashion, is both artefact and artificer of language change and linguistic diversity in the city. Thereby the city constantly makes and remakes identity in a manner that confounds the project of fashioning the 'appropriate citizen'. The lesson for language planning and policy must be that language, in this sense, may not be 'fixed'.

7
Power

Introduction

This chapter studies the tensions between urban regimes, responsible for the imposition of order on urban space and the various groups that comprise city life from the point of view of language issues. Language is situated in relation to the marginalisation of certain groups or communities, and their languages. The range of forms and types of resistance of such language groups, formal, informal, community-based, identity-based and the politics of the 'backyard', are outlined. An analytical description of language as resistance, defined as the means and ability to negotiate the imposition of order, is shown to be consistent with the nature of city life. It is argued that language as a social movement, as protest and as resistance is not wholly anarchic. Instead, it conforms to the cultural logic of the city as an open, diverse and intense entity that is inherently disordering.

Competition and power in the linguistic ecology

While it can be demonstrated beyond any reasonable doubt that competition, or conflict, is central to the function of ecosystems, many in the field of ecolinguistics, however, seek to emphasise non-competitive relationships. It is appropriate at this point to directly confront this issue in order to develop a more complete understanding of the function of power with regard to language in society. Fill (1993: 57–80), for example, contends that ideas of interdependence and co-operation – 'the ties that bind' are much more informative of the nature of human ecology than Darwinian metaphors on the struggle for life. Also, Mühlhäusler's claim that '[f]unctioning ecologies are characterised by predominantly mutually beneficial links and only to a small degree by competitive relationships' (Mühlhäusler, 2001: 1) implies that the existence of competition or conflict renders an ecosystem non-functional. Elsewhere Mühlhäusler (2000) identifies such ecosystems as 'Competitive Ecologies'. This type of ecology is defined by Mühlhäusler as follows:

> The stability of Types 1 and 2 is a result of the relative lack of power of the communities that inhabit these ecologies whilst Type 3 is characterised both by power differential and constant restructuring of the ecology. The link between political and linguistic power is not a necessary one. Before the advent of European nation states, for instance, centralised power and tolerance of linguistic diversity were not mutually exclusive, with Austro-Hungary before 1918 and Yugoslavia before its disintegration after Tito's demise being examples.
>
> (Mühlhäusler, 2000: 327)

In this context, language is related to the asymmetric distribution of power within the competitive or conflictual ecosystem. Of course, Wright (2004) correctly asserts that the toleration of linguistic diversity under totalitarian or absolutist forms of government ought not to surprise. Neither should it be assumed that such tolerance is benign, or even positive, as under such systems the languages of the powerless and the marginal are of little or no consequence whatsoever to authority. While it is in the context of the nation-state (specifically the language situations in contemporary France and ex-Yugoslavia) that Mühlhäusler asserts 'the non-ecological nature' of competitive polities (2000: 345), this insight, by extension, applies to the city. Conflict, whether as understood by Sennett (e.g. 1996) or by Mühlhäusler, is a function of the urban domain. The city, as we have seen earlier in this text, is defined by the proximity of difference, and, more to the point, difference is crosscut by unequal power relations. It is from this that such competition arises. Thus, the position adopted by such ecolinguists is rather problematic as the reality of language–power relationships logically demands that all language situations, to a greater or lesser extent, be reduced to the status 'non-functioning' ecologies.

One can avoid this intellectual *cul-de-sac* in a number of ways. The starting point is to accept that competition or conflict is central to the operation of ecosystems and to recognise that competition is the mechanism whereby agents situated within a given ecosystem seek to gain the means of their survival, of both physical and cultural reproduction. The resources, both material and non-material, necessary to this are understood as the conditions of reproduction and power, understood as the capacity to allocate resources, is therefore the focal point of competition. Power, in this way, fulfils a similar function in all societies. Giddens puts it as follows, for example:

> In all societies, traditional and modern, administrative power is the core of domination generated by authoritative resources, although it is not the only such resource that exists (there is in addition power deriving from control of sanctions and from ideology).
>
> (Giddens, 1985: 46)

By administrative power Giddens means the institutions of the polity. In this case it can be understood as a city government or the range of institutions that, taken together, govern the city. Power, of course, is not of necessity an oppressive source of conflict, it can be both enabling and constraining, it can be the medium of either freedom or oppression but, more than anything, it is the capacity to achieve outcomes (Giddens, 1986: 157–8). The location of, or control over, this capacity is a central issue. There is no natural distribution of power in urban society, but rather the asymmetric distribution of power in the city, as with other forms of societal organisation, is the result of certain types of competition. That is to say that in ecosystems there exists a hierarchy of power. That power may not merely relate to a sense of control or authority over other actors or resources in the ecosystem, but may also relate to the extent to which the ecosystem as a functioning entity is defined by an actor. The notion of 'keystone species' may be a useful ecological analogy. In an ecosystem a species may gain a position of integral importance to the extent that the loss of the keystone species will result in the dramatic transformation of the complete ecosystem. The making and remaking of the city as a social entity is, in part, shaped by the privileged empowerment of dominant groups, classes, sections, interests or values at various historical junctures. The dislocation, or threatened dislocation, of such dominance, whether psychological or physical, results in what Giddens describes as 'power deflation'. The origins of many conflicts are to be found here (Giddens, 1985: 202). At present, this dislocation is very apparent in Northern cities where dramatic movements of migrant populations have transformed the linguistic and cultural fabric of urban life. Language planning and policy may be understood, in this context, as a tool aimed at the integration of such migrants to the 'nation'. This may be focussed on the gateway cities for migrants and take place through the education system, such as in the case of London (e.g. Baker & Eversley, 2000). The tensions that result from the complex interplay of identity, power and institutions may be manifest in competition in various ways. Different degrees of competition exist in ecology, some of which may accrue mutual benefits for the agents, some of which will not. In terms of human ecology, violent conflict is but an extreme form of ecological competition, one that clearly is not mutually beneficial to all agents in the ecosystem. Violence, as an extreme expression of power, may be legal through state sanction. In almost all cases the state possesses a monopoly on legal violence, for example:

> The nation-state, which exists in a complex of other nation-states, is a set of institutional forms of governance maintaining an administrative monopoly over a territory with demarcated boundaries (borders), its rule being sanctioned by law and direct control of the means of internal and external violence.
>
> (Giddens, 1981: 190)

The violence of the state may take many forms other than the physical for, as Bourdieu (1991) points out, symbolic violence, including through language, is a very powerful tool. Nowhere is it exercised more profoundly than in the city. The condition of Francophone gays and lesbians in English-speaking Toronto is powerfully illustrative of this (Labrie & Grimard, 2003) – a point to which we will return later. It is the case, however, that it is through forms of ethnicity that much of this symbolic violence is manipulated (e.g. Mac Giolla Chríost, 2003). The nation-state has been a crucial vehicle in this regard throughout the modern period and its relationship with language remains important in shaping the discourse on linguistic diversity in the city. For example, histories of the nation-state show that language has been a critical element in the negotiation of the condition of modernity and the transition from pre-modern *ethnie* to the modern nation-state. In this context the nation-state is conceived of as a politically empowered ethnic group defined, in large part, by language. Thus, empowerment is realised *via* language and in this sense, as Chomsky puts it, '[q]uestions of language are basically questions of power' (Chomsky, 1979: 191). The transition of Germany to nation-statehood during the 19th century is illustrative of this process and the salience of language in it. The German language, from the Enlightenment onwards, was increasingly regarded by intellectuals and nationalists alike as the most meaningful marker of German ethnic and national identity (Hobsbawm, 1992: 98–9). The form of Romanticism shaped by Humboldt, Herder and Fichte in modern German-speaking Europe defined language as the most important means of informing the world view of the individual. Moreover, the individual speakers of a given language as members of a language community as a whole form a collective historical experience through that language. Thus, it is through each unique language that a historical community, a people, makes sense of its own place in the world, distinct from other peoples. Language, place and people, their past and their destiny, are bound together in an essential and unbreakable bond. Also, the logic of Romanticism determines that from each language arises a nation and for each nation there exists an absolute right to statehood: '[I]t is beyond doubt that, wherever a separate language can be found, there a separate nation exists, which has the right to take charge of its independent affairs and govern itself' (Fichte, 1968: 184). In this way also, the ancient and distinctive origins of the ethnicity of a people may be uncovered through the examination of its language. Concealed within its vocabulary, syntax and grammar is the most intimate self-knowledge and self-understanding of the people as a historically meaningful community: 'The art of tracing verbal roots, and explicating the meanings and synonyms of words and phrases, "made sense" within a larger evolutionary framework in which language was seen as having an intimate and revelatory position within the collective memory and experience' (A. D. Smith, 1986: 181). This view of the relationships between language, people and state was dominant across Europe throughout the modern historical period. The implications of this perspective on the relationship between language and power for pre-modern *ethnies* that do not respond to the challenge of modernity through the gaining of nation-statehood, thereby failing to respond appropriately to the orthodox discourse on nationhood, is status as ethnic minorities within the nation-states of dominant *ethnies*. A history of the 20th century, in particular, shows that such status can result in assimilation, oppression, enforced exclusion or genocide.

It is not a coincidence that the imagery and geographical rhetoric associated with the Romantic ideal of the linguistically homogeneous nation-state finds it most difficult to accommodate the city, given its inherently cosmopolitan nature. When linguistic diversity was recognised at that time it too was conceived of in ruralised, quasi-national spaces – provinces or regions with distinctive cultural identities. It is a feature of the orthodox discourse on language and ethnicity in this period that such peoples and places would benefit from their being assimilated to the superior body of the metropolitan nation-state. The views of Michelet on France, for example, exemplify this ideal. The French Revolution of 1789, according to Michelet, gave birth to France as 'a whole nation, free from all distinction' (Michelet, 1967: 13) and this freedom from distinction meant that the diverse regional identities of France require to be integrated, as a matter of absolute necessity, to French national identity: '[T]his sacrifice of the diverse interior nationalities to the great nationality which comprises them undoubtedly strengthened the latter ... It was at the moment when France suppressed within herself the divergent French countries that she proclaimed her high and original revelations' (Michelet, 1973: 286). This erasure of diversity and difference was not merely useful to the bureaucratic mechanics of the effective administration and governance of the French nation-state but it was, in the eyes of Michelet, an necessary and euphoric condition through which the transcendental national spirit is released:

> Where, then, are the old distinctions of provinces and races of men? Where those powerful and geographical contrasts? All have disappeared: geography itself is annihilated. There are no longer mountains, rivers or barriers between men ... All at once, and without even perceiving it, they have forgotten the things for which they would have sacrificed their lives the day before, their provincial sentiment, local tradition, and legends. Time and space, those material conditions to which life is subject, are no more. A strange *vita nuova*, one eminently spiritual ... is now beginning for France. It knew neither time nor space.
>
> (Michelet, 1967: 444)

Similarly, the English liberal humanist position on diversity in general and linguistic diversity in particular was that it was something which impeded the development and operation of the institutions of the state. If not addressed, it frustrated the coalescence of shared, popular values and common public views, each of which were regarded as necessary features of good governance. From this it was inferred that linguistic diversity was contrary to freedom and democracy. Mill states this classical liberal orthodoxy in the plainest of terms:

> But, when a people are ripe for free institutions, there is a still more vital consideration. Free institutions are next to impossible in a country made up of different nationalities. Among a people without fellow-feeling, especially if they read and speak different languages,

the united public opinion, necessary to the working of representative government, cannot exist.

(Mill, 1972: 361)

The assimilation of such 'different nationalities', including the Welsh or the Scots, to British national identity, or the Bretons and the Basques to French national identity, is not only a matter of benefit to the nation-state but, according to the historical liberal position, accrues a range of benefits to those peoples for whom assimilation is their intended fate, thus:

When proper allowance has been made for geographical exigencies, another more purely moral and social consideration offers itself. Experience proves it possible for one nationality to merge and be absorbed in another: and when it was originally an inferior and more backward portion of the human race the absorption is greatly to its advantage. Nobody can suppose that it is not beneficial to a Breton, or a Basque of French Navarre, to be brought into the current of ideas and feelings of a highly civilised and cultivated people – to be a member of the French nationality, admitted on equal terms to all the privileges of French citizenship, sharing the advantages of French protection, and the dignity and prestige of French power than to sulk on his own rocks, the half-savage relic of past times, revolving in his own mental orbit without participation or interest in the general movement of the world. The same remark applies to the Welshman or the Scottish highlander as members of the British nation.

(Mill, 1972: 395)

Of course, very few would argue today that 'half-savage' minorities need to be drawn from their 'rock' dwellings so that they might avail of the opportunity to expand their rigidly narrow 'mental orbit'. In some quarters, however, a discourse on language, power and identity continues to be articulated wherein the implicit superiority of some *ethnies*, and their associated cultural attributes, is asserted over that of others. Also, in the vocabulary of popular language behaviours of the modern period the differential use of the terms 'ethnic' and 'nation' developed to reflect functions of status and power. For example, the term 'ethnic' evolved as a signal of the lesser value of the attributes of minority cultural groups while 'national' was applied to the attributes of the dominant *ethnie*. According to Isajiw (1980), much of the literature on the subject of ethnicity in the USA assumes that the term 'ethnic' is inevitably associated with the status of 'minority' and in this way, therefore, the historically dominant *ethnie* transcends ethnicity. As a result, the 'ideal' attributes of the dominant *ethnie* become normative and this is mediated through the institution of governance:

> The European nation has, at least in principal, grown up around an 'ideal' of cultural homogeneity, established and reinforced through the state and controlled transmission of literate culture, alongside state control over entry and the acquisition of citizenship; thus the nation represents territorialized cultural belonging, while the state formalizes and controls legal membership.
>
> (Morris, 1997: 194)

The concept of 'territorialized cultural belonging' does not, of course, apply directly to the city for it is not defined by such a sense of place. Rather, the proximity of different worlds in the city and the intensity of city living defy such a possibility. It is in the city, more than any other part of the state, that the meaning of citizenship is most profoundly challenged. It is in the urban context that those furthest from the 'ideal' and 'appropriate' citizen encounter the state. The development of multicultural policies during the last quarter of the 20th century in Canada, and subsequently Australia and elsewhere in the English-speaking North, was aimed at the amelioration of the homogenising effect of policy practices in relation to historically resident minority ethnic groups (e.g. Kymlicka, 1995). While the rhetoric of the multicultural project quickly evolved to embrace the diversity of more recent migrant groups, some commentators suggest that certain inherent contradictions remain (e.g. Baumann, 1996). Favell argues that while particular rights may be assigned to minority ethnic groups and certain resources may be allocated to them through the implementation of multicultural policy, this is merely another form of assimilation:

> [E]thnic minorities are offered cultural tolerance, even 'multicultural' rights and institutions, in exchange for acceptance of basic principles and the rule of law; they are imagined as culturally-laden social groups, who need to be integrated and individualised by a public sphere which offers voice and participation, transforming them from 'immigrants', into full and free 'citizens'; they are to become full, assimilated nationals, in a nation-state re-imagined to balance cultural diversity, with a formal equality of status and membership.
>
> (Favell, 1998: 213–14)

The implication here is that multiculturalism does not enable the trans-formation of the relationship between language and power in which diverse groups, cultures and languages have unequal value ascribed to them by the state. Therefore, rather than contesting the presumed legit-imacy and authenticity of the essential cultural attributes of the domi-nant *ethnie*, multiculturalism also turns upon an essentialist approach to the matter:

> In this set of understandings, 'culture' is: a kind of package (often talked of as migrants' 'cultural baggage') of collective behavioural-moral-aesthetic traits and 'customs', rather mysteriously transmitted between generations, best suited to a particular geographical loca-tions yet largely unaffected by history of a change of context, which instils a discrete quality into the feelings, values, practices, social relationships, predilections and intrinsic nature of all who 'belong to (a particular) it'.
>
> (Vertovec, 1996: 51)

While some significant reworking of the multicultural project has occurred (e.g. King, 2000; May, 2001 & *The Parekh Report*), commentators assert that it persists in its engagement with a simplistic and unprob-lematised modernist conception of the nation-state. Vertovec, for exam-ple, observes that: 'Multiculturalism did away with the expectation of assimilation and acculturation, while the expectation of common attachment to the encompassing nation-state went unchallenged. ... Multiculturalism's relationship to the nation-state ... seems to remain as was' (Vertovec, 2001: 5,6). Equally significant, according to others (Alibhai-Brown, 2000), is the failure of multiculturalism to engage in an explicit and robust manner with postmodern thought and the material conditions of globalisation. It is to this that we turn our attention next.

Globalisation, polity and the remaking of linguistic capital

The condition of postmodernity is characterised by society in a state of flux, instability and fracture. In contrast, society conceived of as stable, bounded and homogeneous is a critical point of reference with regard to understanding Bourdieu's notions of habitus and market, thus: 'The single linguistic community, or the unified linguistic market, to which Bourdieu refers is most clearly represented in and by the homogeneous civic culture of the modern nation-state' (May 2001: 156).

But dynamism is also a feature of Bourdieu's conception of language in society and the erosion of the status of the nation-state as the pre-eminent polity of the modern era by the forces of globalisation is a very significant transformation, one that has broad implications for language in the urban context. The historical conjuncture, or fracture, between the pre-modern and the modern that is critical to A.D. Smith's understanding of the transformation of *ethnies* into nations is explained in terms of discourse and the reshaping of the set of dispositions that constitute the habitus. Under the challenge of globalisation, the erosion of the hegemony of the nation-state as the most authoritative form of polity suggests that it is pertinent to ask whether the present historical conjuncture signals the onset of a decisive assault upon the structuring dispositions of the modern form of habitus.

Globalisation, as outlined by Mac Giolla Chríost elsewhere (2005), is a term often associated with the myriad and rapid changes that much of the world is currently experiencing. The meaning of the term relates to a number of issues, including more extensive global interconnectedness, a reconfiguration of interactions between local and global processes and increasing organisation and exercise of power at a local level. While globalisation can be seen as a threat to local identities and cultures, it can be argued that these may be reinvigorated by the processes associated with globalisation in a number of ways. Also, globalisation may be described as a multidimensional process that incorporates all social relations – cultural, economic and political and, as such, the effects of globalisation can be seen in all aspects of society. Notwithstanding the complexity of globalisation and the diversity of its impact upon society, it may be seen to comprise a number of characteristic features. According to Cochrane and Pain (2000: 15–22), these are as follows:

- Stretched social relations – that is the existence of cultural, economic and political networks of connection that are global in their extent. These transcend nation-state boundaries and are especially manifest in the phenomenon of regionalisation – that is the increased interconnection between states that border on each other. Also, the individual is positioned in this network of interconnection in such a way that apparently local actions might have global consequences.
- Intensification of flows and interactions – this stretching of social relations appears to be related to an increased density of interaction across the globe, in turn implying that the impacts of actions

are greater than before. Also, the density of contemporary communication connects distant actions, decisions, people and events in an immediate shared social space, a space that is virtual rather than physical or territorial.

- Increasing interpenetration of global and local social processes – that is what would ordinarily be understood as distant cultures and societies in conventional geographical terms encounter at a local level with increasing frequency and intensity. The resulting interpenetration of geographies of the local and the global gives rise to increased cultural diversity.
- Development of a transnational, global infrastructure – that is, the formal and informal institutional arrangements that are necessary to the functioning of globalised networks, including transnational or global institutions of economic and political governance. These are expressed as interconnections that transcend nation-state boundaries and function beyond their systems of regulation and control, such as the global financial market with its regulations and rules that other agents have to conform to.

In the context of a globalising world, it has become common currency that the contemporary nation-state is 'too small to cope with the big issues, and too big to cope with the small ones' (Davies, 1997: 1120). That is not to say that the nation-state is no longer a key player in the world of geopolitics but rather that its authority as a sovereign, autonomous and independent political unit is subject to challenge. It now shares the stage with other players both at local and at global levels, including the city in various forms – as polity (Singapore), as global financial powerhouse (London, Tokyo), as global political nerve centre (New York), as centre of global cultural (re-) production (Los Angeles) or as gateway to global migration (Toronto). It is necessary to analyse briefly the nature and extent of that challenge to the nation-state. The point here is that the erosion of the historical hegemony of the nation-state, a process in which the city is but one of a number of actors, has the effect of opening up new spaces for cities in global political, economic and social terms. This in turn impacts upon language, both globally and locally, at macro and micro levels. For much of the modern historical period the map of the world has been organised into discrete geographical units that are simultaneously territorial and political communities – nation-states. This geopolitical framework is widely known as the Westphalian system, following the 17th-century European treaty through which the system is considered to have been inaugurated. According to McGrew (2000:

132–4), this system is defined by five key features – territoriality, sovereignty, autonomy, primacy and anarchy – as follows:

- The legal and political powers of nation-states are limited to discrete territorial borders.
- Within these specific territorial units, nation-state governments claim absolute and exclusive authority over and allegiance from the peoples resident therein as citizens of the nation-state.
- Nation-states function as independent containers (Taylor, 1995a) of political, economic and social activity. Within the borders that separate the domestic sphere of the nation-state from the rest-of the-world outside, the nation-state has the right to self-governance free from interference.
- As they control access to territory and the economic, human and natural resources therein, nation-states dominate global politics, there is no higher authority or greater power than the nation-state.
- In a world of nation-states, it is the function of the nation-state to ensure the security and well-being of its citizens. In the Westphalian system, the norms, principles and practices of nation-states underscore the separation of domestic and international affairs with the former defined by the existence of government as the central institution of political control. In contrast, international affairs are defined by the relative absence of governance.

It is not possible in this study to offer comprehensive critique of this particular view of the nature and function of the nation-state. Other commentators lay emphasis on certain key features over others. For example, Anderson (1995: 69–71) identifies territory, sovereignty and nationalism, largely following Benedict Anderson for whom that nation is construed as 'an imagined political community – and imagined as both inherently limited and sovereign'. The above outline will suffice in order to make a few points in order to relate broadly the nature the evidence relating to the impact of globalisation on the nation-state.

Evidence that globalisation is impacting upon the nation-state is considerable and diverse. For example, one might point to the flows of migration across nation-state boundaries and the contemporary continuity of diaspora communities, sustained in part by new information and communication technologies (ICTs) (e.g. Karim, 1998) but also by increasingly affordable and rapid forms of international transport. Similarly, transnational flows of trade and investment or of environmental pollution could equally be presented as evidence of the erosion of the capacity of the nation-state to determine or shape events in a globalising world. Also, the global reach of new technologies along with their historically unprecedented rate of uptake by comparison with previous communications technologies and their accessibility to agents other than the nation-state could be cited (e.g. Appadurai, 1995). One could add that increasing accessibility to and identification with global icons – both people and products – undermines the notions of national identity and culture that are central to the nation-state. The emergence of new forms of governance such as the Scottish Parliament of the Autonomous Community of Catalonia, the growth of supranational institutions of governance such as the World Trade Organisation, the North Atlantic Treaty Organisation and the United Nations, as well as the increasing salience of non-governmental organisations (NGOs) such as Greenpeace, the Red Cross or Oxfam as agents in the global political landscape appear to serve notice on the hegemony of the nation-state. In short, globalisation marks a shift in the geography of local and global socio-political relations. As a process that is multidimensional, the associated geographies are, rather unsurprisingly, both complex and overlapping.

The evidence for the impact of globalisation on the nation-state can be interpreted in a number of ways. The three predominant approaches to globalisation are described as traditionalist, globalist and transformationalist (Held, 2000) and from each of these different insights can be drawn. Those scholars who hold to the traditionalist position on globalisation caution against what they regard as the excessive claims made by others for globalisation and its impact. According to this critique of globalisation, the nation-state remains the key agent in the global political landscape. The hegemony of nation-state is hierarchical, and the USA, as the world's largest economy, the most dominant military power and pre-eminent in the field of space technology, fulfils the role of hegemon. Thompson (2000) deploys evidence relating to international trade, international finance and multinational corporations to argue that the extent of globalisation in the world economy is limited. For example, he notes that patterns with regard to the internationalisation of trade display considerable continuity throughout the course of the 20th century. For Thompson, therefore, the socio-political system continues to operate in the interest of nation-states and their geostrategic concerns. He also argues that while nation-states are still powerful they do not fully exercise that power. This, he contends, is because the rhetoric rather than the reality of globalisation has weakened the political will of nation-states to do so. Other global economic patterns cannot, however, be explained away as rhetorical flourishes. The emergence of transnational corporations, while not a quantitative change, represents a significant qualitative shift in the global economy. The dislocation of global corporations from a single nation-state as 'home' is a substantial erosion of the economic sovereignty and autonomy of the nation-state. Similarly, the trilateral economic regionalisation centred on North America, Europe and Japan and embracing considerable triad interdependency and integration is not easily accounted for by the traditionalist approach.

For proponents of the globalist perspective on globalisation, the nation-state has been superseded, for in the contemporary political economy, global corporate and financial capital is the key agent. Power, therefore, is not exclusive to the nation-state but is instead exercised by a global cosmocracy, a transnational business community. In this context, power is exercised through the networked infrastructure of global markets, driven by new ICTs, and in the interests of global capital. As a result, the capacity of nation-states is severely constrained as they are simultaneously too small to exercise authority over global capital and too big to protect the interests of their citizens from the challenges of a globalising economy. However, others underline the limited penetration of the new technologies that are central to the globalist position. For example, Everard (2000) shows that the geography of the Internet is not global, many parts of the world remain excluded from this networked society as the cost of new technologies render them inaccessible to billions of citizens. Also, A.D. Smith points to the failure of the globalisation of culture as an ideological process that engages with a sense of community that is meaningful to individuals (1995: 6 & 160) – globalisation does not explain the rise of ethno-nationalism in post-Soviet Europe. It is this very sense of community that serves so powerfully to authenticate and legitimise the nation-state and, for A.D. Smith, it is in this absence that the paradox of fragmentation and globalisation that characterises contemporary socio-political shifts arises.

Transformationalists seek to draw from the insights of both the traditionalist and globalist perspectives in delineating a more comprehensive approach to globalisation. McGrew outlines their approach in the following terms:

> For transformationalists these three accounts of global governance are considered complementary rather than contradictory; each offers an insight into a particular dimension of global power relations.

Indeed they correspond to the three principal structures that inter-
sect to define the form of contemporary global governance and
world order: Geo-politics and the inter-state system; the system of
global capitalist production; the global social system.

(McGrew, 2000: 160–1)

According to the transformationalist approach, the key agents of
globalisation are epistemic communities, NGOs and social movements.
They exercise power through diverse social forces in a polyarchic manner and in the interests of myriad sectional and collective concerns.
Given the nature of epistemic communities, it is not unexpected that
for transformationalists power is exercised through the application of
knowledge and technical deliberation. The exercise of power is also
characterised by the mobilisation of communities across boundaries
and is marked by transnational coalition building and multilayered
global governance as responses to the erosion of the authority of the
nation-state and the necessity of engaging with the social, economic
and environmental issues that transcend Westphalian concepts of sovereignty and autonomy. The transformationalist approach, therefore,
seeks to avoid the determinism of both the globalist and traditionalist
positions while at the same time drawing from them in constructing
a coherent theoretical position that weaves together notions of state
power, corporate power and people power. Despite the coherence of
the transformationalist position, it would appear to be of limited application beyond Europe (Held, 2000: 169–77). The emergence of multilayered governance, central to the transformationalist position, is most
apparent in Europe where the development of the European Union
has been accompanied by new and diverse forms of regional and local
government. In much of the rest of the world, evidence for the emergence of alternative polities to the nation-state, whether above, below
or alongside it, is less obvious.

The organisation of the world into discrete geopolitical units that
characterises the Westphalian ideal has been undermined by new conceptions of political community and space. The emergence of multiple
layers of governance, trans-border communities of interest and transnational social, economic and environmental problems, all challenge the
notion of territoriality that is fundamental to the modern nation-state.
Rather than rendering the nation-state redundant, it is more useful to
consider that the role of the nation-state and the nature of its sovereignty and autonomy has been changed. One of the impacts of globalisation has been to coos nation-state sovereignty to be redefined. In a

world of multilayered governance, nation-state sovereignty is not absolute but negotiable, as public power and authority is increasingly shared. The autonomy of the nation-state has been similarly reconfigured; it is no longer exclusive but rather is embedded in multilateral collaboration and co-operation among diverse polities which include the nation-state. In this sense, the nation-state is a more and not a less important player as it is required to be more active – a reflexive state – in a globalising world that appears increasingly anarchic, in which a multiplicity of polities, authorities, organisations, movements and ideologies contest and lay claim to the allegiances and identities of its citizens. But what are the implications of all of this for language? Taken as a whole, this erosion of the nation-state in a globalising world opens up new spaces for language, in which the city is a central player. In such a context, a given language is not the singular emblem of the nation-state nor is it the exclusive means of access to the resources of the state and to citizenship. Rather, the globalising city appears to be empowering of and to be empowered by linguistic diversity. Some research is beginning to uncover certain aspects of the relationship between language and the contemporary urban context and it is to this that we turn to next.

Language in the globalising city: Transnationalism, sustainability, symbolic violence

Transnational movements have certain implications for language in the context of their alteration by the time-space compression that defines the current form of globalisation (Anderson, 1995: 79–82). Transnational movements are both the product of and catalysts for contemporary globalisation processes. A single such movement may be characterised as a network of interest that transcends the borders of nation-states. Cochrane puts it as follows: 'Transnational movements consist of social, cultural and political networks which cross the territorial boundaries of existing states, generally with concerns wider than those specified by the boundaries of national politics' (Cochrane, 1995: 266). It is in this boundary-crossing that transnational movements open up new spaces for language. That the discrete territoriality of nation-states has been made increasingly porous by the activities of transnational movements has implications for language. For example, new ICTs penetrate nation-state borders to an extent that no previous similar technology has done (Appadurai, 1995). The virtual simultaneity of the electronic transfer of capital, news, ideas and information, irrespective of the geographies of the nation-state, mean that this particular transnational shift has enormous potential to severely erode the power of the nation-state and allow for existence of cultural diversity to greater extent that before. According to Karim (1998), the flows of migration across nation-state boundaries and the contemporary continuity of global diaspora communities are sustained, in part, by new ICTs. That said, as Everard (2000) points out, the penetration of the ICT revolution in global terms is rather limited in its extent. Many parts of the world remain excluded from this networked movement as, in large part, the cost of the new technologies is prohibitive for many. Sustainability of migrant languages is also enabled by transnationalist shift, as ease of physical movement of peoples across the globe has accelerated. This means that, as in the case of Turkish in the cities of the urban North for example, some commentators can reasonably suggest that minority languages may be sustained at a great distance from their 'homeland':

> [T]he Turkish community members in Australia have diverse vitalities with regard to demographic factors, sociostatus factors, and institutional support factors. On the whole they do not constitute a large population; however, the fact that they are concentrated in certain suburbs in two major cities (Melbourne and Sydney) provides them with a strong community network … In spite of immense geographic distance, contact with the homeland is commonly maintained.
>
> (Yağmur, 2004: 126)

In Western Europe the numbers of Turkish speakers are much greater, calculated at just over 2.5 million (Yağmur, 2004: 128), and are heavily concentrated in urban Germany and the Netherlands. The ethnolinguistic vitality of Turkish is sustained by the continued flow of migration:

> Even though EU countries put strict restrictions on accepting new immigrants from Turkey, a trend of increasing immigration is observed by way of family formation (second-generation migrants marrying someone from the homeland.) This constant flow of new first-generation immigrants from Turkey enhances first-language maintenance in the domestic context.
>
> (Yağmur, 2004: 128–9)

Its vitality is also sustained by the fact that Turkish speakers in Europe can avail of an impressively wide variety of media in their language, including the major Turkish newspapers, magazines and TV channels. Studies of the patterns of actual use of the Turkish language among this

Table 7.1 Language use among Turkish speakers in Australia and Germany (adapted from Yağmur, 2004)

Questionnaire item	Turkish speakers in Australia	Turkish speakers in Germany
Amount of contact with relatives in Turkey	2.80	3.33
Difficulty in speaking Turkish when in Turkey	1.97	2.07
Difficulty in understanding Turkish when in Turkey	1.62	1.33
Participation in Turkish community organisations	1.85	1.53
Language mixing	2.65	3.20

Notes: Scale 1 = very little, 5 = very much

diaspora, specifically in Germany and in Australia, reveal something of the depth of this vitality (Table 7.1). Turkish speakers are understood to maintain fairly substantial levels of contact with relatives in Turkey and, in spite of considerable levels of language mixing (English-Turkish, German-Turkish), levels of ability to speak and to understand Turkish appear to be sustained over the medium term. The data from the Turkish speaking communities in Australian and in Germany cases are broadly comparable, but a significant difference is apparent with regard to perceptions of the sustainability of Turkish language and its associated culture. In short, much more positive attitudes are prevalent in Germany in relation to this issue. The difference of perception on this matter is interesting in that the policy project of multiculturalism is pursued in Australia while, in contrast, the policy approach in Germany is rather exclusionist in many regards. For example, Turkish speakers are on the one hand readily granted 'guest worker' status so as to enable them to undertake various sorts of employment that native-born Germans are less ready to undertake, while on the other hand their pathway to German citizenship is fraught with many challenges. The idea of the appropriate German citizen continues to be heavily influenced by notions of authentic biological ethnicity, although the simple fact of the candidature of Turkey to join EU is changing the landscape, despite the enormous political difficulties relating to that particular project. This suggests *prima facie* that simple mathematics has a greater impact upon attitudes than has public policy. But, while numbers may well prevail in some respects, the symbolic violence of inimical policy brings about its own resistance, thereby sustaining alternative allegiances to that demanded by the host state. This is reinforced by the contemporary form of globalisation.

According to Vertovec (2001), transnational movements challenge the sovereignty of the nation-state by making competing claims on the allegiance of citizens to the extent that citizenship has been transformed, representing a shift towards a new kind of cosmopolitanism. For example, according to Layton-Henry (2002) and Brandt and Layton-Henry (n.d.), contemporary transnational communities have transformed the nature of citizenship whereby nation-states are no longer the sole arbiters of an exclusive form of citizenship. In their examination of three urbanised, transnational ethnic groups – the Hongkong Chinese in Toronto and Vancouver in Canada, the African Caribbean in London and Birmingham in the UK and the Turks in Berlin and Cologne in Germany – they show how multiple identifications pertain to contemporary forms of citizenship. In addition to such transnational ethnic identifications eroding the monopoly of the nation-state to national identity, they argue that other polities, such as the European Union, now offer coherent and politically meaningful forms of citizenship. They also suggest that the highly mobile and flexible international labour migration has caused nation-states to themselves erode distinctions between the citizen and the alien non-citizen. Although, as has already, been noted in Chapter Six of this work, there has been a reaction to this in many of the English language states of the developed North, demanding competence in English as a condition of citizenship. Other commentators (e.g. Beeley, 1995) point to the emergence of transnational religious movements as competing foci for the allegiance of people. The increasing globalisation and politicisation of Islam may be suggestive of the emergence of an alternative form of citizenship. While Beeley (1995) previously suggested that Islam continues to operate largely within the nation-state system, it would appear to be the case, post 9/11 in particular, that it has become increasingly influential as a transnational movement connecting people and communities within and between nation-states. Again, globalising cities are critical sites in this. This can be seen in the changing geography of the city of Toronto, for example, where Greektown on the Danforth, has been commodified by the city government as a tourist destination with a discrete ethnic identity. Among other things, tourists are encouraged to try to identify some of the specific locations in this past of the city that appeared in the film *My Big Fat Greek Wedding* (e.g. see the website www.greektowntoronto.com). Despite the commodification, an Islamic or Arabic cultural repertoire is an increasing presence in this particular 'Greek' part of the city. This, as evidenced during fieldwork by the author in this city during April 2006, takes the form of a mosque, food preparation workshops and retail outlets, but in this case the specific ethnic form is not a marketable commodity. There is no geography of the Hollywood feature film to amuse the tourist gaze. In contrast, the Irish language in Belfast has made the transition from the language of an alienated, ethnic ghetto to the emblematic product of a Gaeltacht quarter – a potential engine of economic growth based upon the cultural industries and including tourism (Dutton, 2004; Mac Giolla Chríost, 2005).

Being there is not enough to belong and claims to citizenship are far from straightforward. For example, Yağmur (2004: 132) notes that despite the fact that there are around 2 million Turkish speakers in residence in Germany and around a quarter million Turkish speakers resident in the Netherlands when citizenship was made more accessible to Turkish migrants across Europe as a whole towards the end of the 1990s, almost equal numbers applied from each – 24,682 for Germany and 22,179 for the Netherlands. This, it is suggested, is explained by the fact that Turkish speakers in Germany are less keen to apply for citizenship as it would mean renouncing Turkish citizenship rather than attaining dual citizenship. It is noted by commentators elsewhere that there is a 'bottom-up push for pluralism' (Extra & Yağmur, 2005: 18). They assert that the people of Europe 'no longer identify exclusively with nation states, but give increasing evidence of multiple affiliations' (Extra & Yağmur, 2005: 19). In their research upon multilingualism in a number of European cities (Gothenburg, Hamburg, the Hague, Brussels, Lyon and Madrid), they found that Turkish was identified as the immigrant minority language with the greatest capacity to sustain itself as it was extensively used at home and between generations within the family, as well as having very high numbers of speakers (Extra & Yağmur, 2005; Extra & Yağmur, 2004). The various data from Amsterdam may be drawn together and deployed here so as to illustrate the point (Table 7.2). The immigrant minority languages examined by Extra and Yağmur were assessed according to the four principal dimensions pertaining to linguistic vitality, namely

- language proficiency – the extent to which the language is understood;
- language dominance – the extent to which the language is spoken best;
- language choice – the extent to which the language is commonly spoken at home with the mother and
- language preference – the extent to which the language is spoken as a matter of preference.

(Extra & Yağmur, 2004: 34)

Table 7.2 Language vitality index for top ten immigrant minority languages in urban Europe according to vitality (adapted from Extra & Yağmur, 2004)

Language	Number of speakers of primary school age	Proficiency	Choice	Dominance	Preference	Vitality
Turkish	4,789	96	86	56	50	72
Somali	288	92	88	57	53	72
Farsi	131	92	84	54	53	72
Chinese	419	94	82	52	48	68
Urdu/Pakistani	547	94	80	46	51	68
Berber	2,769	94	83	43	42	66
Serbian/Croatian/Bosnian	116	84	62	43	52	62
Papiamentu	893	87	58	40	46	58
Akan/Twi/Ghanese	152	89	69	37	33	57
Arabic	2,740	89	60	38	42	57

Their evidence suggests that there is a post-imperial context to explaining the relative vitality of certain immigrant minority languages in Amsterdam, and therefore linguistic diversity in Northern European cities in general. They note that languages that had been in contact with Dutch during colonisation, such as Hindi and Sranan Tongo in Surinam, and Moluccan Malay and Javanese in Indonesia, tend to have lower levels of vitality in post-imperial Amsterdam. Also, other European languages such as English, French and German have similarly low levels of vitality (Extra & Yağmur, 2004: 34–5).

The transnational migrant is not uniquely drawn to the globalising city. The linguistic situation of other diverse groups reveals different aspects again of the impact of the urban condition upon language, in particular the operation of Bourdieu's notion of symbolic violence at the interface of sexual and linguistic identities. Cites are attractive to gays and lesbians as arenas of sexual emancipation, but also as places that offer the means of 'la création de nouvelles communatés linguistiques ... et de nouvelles formes de reproduction sociale, culturelle et linguistique dans ses sociétés en mutation' [the creation of new linguistic communities ... and new forms of social, cultural and linguistic reproduction in these societies of change] (Labrie & Grimard, 2003: 118). But, these cities are also the sites of symbolic violence in terms of both sexual and linguistic identity (Labrie & Grimard, 2002: 125) if the case of immigrant Francophone gays and lesbians in the city of Toronto is typical. These groups adopt various strategies of resistance (Labrie & Grimard, 2002: 118) to which social and geographical mobility is crucial as is the fundamental restructuring of basic language behaviours, for example:

> Les pratiques langagières sont alors transformées, ce qui peut aussi bien vouloir dire l'immersion complete dans un environnement anglo-dominant au point de destructurer sa façon de parler français, ou comme certains l'experiment "d'en perdre son français", que la découverte d'un milieu de vie plus francophone que jamais. Sur le plan identitaire, la plupart développent un sentiment aigu d'identité axé sur leur people d'origine: québécois ou acadien, par exemple, avec un rapport ambigu au milieu d'origine qu'ils idéalisent en reference à l'usage preponderant de la langue français et à la convivialité des modes de sociabilité, où ils aimeraient retourner, mais à la condition de preserver les acquis de la mobilité sociale. [The language practices are then transformed, and one is able also to speak of the complete immersion in an Anglo-dominant environment to

the point of the destruction of behaviours with regard to the speaking of French, or a certain experimentation with 'losing one's French', whereby a better, more Francophone life than ever before is discovered. Most individuals develop in this identity plan a pointed sense of identity, centred on their people of origin: québécois or acadien, for example, with an ambiguous rapport with place of origin which they idealise through reference to the preponderance of the use of the French language and the conviviality of the styles of sociability, to where they would like to return, but on the condition of preserving their acquired social mobility]

(Labrie & Grimard, 2002: 134)

While the experience of being subject to symbolic violence has, in some ways, an inimical impact upon the marginal and the minoritised, upon difference, the act of responding to symbolic violence also has the potential to become a process of empowerment. The act of 'losing one's French', for example, begins as a strategic reaction to English as the dominant language of the city and is an adaptation that enables social mobility. But this action evolves into a means of recovering the language but now remade 'better' than the original as it allows for the emancipation of the individual from that which they had been before. One outcome of this process is the construction of an ambiguous relationship with that state of origin, a place and a sense of self, to which the newly made urban denizen may desire to return but cannot. At least, not without sacrificing that which the city has enabled them to become. Beyond the self, the challenge posed by the various expressions of symbolic violence invites some to seek to remake urban society and others to lever from that society the capital that enables choice, the resources that empower:

La ville, au contraire, est critiquée en raison de l'importance prédominante accordée au travail, de la rapidité de son rythme de vie et de la froideur de ses modes de sociabilité, mais probablement, aussi et surtout, en raison des formes de violence symbolique qui y sont pratiquées et que les gais et lesbiennes francophones continuent à ressentir en tant que francophones dans un milieu anglo-dominant, en particulier dans les circles gais et lesbians, et en tant que gais ou lesbiennes dans des circles hétéronormatifs, que ce soit dans le monde francophone ou dans celui du travail. Tel que mentionné plus haut, pour échapper à cette violence symbolique, quelques-uns tenteront de transformer la société en se servant de

leur capital symbolique et materiel, qu'il s'agisse de moyens finan-
ciers, de respectabilité sociale, d'expertise professionnelle ou linguistique. Enfin, celui ou celle qui desire s'adapter et se fonder dans la
société anglo-dominante a toujours la possibilité de se servir de la
langue français comme capital de seduction. [The city, in contrast, is
to be criticised by reason of the overwhelming importance attached
to work, the rapidity of the rhythm of life and the coldness of the
styles of sociability but probably, above all, because of the forms of
symbolic violence that are practiced and which Francophone gays
and lesbians continue to experience as a result of being Francophones
in an Anglo-dominant milieu, in particular in the gay and lesbian circles, and as a result of being gays and lesbians in hetero-normative circles, whether in the Francophone world or in their workplace. As
mentioned previously, in order to escape from this symbolic violence,
some attempt to transform society so as to help their symbolic and
material capital. This is a matter of financial means, social respectabil-
ity, and professional or linguistic expertise. Lastly, whomsoever
wishes to adapt and to establish themselves in the Anglo-dominant
society always have the possibility of benefiting from the French language as capital in seduction]

(Labrie & Grimard, 2002: 134)

Here, the shifts to and from English and French can be read at a number of levels and be shown to illustrate that language is a calculation in
the geometry of power that shapes much of the urban society. Linguistic
diversity is a resource that might be mined by many agents in the
city – minoritised language communities, policy actors in urban regimes,
the individual. Its peculiar power transcends matters of mere communication as it is intimately woven into the ever-changing fabric of place
and identity in the city. Here, more than in any other context, language's making of, and its own construction from, the social world are
together at their most dynamic in social terms, their most intellectually
challenging, and their most revealing of the human condition.

Conclusions

Language shapes the chaotic patterning of identity and power in the
city space while at the same time being itself shaped by the city. The
management of linguistic diversity through various practices in language planning and policy is a critical feature of city governance. At its

most productive this relationship between diverse language communities, language planning and government takes the form of a coalition of interest, an active engagement on the part of all players with the capacity to act on behalf of linguistic diversity, and a sense of the shared ownership of the urban domain. In such a context the activity associated with language planning and policy therefore becomes enabling and inclusive rather than constraining and exclusive through focussing upon power as a function of social production rather than as an issue of social control. It is in this way that linguistic diversity, multiculturalism, citizenship and governance ought to relate to each other in the city.

8
Conclusions

The epistemological and ontological shifts made by this book impact upon both the study of language and the study of the city in a number of disciplinexs. This impact comprises the following:

- How, and the extent to which, the city and language shape and are shaped by one another.
- How, the city, along with the various social processes which operate through it and in it, affects the status and use of language at the societal level and the relationship of that to patterns of language use in specific, local, city sites.
- The implications of this for the study of language in social context on one hand, and on the other hand, its implications for the study of the city.
- And the implications of this for the practice of language planning and policy in urban contexts – research to make urban practices in language diversity observable so as to inform social policy, not merely 'administered' language (Coulmas, 2005) – oral, spontaneous, language 'of the street' but also 'unadministered' language – language resulting from 'purposeful intervention in the course of language development' (Coulmas, 2005: 3) through education, corpus planning etc.
- And, in addition, the extent to which sociolinguistics is necessarily urban, and the implications of this for the further development of the discipline and for the direction of empirical research in the field.

Cities are in a constant state of change and are actively engaged in the continuous reconstruction of space. Different groups in the city make various contested claims to that space and language is part of the tension that arises from this. More particularly, language relates to the multiple, everyday social practices that are necessary to the mundane negotiation of the condition of being in the city (Jarvis, Pratt & Wu, 2001). This has a variety of implications for language planning and policy. While one may not necessarily go as far as Castells in claiming that the meaning of the city depends on its governance (2002: 557), it is reasonable to assert that language planning and policy as a function of city governance must be more central to everyday, ordinary life of cities. It is not, therefore, a question of grand ideology, even though cities function as gateways to the nation-state through the integration and assimilation of global migrants and others, but rather it is a matter of access to citizenship, and to the public body in general. The city is a critical site for the unequal and uneven impact of the contemporary form of globalisation – in economic, political and cultural terms. Language planning and policy can make a positive contribution to the lives of the most marginal peoples in the world economy, as well as play a role in helping to sustain the global linguistic diversity. Today, it is cities that are the most linguistically diverse sites in world. The agenda has become more urgent in recent years, as Coulmas points out:

> As a result of post-colonial mass migration, sizeable immigrant groups have formed in the metropolitan centres of those countries of the northern hemisphere which in the 19th century established largely monolingual regimes, not least because industrial society made horizontal nationwide communication necessary. National language regimes thus came into existence. Since these regimes are predicated on the ideology that language is a birthright and a vital marker of identity, and since the European societies in question recognize equality and freedom of choice as basic values, it has become increasingly difficult to restrict the use of community languages, including the languages of autochthonous minorities which were formerly a target of strong discrimination. Thus, ironically, in combination with progressing democratisation, monolingual language regimes have become instrumental in their own undoing. All Western countries as well as Japan are faced with increasing linguistic pluralism in urban centres and, calls for deregulation notwithstanding, feel compelled to introduce more language regulations targeted especially at immigrant communities.
>
> (Coulmas, 2005: 12)

The contemporary form of globalisation intensifies tensions between ethnic identities – defined by their specificity, historicity and autonomy.

Understanding the role of language in this area demands that we attend to the multiple, diverse and contingent identities associated with the city. Here, circumventing the primordial versus social constructivist debate as pertains to ethnicity through the application of the notion *ethnie* allows the craft of language planning to escape from the intellectual *cul-de-sac* of this dichotomy. For urban regimes, linguistic diversity and cultural plurality more generally ought to be recognised as the inevitable consequences of the condition of the city. The expression of difference in social practice along with the negotiation of competition and conflict therefore can be understood as an energising and inclusive project (Sennett, 2002; 1996; 1976). The implication of this is that the engagement with the reality of difference by urban regimes and not merely the management of difference as a commodity (e.g. Heller, 2003) is a necessity. In this way, linguistic diversity and difference are accommodated in the context of the fabric of city as a socially integrated whole (e.g. Fanstein, 2004; 2000).

For language planning and policy, the city is a necessary feature of the late 20th century turn in the discipline towards 'the new world order, postmodernism, and linguistic human rights' (Ricento, 2000). But, the nature of the city itself as a problematised entity in which language is situated must also be recognised. Thus, it is a requirement of the discipline that it engages with city and urban planners in order to effectively accommodate the urban condition to language planning and policy. The nature of city helps to provide 'a more complete explanation of language behaviour' (Ricento, 2000: 208–9) but this has, in the past, been taken for granted by sociolinguists. Those classical sociolinguistic studies in the English-speaking academic world which profoundly shaped the emergence and development of sociolinguistics as a distinctive area of scholarly activity in the period from the mid-1960s until the late 1980s can now be seen to be inadequate in a number of very important ways. For, not only were they markedly uncritical of social structure, but they also rendered the city and, more importantly, the urban condition invisible to their understanding of language and society. More recently, the work of French sociolinguists in particular, however, is beginning to open up the area for a different type of approach. 'La sociolinguistique urbaine existe-t-elle? Autrement dit, se distinguée t-elle, sur les plans conceptuels et méthodologiques, d'une sociolinguistique "non-urbaine"?' [Does urban sociolinguistics exist? To put it another way, what marks it out, in the conceptual and methodological terms, from a 'non-urban' sociolinguistics?] (Bulot, 2002: 8). The answer is, it would appear, that 'la sociolinguistique urbaine est une sociolinguistique *en* et *de* crise' [urban sociolinguistics is a sociolinguistics in and of crisis] (Bulot, 2002: 9). The crisis is a matter of epistemology, it is conceptual – that is, how to approach language in urban places and in urban space. Such a re-examination of language in the city is nothing less than an invitation to forge a new domain for sociolinguistics, central to which is the reclamation of the 'social' in sociolinguistics:

> Dans une intervention à un colloque d'ethnologie, Pierre Bourdieu rappelait que, pour Durkheim, l'inconscient était l'oubli de l'histoire, et il ajoutait; "Je pense que l'inconscient d'une discipline c'est son histoire; l'inconscient ce sont les conditions sociales de production occultées, oubliées". Toute approche épistémologique serait ainsi, d'un certain point de vue, une quête historique, une plongée dans l'inconscient d'une science, et dans celui de la sociolinguistique nous rencontrons donc, aux origines même de cette science, la ville. Et celle-ci nous donne à voir toute la complexité sociale que la linguistique se devrait de prendre en compte. Vaste programme, je sais. Mais combien excitant. [During an intervention at an ethnological colloquium, Pierre Bourdieu recalled that, according to Durkheim, the subconscious was the forgotten of history, and he added; "I think that the subconscious of a discipline is its own history, the subconscious is the hidden, forgotten social conditions of production". Each epistemological approach will be, in this way, of a certain point of view, an historical collection, a leap into the subconscious of a science. In the case of sociolinguistics we encounter the same origins of the science, that is, the city. And this makes us see the full social complexity of linguistics that merit being accounted for. It is a vast programme, I know. But, exciting.]
>
> (Calvet, 2002: 52)

What, specifically, however, is the way forward? Let us sketch out some of the key issues here, based upon the understanding that this is not the final statement on the nature and implications of linguistic diversity in the city but rather it is merely to open up, from a new perspective, the relationship between language and society. Notwithstanding the years that have passed since Jackson's (1989: 155–70) insight about the necessity of recognising the active role of language in constructing the social world, there remains considerable scope for exploring the cross-fertilisation of sociolinguistics/language planning and urban planning. The urbanisation of the global population, involving complex, sometimes dramatic, flows of people within and between countries, creates socially diverse, and divided, cities. In the North, 'cities are increasingly becoming a site of aggregation and representation of different interests' (Le Galès, 2005: 243), key loci in a complex web of governance within which an order related to scale is less and less evident (Newman & Thornley, 2005). This project will examine a little considered aspect of urban governance: its engagement with linguistic diversity. Language remains a potent marker of difference, with linguistic difference often elided with, or subsumed within, ethnic-racial differences (see, e.g., *The Parekh Report*, 2000). The management of diversity has long been a task of urban governance (Cochrane, 1999). However, over recent decades the context within which it has been undertaken have created new challenges and tensions. Under the conditions of the contemporary form of globalisation, cultural difference, of which linguistic diversity is a central feature, is reshaping the social fabric of cities of all sizes and in all parts of the world. This is reflected in new, or renewed, forms of cultural identity, of cultural division in urban labour markets, of political mobilisation, of conflict and cohesion (Eade & Mele, 2002).

Within urban planning, the discussions of how the state and planners more generally should understand and respond to cultural mix in cities have rarely made references to language and its significance (e.g. Sandercock, 2003). The implication is that language is a neutral and inert medium for the transmission of culture. This attitude is reminiscent of discredited notions of how to understand the spatiality of social processes, and is just as misguided. Language is an ever-changing artefact that is both shaped by and helps shape social life, sometimes contributing to, sometimes undercutting, constructions of identity and Otherness. Taking full account of language, for example, can enrich discussions of cultural hybridity. It is important to understand why, and in what ways, being able to speak a particular language may (or may not) play a part in the construction (whether successful or not) of social identities as bases for popular mobilisation or, indeed, governance. In brief, how is linguistic diversity implicated in urban management of the 'mongrel city' (Sandercock, 2003)? Reviews of urban policies which omit any reference to language or linguistic diversity (e.g. Le Galès, 2005: 245) are illustrative of the inability of existing analyses to address this question. The sociolinguistic literature which partly underpins language planning provides a basis on which to construct an answer to the question.

The discipline of language planning and policy remains dominated by a concern with language issues in 'national contexts' (Kaplan & Baldauf,

1997: 324–40). That is to say that the nation-state is the focal point of the craft of language planning and policy. Also, that is despite the fact that in sociolinguistics more generally the city is recognised as being 'innovative, unstable linguistically' (Wardhaugh, 2001: 136) and thereby central to understanding linguistic variation and change (see, e.g., Bulot, 2002a, 2002b; Calvet, 2002). Typically, studies in language planning have concentrated on individual languages, or the relationship of a single minority language to a dominant one (e.g. Fishman, 1994; Kaplan & Baldauf, 1997; Levine, 1990). They have tended to ignore the broader cultural politics within which language use is embedded (e.g. Extra & Yağmur 2004), and have often prioritised small settlements, often in rural areas despite, in some cases, the empirical geography of the language (Aitchison & Carter, 2000; Nettle & Romaine, 2000). This, in some ways, reflects historical concerns with the modernist project of nation-state building and its associated emphasis on the desirability and efficacy of a single language for state and citizen (Ricento, 2000; May, 2001; Wright, 2004). In this historical context, the city has tended to severely reduce the extent of linguistic diversity (Withers, 1984). In some societies the language policies have been very oppressive, giving the cities a distinctive, marked geography of language (Christopher, 2004; Williams & Van der Merwe, 1996). Moving beyond this modernist paradigm is a critical challenge for language planning and policy in the 21st century. Developing the scope and subtlety of language planning by using – and extending – the findings of urban planning and associated disciplines into the governance and cultural politics of cities, for example, the potential for 'the other' to transform 'the centre', whether partially or completely (e.g. Sassen, 1996) is a necessary response.

For language planning and policy practitioners, policy-related outcomes include comprehending the extent to which linguistic diversity might be sustainable in urban contexts – sustainable in the sense that it contributes to the 'holding together' (Sandercock, 2003) of the city so that difference become a force for cohesion rather than division. Also, now subject to scrutiny is the nature of the contemporary challenge to multiculturalism as a policy project and the implications of that challenge to late modern framings of the normative citizen and of citizenship from the perspective of urban linguistic diversity. The contested notion of multiculturalism (e.g. Mitchell, 1996) may provide a common focus to new research in this area in the future. The policy project of multiculturalism has recently been challenged on a number of fronts, including in the UK by the current chair of the Commission for Racial Equality and chair designate of the newly created Commission for Equality and Human Rights (Phillips, 2005). The intellectual concerns relating to language in the city are stimulated by this challenge.

The new context for managing urban linguistic diversity raises a number of issues which merit our attention. First of all, social diversity – and, especially, cultural diversity – has been valorised within the ubiquitous place marketing associated with urban entrepreneurialism. If cities are increasingly sites of consumption (Zukin, 1991; 1995), then ethnolinguistic groups have potential value as both symbols of the sophistication of a city's 'product', and also as contributors to the city's commodified cultural packages. We may reasonably hypothesise that these two functions may represent diversity differently: while place marketing can afford to feature the authentically different (if carefully chosen), there is a considerable literature which shows how cultural practices – from religious to culinary – are modified, indeed invented, for the consumption of the tourist (Shaw *et al.*, 2004). Such apparent deformations under the pressures of commodification, however, can also be sites of resistance for cultural minorities. Yet, if cultural diversity is valorised by governance agencies, it is also represented as potentially threatening – to social order in general, and in particular to the (often mobile) urban middle classes who are central to the project of 'regenerating' Northern cities through state-sponsored gentrification (Smith, 2001; Lees, 2004). More particularly, linguistic diversity is portrayed as potentially threatening. For example, the project of constructing proper British citizens has at its heart the fostering of linguistic competence in English: the language is to be the vehicle for a set of attitudes and behaviours which will help guarantee social order (Life in the UK Advisory Group, 2003). It is clear that the management of linguistic diversity is at the front line of the construction of the appropriate British citizen and that the urban is a crucial focus for the interplay of policies from throughout the web of governance. Similar projects are underway elsewhere in Europe and North America. Here is a tension which threatens the project of creating orderly, manageable cities which can act (it is hoped) as motors of regional or national economies: on the one hand urban governance seeks to promote and valorise linguistic diversity; on the other hand it both fears and attempts to manage it. Understanding the management of this tension relates to how 'threatening' manifestations and outcomes of linguistic diversity are constructed and understood by agencies of urban governance, how authorities engage with minority language groups within formal and informal structures of urban governance, and how the interplay of policies at different scales is negotiated in the urban context.

A second set of changes in the context of urban linguistic diversity revolves around the projects and aspirations of the linguistic communities themselves. The emancipatory and empowering potential of cities may be more often thwarted than realised in practice (Amin, Massey & Thrift, 2000; Lees, 2004) but it seems inevitable that for many linguistic groups – for better or for worse – multilingual cities will become central to their languages' survival. Historically, linguistic diversity has been anchored by geographical 'homelands' where a language might be used as the medium of daily life. The creation and sustaining of such 'homelands' remains among the (often disputed) goals of some political and governmental organisations dedicated to promoting languages considered under threat (May, 2001). This strategy may be inadequate for more than one reason. First, if regional cities with associated linguistic 'homelands' are to compete for globally mobile investment, and personnel, then new languages – and especially 'global' languages – will also be attracted. Secondly, the economic, and indeed symbolic, dominance of cities means that exclusively rural 'heartlands' are unlikely to support viable communities – young people need, and often want, to live in cities, for example. In these circumstances, creating and maintaining linguistic networks or enclaves in cities may be central to a language's future. Also, the contemporary form of globalisation has intensified and stretched the diasporic experiences of mobile peoples, creating relations within cities which in part may be shaped by, and help shape, relations 'stretched' far outside the city (Smith, 2001). One particular product of this is the reformation of culture, identified by some commentators as a state of 'trans-culturalism', whereby culture is no longer 'in place' but rather is 'in the making'. Another feature of these changes is the complex interlocking of senses of rootedness and cosmopolitanism, something that is manifest in dualities of identity and citizenship (Appadurai, 1996). These various dynamics resulting from the globalisation of culture have implications both for the function of language in the social construction of space and in the making and articulation of sense of identity. The responses of different language communities and, indeed, of individual speakers to this state of being 'in between' varies (Penninx, Martiniello & Vertovec, 2004; Rogers & Tillie, 2001). The limited literature that is relevant suggests that adaptations by linguistic groups to the multilingual city will vary according to a number of factors. These include, in particular, the status of the language in the country of which the city is a part, the constitutional status/role of the city and the extent to which linguistic identity is predicated upon another source of identity – religious, political or ethnic

(Penninx *et al.*, 2004; Rogers & Vertovec, 1995). Interrogating the source, nature and impact of these varying adaptations implies the examination of the effects that being constructed as 'Other' have on linguistic minorities, the nature of linguistic (including attitudinal) adaptations being made by language groups, and the consequences of these adaptations for the social and cultural identity of both the 'mobile subjects' and the 'locals'.

Thirdly, the complex set of relationships between the languages of a city – be they 'global' or 'arterial' languages, the language of a nation-state, minority autochthonous languages or the languages of immigrant communities – is shaped by the inequality of power in the encounters between these languages and their speakers. For example, some languages are privileged as official languages of the state; others are protected as local, minority vernaculars. This has, as a consequence, implications for linguistic identity and is an important factor in the shaping of cultural hybridity. It has implications also for language planning and policy approaches and responses to linguistic diversity including assimilation, separatism, ghettoisation, multiculturalism, interculturalism and cosmopolitanism. In the English speaking cities of the North we can speak of a dominant project of multiculturalism (*The Parekh Report*, 2000; Kymlicka, 1995), understanding that contested term as involving conscious strategies to improve the situation of culturally different groups without assimilation or exclusion from citizenship, and relating to the delivery of group-specific services, recognition of group rights, and the political inclusion of group representation. It is challenged by the radical consequences of this movement of language through space, its role in the localisation of social and cultural relations in a globalising world, and the ways in which language speakers, as mobile subjects, are made 'stable'. Also, it is the case that the policy and planning family does not function as an integrated whole in relation to the management of linguistic diversity in the city. Some policy and planning practices, operating from different functions of urban government, have outcomes for linguistic diversity that are diametrically opposed. For example, educational policies may attempt to promote a widely shared official language, while urban planning policies may valorise linguistic diversity by recognising and prioritising ethnolinguistic groups as recipients of grants or other support. The geometry of power that exists in the city has uneven and unequal outcomes both across different language communities and within specific language networks. These suppositions invite the study of how some minority language groups network within formal and informal structures of urban governance, what the implications of the various adaptations made by migrants and locals for language planning and policy are, how the functions of urban government relate to each other in policy and planning practices with regard to linguistic diversity, and what role agencies of language planning and policy might potentially play in the management of sustainable linguistic diversity in the city.

So, the impact of the city on language is profound; equally, language and, more precisely, linguistic diversity substantially make and remake society through the city. The intellectual challenge posed by this agenda must be met by city and urban planning, sociolinguistics, and language planning and policy. And, it is a matter of necessity. Given that the greater part of humanity will be urban-dwellers before very long (perhaps already will be by the time this text appears in print) and that the power and influence of the city is set to increase substantially in the foreseeable future, superseding that of nation-states in many regards (e.g. United Nations – Habitat, 2006), the task identified here is more than exciting – it is, in the most absolute terms, fundamental.

Bibliography

Aitchison, J.W. & Carter, H. (1987). 'The Welsh language in Cardiff: a quiet revolution', *Transactions of the Institute of British Geographers* new series 12, pp. 482–492.

Aitchison, J. & Carter, H. (1994). *A Geography of the Welsh language 1961–1991*, Cardiff: University of Wales Press.

Aitchison, J. & Carter, H. (2000). *Language, Economy and Society: The Changing Geography of the Welsh Language in the 20th Century*, Cardiff: University of Wales Press.

Alexander, L. (2006). 'Sen. Alexander introduces Senate resolution on National Anthem', press release accessed from http://alexander.senate.gov/ (site accessed 19 May 2006).

Alibhai-Brown, Y. (2000). *After Multiculturalism*, London: The Foreign Policy Centre.

Allen, J. (1999a). 'Cities of power and influence: settled formations'. In Allen, J., Massey, D. & Pryke, M. (eds.), *Unsettling Cities: Movement/Settlement*, London: Routledge, pp. 181–227.

Allen, J. (1999b). 'Worlds within cities'. In Massey, D., Allen, J. & Pile, S. (eds.), *City Worlds*, London: Routledge, pp. 53–97.

Allen, J.P. (2002). 'The Tortilla-Mercedes divide in Los Angeles', *Political Geography* 21(5), pp. 701–709.

Allen, J., Massey, D. & Pryke, M. (eds.) (1999). *Unsettling Cities: Movement/Settlement*, London: Routledge.

Amin, A. & Graham, S. (1999). 'Cities of connection and disconnection'. In Allen, J., Massey, D. & Pryke, M. (eds.), *Unsettling Cities: Movement/Settlement*, London: Routledge, pp. 7–47.

Amin, A., Massey, D. & Thrift, N. (2000). *Cities for the Many not the Few*, Bristol: Policy Press.

Anctil, P. (1984). 'The double majority and ethnocultural multiplicity in Montreal', *Recherches Sociographiques* 25(3), pp. 441–456.

Anderson, J. (1995). 'The exaggerated death of the nation-state'. In Anderson, J., Brook, C. & Cochrane, A. (eds.), *A Global World? Re-ordering Political Space*, Oxford: Oxford University Press, pp. 65–112.

Appadurai, A. (1995). 'The production of locality'. In Fardon, R. (ed.), *Counterworks: Managing the Diversity of Knowledge*, London: Routledge, pp. 204–205.

Appadurai, A. (1996). *Modernity at Large: Cultural Dimensions of Globalization*, Minneapolis, MN: University of Minnesota Press.

Backhaus, P. (2005). 'Signs of multilingualism in Tokyo – a diachronic look at the linguistic landscape', *International Journal of the Sociology of Language* 175/176, pp. 103–121.

Baker, C. & Jones, S.P. (1998). *Encyclopedia of Bilingual Education and Bilingualism*, Clevedon: Multilingual Matters.

Baker, P. & Eversley, J. (eds.) (2000). *Multilingual Capital: The Languages of London's Schoolchildren and Their Relevance to Economic, Social and Educational Policies*, London: Battlebridge Publications.

Barth, F. (1969). *Ethnic Groups and Boundaries: The Social Organisation of Cultural Difference*, Boston, MA: Little, Brown & Co.

Barth, F. (1984). 'Problems in conceptualizing cultural pluralism, with illustrations from Somar, Oman'. In Maybury-Lewis, D. (ed.), *The Prospects for Plural Society*, Washington, DC: American Ethnological Society, pp. 77–87.

Barth, F. (1989). 'The analysis of culture in complex societies', *Ethnos* 54, pp. 120–142.

Barth, F. (1998 [reprint of Barth 1969 with new preface]). *Ethnic Groups and Boundaries: The Social Organisation of Cultural Difference*, Prospect Heights, IL: Waveland.

Baumann, G. (1996). *Contesting Culture: Discourses of Identity in Multi-Ethnic London*, Cambridge: Cambridge University Press.

Bauman, R. (2003). *Voices of Modernity: Language Ideologies and the Politics of Inequality*, Cambridge: Cambridge University Press.

BBC News (2006). 'US Senate in wrangle over English', http://bbc.co.uk/ (site accessed 19 May 2006).

Beeley, B. (1995). 'Global options: Islamic alternatives'. In Anderson, J., Brook, C. & Cochrane, A. (eds.), *A Global World? Re-ordering Political Space*, Oxford: Oxford University Press, pp. 167–207.

Benton-Short, L., Price, M. & Friedman, S. (2004). *Global perspective on the connections between immigrants and world cities*, Occasional Paper Series, George Washington Centre for the Study of Globalization CSGOP-04-32.

Bhabha, H. (1994). *The Location of Culture*, London: Routledge.

Block, D. (2006). *Multilingual Identities in a Global City: London Stories*, Houndmills & New York: Palgrave Macmillan.

Blommaert, J. (2003). 'Commentary: a sociolinguistics of globalization', *Journal of Sociolinguistics* 7(4), pp. 607–623.

Boas, F. (ed.) (1911). *Handbook of American Indian languages*, Washington, DC: Smithsonian Institution.

Bourdieu, P. (1977). *Outline of a Theory of Practice*, Cambridge: Cambridge University Press.

Bourdieu, P. (1990). *The Logic of Practice*, Stanford: Stanford University Press.

Bourdieu, P. (1991). *Language and Symbolic Power*, Cambridge: Polity Press.

Brandt, B. & Layton-Henry, Z. (n.d.). *Transnational Communities and the Transformation of Citizenship*. http://www.transcomm.ox.ac.uk.

Bulot, T. (2001). 'Ségrégation et urbanisation linguistique: l'altérité urbaine définie ou l'étranger est une personné', *Diverscité Langues* VI. http://www.teluq.uquebec.ca/diverscite Télé Université du Québec.

Bulot, T. (2002a). 'La sociolinguistique urbaine: une sociolinguistique de crise? Premières considérations', *Marges Linguistiques* 3, pp. 8–10.

Bulot, T. (2002b). 'La double articulation de la spatialité urbaine: "espaces urbanises" et "lieux de ville" en sociolinguistique', *Marges Linguistiques* 3, pp. 91–105.

Bulot, T., Bauvois, C. & Blanchet, P. (eds.) (2001). *Sociolinguistique urbaine. Variations linguistiques: images urbaines et sociales*, Rennes: Presses Universitaires de Rennes.

Bulot, T. & Tsekor, N. (eds.) (1999). *Langue urbaine et identité (Langue et urbanisation à Rouen, Venise, Berlin, Athènes et Mons)*, Paris: L'Harmattan.

Burholt, V. (2004). 'The settlement patterns and residential histories of older Gujaaratis, Punjabis and Sylhetis in Birmingham, England', *Ageing and Society*, 24(3), pp. 383–409.

Burkeman, O. (2006). 'Migrants take protest to LA streets', *The Guardian*, Monday, 27 March 2006.

Calvet, L.-J. (2002). 'La sociolinguistique et la ville; hazard ou nécessité?' *Marges Linguistiques* 3, pp. 46–53.

Calvet, L.-J. & Moussirou-Mouyama, A. (eds.) (2000). 'Le plurilinguisme urbain' Institut de la Francophonie/Didier Erudition.

Cameron, D. (1990). 'Demythologizing sociolinguistics: Why language does not reflect society'. In Joseph, J.E. & Taylor, T.J. (eds.), *Ideologies of Language*, London: Routledge, pp. 79–93.

Castells, M. (1989). *The Informational City: Information Technology, Economic Restructuring and the Urban-Regional Process*, Oxford: Blackwell.

Castells, M. (1996). *The Information Age: Economy, Society and Culture. Vol.1. The Rise of the Network Society*, Oxford: Basil Blackwell.

Castells, M. (1997). *The Information Age: Economy, Society and Culture. Vol.2. The Power of Identity*, Oxford: Basil Blackwell.

Castells, M. (2002). 'Local and global cities in the network society', *Tijidschrift voor Economische en Sociale Geografie* 93(5), pp. 548–558.

Chambers, D. (1999). 'Women's experiences and negotiations of suburban planning'. In Pile, S., Brook, C. & Mooney, G. (eds.), *Unruly Cities?Order/Disorder*, London: Routledge, pp. 50–52.

Cheshire, J. (1978). 'Variation in the use of "ain't" in an urban British English dialect', *Language and Society* 10, pp. 365–381.

Cheshire, J. (1982). 'Linguistic variation and social function'. In Romaine, S. (ed.), *Sociolinguistic Variation in Speech Communities*, London: Edward Arnold, pp. 153–175.

Chomsky, N. (1979). *Language and Responsibility*, London: Harvester.

Christopher, A.J. (2004). 'Linguistic segregation in urban South Africa', *Geoforum* 35(2), pp. 145–156.

Cochrane, A. (1995). 'Global worlds and worlds of difference'. In Anderson, J., Brook, C. & Cochrane, A. (eds.), *A Global World? Re-ordering Political Space*, Oxford: Oxford University Press, pp. 249–279.

Cochrane, A. (1999). 'Administered cities'. In Pile, S., Brook, C. & Mooney, G. (eds.), *Unruly Cities? Order/Disorder*, London: Routledge, pp. 299–344.

Cochrane, A. & Pain, K. (2000). 'A globalizing society?' In Held, D. (ed.), *A Globalizing World? Culture, Economics, Politics*, London: Routledge, pp. 5–45.

Connor, W. (1978). 'A nation is a nation, is a state, is an ethnic group, is a...' *Ethnic and Racial Studies* 1, pp. 377–400.

Cooper, R.L. (1974). 'Choosing a lingua franca in an African capital', *Language in Society* 3(1), pp. 147–154.

Cooper, R.L. (1982). 'A framework for the study of language spread'. In Cooper, R.L. (ed.), *Language Spread: Studies in Diffusion and Social Change*, Bloomington: Indiana University Press & Washington, DC: Center for Applied Linguistics, pp. 5–36.

Cooper, R.L. (1989). *Language Planning and Social Change*, Cambridge: Cambridge University Press.

Coulmas, F. (2005). 'Changing language regimes in globalizing environments', *International Journal of the Sociology of Language* 175/176, pp. 3–15.

Coupland, N. (2003). 'Introduction: sociolinguistics and globalisation' *Journal of Sociolinguistics* 7(4), pp. 465–472.

Coupland, N. & Jaworski, A. (eds.), (1997). *Sociolinguistics: A Reader and Coursebook*, Houndmills: Macmillan.

Creech, R.L. (2005). *Law and Language in the European Union: The Paradox of a Babel 'United in diversity'*, Netherlands: Europa Law Publications.

Crystal, D. (1987). *The Cambridge Encyclopedia of Language*, Cambridge: Cambridge University Press.

Crystal, D. (2001). *Language and the Internet*, Cambridge: Cambridge University Press.

Crystal, D. (2003). *English as a Global Language*, Cambridge: Cambridge University Press.

Dafis, C. (1975). 'The manifesto' *Planet* 26/27 1974/75, pp. 77–136.

Davies, N. (1997). *Europe: A History*, London: Pimlico.

Davis, M. (1994). *Beyond Bladerunner: urban control: the ecology of fear*, Pamphlet 23, Open Magazine Pamphlet Series.

De Baroid, C. (1990). *Ballymurphy and the Irish War*, London: Pluto Press.

DeBernardi, J. (1994). 'Social aspects of language use'. In Ingold, T. (ed.), *Companion Encyclopedia of Anthropology: Humanity, Culture and Social Life*, London: Routledge, pp. 861–890.

De Klerk, V. (2002). 'Changing names in the "new" South Africa: a diachronic survey', *Names* 50(3), pp. 201–221.

De Klerk, V. & Lagonikos, I. (2004). 'First-name changes in South Africa: the swing of the pendulum', *International Journal of the Sociology of Language* 170, pp. 59–80.

Dittmar, N. (1976). *Sociolinguistics: A Critical Survey of Theory and Application*, London: Arnold.

Dorier-Apprill, E. & Van Den Avenne, C. (2002). 'Usages toponymiques et pratiques de l'espace urbain à Mopti (Mali)', *Marges Linguistiques* 3, pp. 151–158.

Duranti, A. (1997). *Linguistic Anthropology* Cambridge: Cambridge University Press.

Dutton, C. (2004). *Gaeltacht Quarter. The establishment of a development board and related issues. Final report to the Department of Culture, Art and Leisure, the Department of Social Development and the Department of Enterprise, Trade and Investment.* [Northern Ireland]

Eade, J. & Mele, C. (eds.) (2002). *Understanding the City*, Oxford: Blackwell.

Eagleton, T. (1991). *Ideology*, London: Verso.

Eagleton, T. (1996). *The Illusions of Postmodernism*, London: Routledge.

Eastman, C. (1983). *Language Planning: An Introduction*, San Francisco: Chandler and Sharp.

Eley, G. (1992). 'Culture, Britain and Europe', *The Journal of British Studies* 31(4), pp. 415–425.

Elke, L. (2002). 'Espaces linguistiques à Montréal', *Marges Linguistiques* 3, pp. 137–150.

Eriksen, T.H. (1993). *Ethnicity and Nationalism: Anthropological Perspectives*, London: Pluto.

Everard, J. (2000). *Virtual States: The Internet and the Boundaries of the Nation-State. Technology and the Global Political Economy*, London: Routledge.

Extra, G. & Yagmur, K. (2004). 'Multilingual cities project on immigrant minority languages in Europe', *Babylonia* 1(04) pp. 32–35, www.babylonia-ti.ch.

Extra, G. & Yagmur, K. (2005). 'Sociolinguistic perspectives on emerging multilingualism in urban Europe', *International Journal of the Sociology of Language* 175/176, pp. 17–40.

Fanstein, S.S. (2000). *The City Builders*, Lawrence, KS: University Press of Kansas.
Fanstein, S.S. (2004). *Cities and diversity: should we want it? Can we plan for it?* Conference Paper, Leverhulme International Symposium: The Resurgent City, London School of ECONOMICS, 19–21 April 2004.
Fasold, R. (1990). *The Sociolinguistics of Language*, Oxford: Blackwell.
Fat, L.C. (2005). 'A dialect murders another dialect: the case of Hakka in Hong Kong' *International Journal of the Sociology of Language* 173, pp. 23–35.
Favell, A. (1999). 'To belong or not to belong: The postcolonial question'. In Favell, A. & Geddes, A. (eds.), *The Politics of Belonging: Migrants and Minorities in Contemporary Europe*, Aldershot: Ashgate, pp. 209–223.
Fichte, J. (1968). *Addresses to the German Nation*, New York: Harper & Row.
Fill, A. (1993). *Ökolinguistik: eine einführung*, Tübingen: Gunter Narr.
Fill, A. & Mühlhäusler, P. (eds.) (2001). *The Ecolinguistics Reader: Language, Ecology and Environment*, London: Continuum.
Fischer, S.R. (1999). *A History of Language*, London: Reaktion Books.
Fishman, J.A. (1991). *Reversing Language Shift: The Theoretical and Empirical Foundations of Assistance to Threatened Languages*, Clevedon: Multilingual Matters.
Fishman, J.A. (1994). 'Critiques of language planning: A minority languages perspective', *Journal of Multilingual and Multicultural Development* 15, pp. 91–99.
Frist, B. (2006). 'Frist, Alexander vote for Inhofe amendment declaring English the national language of the United States', press release accessed from http://frist.senate.gov/ (site accessed 19 May 2006).
García, O. & Fishman, J.A. (eds.) (2002). *The Multilingual Apple: Languages in New York City*, Berlin: Mouton de Gruyter.
Garner, R. (2006). 'Pioneering project to teach in pupils' own language is scrapped', *The Independent*, Wednesday, 22 February 2006, p. 13.
Gasquet-Cyrus, M. (2003). 'Sociolinguistique urbaine ou urbanisation de la sociolinguistique?' *Marges Linguistiques* 3, pp. 54–71.
Geertz, C. (1973). The Interpretation of Cultures, New York: Basic Books.
Giddens, A. (1976). New Rules of Sociological Method: A Positive Critique of Interpretive Sociologies, London: Hutchinson.
Giddens, A. (1981) *Contemporary Critique of Historical Materialism. Vol.1 Power, Property and the State*, London: Macmillan.
Giddens, A. (1984). *The Constitution of Society*, Cambridge: Polity Press.
Giddens, A. (1985). *Contemporary Critique of Historical Materialism. Vol.2 The Nation-State and Violence*, Cambridge: Polity.
Giddens, A. (1986). *Sociology. A Brief But Critical Introduction*, Basingstoke: Macmillan.
Gilbert, A. (1999). 'Work and poverty during economic restructuring: the experience of Bogotá, Colombia'. In Allen, J., Massey, D. & Pryke, M. (eds.), *Unsettling Cities: Movement/Settlement*, London: Routledge, pp. 266–269.
Giles, H., Bourhis, R.Y. & Taylor, D.M. (1977). 'Towards a theory of language in ethnic group relations'. In Giles, H. (ed.), *Language, Ethnicity and Intergroup Relations*, pp. 307–348.
Glazer, N. & Moynihan, D. (1975). *Ethnicity: Theory and Experience*, Cambridge MA: Harvard University Press.
Gumbel, A. (2006). 'Millions take to streets to demand immigrants' rights', *The Independent*, Tuesday, 11 April 2006, p. 22.
Haarmann, H. (1986). *Language in Ethnicity: A View of Basic Ecological Relations*, Berlin, New York, Amsterdam: Mouton de Gruyter.

Hall, S. (1992). 'The question of cultural identity'. In Hall, S., Held, D. & McGrew, T. (eds.), *Modernity and its Futures*, Cambridge: Polity Press, pp. 274–325.

Hall, S. (1996). 'Who needs identity? In Hall, S. & duGay, P. (eds.), *Questions of Cultural Identity*, London: Sage, pp. 1–17.

Hannerz, U. (1990). 'Cosmopolitans and locals in world culture'. In Featherstone, M. (ed.), *Global Culture: Nationalism, Globalisation and Modernity*, London: Sage, pp. 237–253.

Hannerz, U. (1996). *Transnational Connections: Culture, People, Places*, London: Routledge.

Haugen, E. (1959). 'Planning for a standard language in modern Norway', *Anthropological Linguistics* 1(3), pp. 8–21.

Haugen, E. (1972). *The Ecology of Language*, Stanford: Stanford University Press.

Haugen, E. (1983). 'The implementation of corpus planning. Theory and practice'. In Cobarrubias, J. & Fishman, J.A. (eds.), *Progress in Language Planning*, The Hague: Mouton, pp. 269–289.

Held, D. (ed.) (2000). *A Globalizing World? Culture, Economics, Politics*, London: Routledge.

Heller, M. (2003). 'Globalization, the new economy, and the commodification of language and identity', *Journal of Sociolinguistics* 7(4), pp. 473–492.

Hernandez, D. (2005). 'Something to shout about – "El Grito"', *Los Angeles Times* Saturday, 17 September 2005, B3.

Hibbert, L. (2004). 'Globalization, the African Renaissance, and the role of English', *International Journal of the Sociology of Language* 170, pp. 81–93.

Hinchliffe, S. (1999). 'Cities and natures; intimate strangers'. In Allen, J., Massey, D. & Pryke, M. (eds.), *Unsettling Cities: Movement/Settlement*, London: Routledge, pp. 137–180.

Hobsbawm, E.J. (1992). *Nations and Nationalism Since 1780: Programme, Myth and Reality*, Cambridge: Cambridge University Press.

Hobsbawm, E.J. & Ranger, T. (eds.) (1983). *The Invention of Tradition*, Cambridge: Cambridge University Press.

Huntington, S. (2004). *Who are We: The Challenges to America's National Identity*, New York: Simon & Schuster.

Isajiw, W. (1980). 'Definitions of ethnicity'. In Goldstein, J. & Bienvenue, R. (eds.), *Ethnicity and Ethnic Relations in Canada*, Toronto: Butterworth, pp. 5–17.

Jackson, P. (1989). *Maps of Meaning*, London: Unwin Hyman.

Jacobs, J. (1999). 'The generators of diversity'. In Pile, S., Brook, C. & Mooney, G. (eds.), *Unruly Cities? Order/Disorder*, London: Routledge, pp. 339–340.

Jameson, F. (1975). 'Beyond the cave: demystifying the ideology of modernism', *Bulletin of the Midwest Modern Language Association* 8(1), pp. 1–20.

Jameson, F. (1991). *Postmodernism, or the Cultural Logic of Late Capitalism*, Durham: Duke University Press.

Jarvis, H., Pratt, A. & Wu, C. (2001). *The Secret Life of Cities*, London: Pearson.

Jones, R.P. (1998). *The myth of coloured identity(?): an examination of the Coloured community of Wentworth*, unpublished MA thesis, Department of Geographical and Environmental Sciences, University of Natal, Durban.

Kachru, B.B. (1992, 2nd ed.). *The Other Tongue: English Across Cultures. English in Global Context*, Champaign, IL: University of Illinois Press.

Kamwangamalu, N.M. (2001). 'Ethnicity and language crossing in post-apartheid South Africa', *International Journal of the Sociology of Language* 152, pp. 75–95.

Kamwangamalu, N.M. (2004). 'Language, social history, and identity in post-apartheid South Africa: a case study of the "Colored" community of Wentworth', *International Journal of the Sociology of Language* 170, pp. 113–129.

Kanani, D. (2003). 'Ieithoedd Cymru – angen dweud mwy', *Golwg* 15(25) p. 26.

Kaplan, M., Goldstein, K. & Hale, M. (2005). *Spanish-language TV coverage of the 2004 campaigns*, Los Angeles: Lear Center Local News Archive USC Annenberg School for Communication and the University of Wisconsin.

Kaplan, R.B. & Baldauf, R.B. (1997). *Language Planning: From Practice to Theory*, Clevedon: Multilingual Matters.

Karim, K.H. (1998). *From Ethnic Media to Global Media: Transnational Communication Networks among Diasporic Communities* WPTC-99-02. http://www.transcomm.ox.ac.uk.

Katsuragi, T. (2005). 'Japanese language policy from the point of view of public philosophy', *International Journal of the Sociology of Language* 175/176, pp. 41–54.

King, A.D. (ed.) (1996). *Re-presenting the City: Ethnicity, Capital and Culture in the 21st Century Metropolis,*New York: New York University Press.

King, A.D. (1974). 'The language of colonial urbanization', *Sociology* 8(1), pp. 81–110.

King, D. (2000). *Making Americans: Immigration,Race and the Origins of the Diverse Democracy*, Cambridge, MA: Harvard University Press.

Kloss, H. (1967). 'Abstand languages and Ausbau languages', *Anthropological Linguistics* 9, pp. 29–41.

Kloss, H. (1977). *The American Bilingual Tradition*, Rowley, MA: Newbury House.

Kroeber, A.L. (1963). *Anthropology: Culture Patterns and Processes*, New York: Harbinger Books.

Kymlicka, W. (1995). *Multicultural citizenship: A Liberal Theory of Minority Rights*, Oxford: Clarendon Press.

Labov, W. (1966). *The Social Stratification of English in New York City*, Washington, DC: Center for Applied Linguistics.

Labov, W. (1972). *Language in the Inner City: Studies in the Black English Vernacular*, Oxford: Basil Blackwell.

Labov, W. (1977). 'The linguistic consequences of being Lame', *Actes de la recherché en sciences socials* 17–18, pp. 113–129.

Labov, W. (1978). *The Origins of Linguistic Change*, International Sociological Association.

Labrie, N. & Grimard, M. (2003). 'La migration de gais et lesbiennes francophones à Toronto: de la stigmatisation à la mobilité' sociale', *Marges Linguistiques* 3, pp. 118–136.

Landry, R. & Bourhis, R.Y. (1997). 'Linguistic landscape and ethnoliguistic vitality', *Journal of Language and Social Psychology* 16(1), pp. 23–49.

Layton-Henry, Z. (2002). *Transnational Communities, Citizenship and African-Caribbeans in Birmingham* WPTC-02-07. http://www.transcomm.ox.ac.uk.

Leclerc, J. (2001). 'Index par politique linguistique' in *L'aménagement linguistique dans le monde Québec, TLFQ, Université Laval* accessed from http://www.tlfq.ulaval.ca/axl/monde/index_politique-lng.htm (site accessed 30 January 2006).

Lees, L. (ed.) (2004). *The Emancipatory City?* London: Sage.

Le Galès, P. (2005). 'Elusive urban policies in Europe'. In Kazopov, Y. (ed.), *Cities of Europe*, Oxford: Blackwell, pp. 235–254.

Levine, M. (1990). *The Reconquest of Montreal: Language Policy and Social Change in a Bilingual City*, Philadelphia, PA: Temple University Press.

Liddicoat, A.J. (2006). *Current Issues in Language Planning. Special Issue on Micro Language Planning* 7(2&3).

Life in the UK Advisory Group (chair B. Crick) (2003). *The New and the Old*, London: Home Office.

Logan, J.R. (2003). *How Race Counts for Hispanic Americans*, Albany, NY: Lewis Mumford Center, University at Albany.

Louw, P.E. (2004). 'Political power, national identity, and language: the case of Afrikaans', *International Journal of the Sociology of Language* 170, pp. 43–58.

Macaulay, R.K.S. (1977). *Language, Social Class and Education: A Glasgow Study*, Edinburgh: Edinburgh University Press.

Mac Giolla Chríost, D. (1996). 'Northern Ireland: Culture clash and archaeology'. In Atkinson, J.A., Banks, I. & O'Sullivan, J. (eds.), *Nationalism and Archaeology*, Glasgow: Cruithne Press, pp. 128–134.

Mac Giolla Chríost, D. (2001). 'Implementing Political Agreement in Northern Ireland: Planning Issues for Irish Language Policy', *The Journal of Social and Cultural Geography* 2(3), pp. 297–313.

Mac Giolla Chríost, D. (2003). *Language, Identity and Conflict*, London & New York: Routledge.

Mac Giolla Chríost, D. (2005). *The Irish Language in Ireland from Goídel to Globalisation*, London & New York: Routledge.

MacKenzie, A., Ball, A.S. & Kirdee, S.R. (1998). *Ecology*, Oxford: BIOS Scientific Publishers.

Maguire, G. (1991). *Our Own Language: An Irish Initiative*, Clevedon: Multilingual Matters.

Maher, J.C. (1996). *Multilingual Japan*, Clevedon: Multilingual Matters.

Maher, J.C. (2005). 'Metroethnicity, language, and the principle of Cool', *International Journal of the Sociology of Language* 175/176, pp. 83–102.

Mair, C. (2003). *The Politics of English as a World Language: New Horizons in Postcolonial Studies*, Cambridge: Cambridge University Press.

Malotki, E. (1983). *Hopi Time: A Linguistic Analysis of the Temporal Concepts of the Hopi Language*, Amsterdam: Mouton.

Mandelbaum, D. (ed.) (1949). *Selected Writings of Edward Sapir in Language, Culture and Personality*, London: Cambridge University Press.

Massey, D. (1999). 'Cities in the world'. In Massey, D., Allen, J. & Pile, S. (eds.), *City worlds*, pp. 99–156.

Massey, D., Allen, J. & Pile, S. (eds.) (1999). *City Worlds*, London: Routledge.

May, S. (2001). *Language and Minority Rights: Ethnicity, Nationalism and the Politics of Language*, Harlow: Longman.

McArthur, T. (2003). *The Oxford Guide to World Englishes*, Oxford: Oxford University Press.

McCain, J. (1998). 'McCain introduces English-plus resolution', press release accessed from http://mccain.senate/gov/ (site accessed 19 May 2006).

McDowell, L. (1999). 'City life and difference: negotiating diversity'. In Allen, J., Massey, D. & Pryke, M. (eds.), *Unsettling Cities: Movement/Settlement*, London: Routledge, pp. 95–135.

McGrew, A. (1995). 'World order and political space'. In Anderson, J., Brook, C. & Cochrane, A. (eds.), *A Global World? Re-ordering Political Space*, Oxford: Oxford University Press, pp. 11–64.

McGrew, A. (2000). 'Power shift: from national government to global governance?' In Held, D. (ed.), *A Globalizing World? Culture, Economics, Politics*, London: Routledge, pp. 127–167.

McIntosh, R.P. (1985). *The Background of Ecology: Concept and Theory*, Cambridge: Cambridge University Press.

McLaughlin, F. (2001). 'Dakar Wolof and the configuration of an urban identity', *Journal of African Cultural Studies* 14(2), pp. 153–172.

McLaughlin, E. & Muncie, J. (1999). 'Walled cities: Surveillance, regulation and segregation'. In Pile, S., Brook, C. & Mooney, G. (eds.), *Unruly Cities? Order/Disorder*, London: Routledge, pp. 103–148.

Michelet, J. (1967). *History of the French Revolution*, Chicago: University of Chicago Press.

Michelet, J. (1973). *The People*, Urbana, IL: University of Illinois Press.

Mill, J.N. (1972). *Considerations on Representative Government*, London: J.M.Dent.

Milroy, L. (1987). *Observing and Analysing Natural Language: A Critical Account of Sociolinguistic Method*, Oxford: Basil Blackwell.

Milroy, J. (1992). *Linguistic Variation and Change: On the Historical Sociolinguistics of English*, Oxford: Basil Blackwell.

Mitchell, K. (1993). 'Multiculturalism, or the united colours of capitalism?' *Antipode* 25, pp. 263–294.

Mitchell, K. (1996). 'In whose interest? Transnational capital and the production of multiculturalism in Canada'. In R. Wilson & W. Dissanayake (eds.), *Global/Local: Cultural Production and the Transnational Imaginary*, Durham, NC: Duke University Press, pp. 219–251.

Monmonier, M. (1991). *How to Lie with Maps*, Chicago: Chicago University Press.

Mooney, G. (1999). 'Urban "disorders"'. In Pile, S., Brook, C. & Mooney, G. (eds.), *Unruly Cities? Order/Disorder*, London: Routledge, pp. 53–102.

Mooney, G., Pile, S. & Brook, C. (1999). 'On orderings and the city'. In Pile, S., Brook, C. & Mooney, G. (eds.), *Unruly Cities? Order/Disorder*, London: Routledge, pp. 345–367.

Morris, L. (1997). 'Globalization, migration and the nation-state: The path to a post-national Europe?' *British Journal of Sociology* 48(2), pp. 192–209.

Mühlhäusler, P. (1996) *Linguistic Ecology: Language Change and Linguistic Imperialism in the Pacific Region*, London: Routledge.

Mühlhäusler, P. (2000). 'Language planning and language ecology', *Current Issues in Language Planning* 1(3), pp. 306–367.

Mühlhäusler, P. (2001). 'Ecology of languages', *Current Issues in Language Planning*. Themes Issue 'Language planning and language ecology'. http://cilp.arts.usyd.edu.au.

Naga, R. (1997). 'Communal places and the politics of multiple identities' *Ecumene* 4(1), pp. 7–13.

Nagel, J. (1994). 'Constructing ethnicity: Creating and recreating ethnic identity and culture', *Social Problems* 41, pp. 152–176.

Nettle, D. & Romaine, S. (2000). *Vanishing Voices: The Extinction of the World's Languages*, Oxford: Oxford University Press.

Newman, P. & Thornley, A. (2005). *Planning World Cities: Globalization and Urban Politics*, Houndmills & New York: Palgrave Macmillan.

Ngom, F. (2004). 'Ethnic identity and linguistic hybridisation in Senegal', *International Journal of the Sociology of Language* 170, pp. 95–111.

Noguchi, M.G. (2005). 'Politics, the media, and Korean language acquisition in Japan', *International Journal of the Sociology of Language* 175/176, pp. 123–156.

Ó Colchúin, D. (2006). 'Béarla, le bhur dtoil' *Beo* 66. http://www.beo.ie (site accessed 16 October 2006).

Odum, E.P. (1975). *Ecology: The Link between the Natural and the Social Sciences*, London: Holt Rinehart & Winston.

Ó Gairbhí, S.T. (2006). 'Seimineár faoi dhearcadh inimirceoirí i leith na Gaeilge' *Foinse*, 29 October 2006, p. 4.

O'Reilly, C. (1999). *The Irish Language in Northern Ireland: The Politics of Culture and Identity*, London: Macmillan.

O'Reilly, C. (ed.) (2001). *Language, Ethnicity and the State Volume 1: Minority Languages in the European Union*, Houndmills: Palgrave Macmillan.

Owen, D.F. (1980). *What is Ecology?* Oxford: Oxford University Press. *The Parekh Report*, Runnymede Trust/Commission on the future of multi-ethnic Britain (2000), *The Future of Multi-ethnic Britain*, London: Profile Books.

Penninx, R., Martiniello, M. & Vertovec, S. (eds.) (2004). *Citizenship in European Cities: Immigrants, Local Politics and Integration Policies*, Aldershot: Ashgate.

Phan, A. (2005). 'Vietnamese lose all, this time to Katrina', *USA Today*, Friday, 16 September 2005 11A.

Phillips, T. (2005). 'What now for multiculturalism?' *Connections* Winter 2004/05.

Phillipson, R. (1992). *Linguistic Imperialism*, Oxford: Oxford University Press.

Pile, S. (1999a). 'What is a city?' In Massey, D., Allen, J. & Pile, S. (eds.), *City Worlds*, London: Routledge, pp. 3–52.

Pile, S. (1999b). 'The heterogeneity of cities'. In Pile, S., Brook, C. & Mooney, G. (eds.), *Unruly Cities?Order/Disorder*, London: Routledge, pp. 7–52.

Pile, S., Brook, C. & Mooney, G. (eds.) (1999). *Unruly Cities? Order/Disorder*, London: Routledge.

Pinch, P. (2000). *Understanding Cities*, Milton Keynes: The Open University.

Pinker, S. (1994). *The Language Instinct*, New York: W. Morrow & Co.

Pred, A. (1990). *Lost Words and Lost Worlds: Modernity and the Language of Everyday Life in Late 19th Century Stockholm*, Cambridge: Cambridge University Press.

Pryke, M. (1999a). 'City rhythms: Neo-liberalism and the developing world'. In Allen, J., Massey, D. & Pryke, M. (eds.), *Unsettling Cities: Movement/Settlement*, London: Routledge, pp. 229–269.

Pryke, M. (1999b). 'On the openness of cities'. In Allen, J., Massey, D. & Pryke, M. (eds.), *Unsettling Cities: Movement/Settlement*, London: Routledge, pp. 321–338.

Pueyo, M. & Turull, A. (2003). *Diversitat i política lingüística en un món global* Barcelona: Editorial Universitat Oberta Catalonia.

Puigdevall i Serralvo, M. (2006). *The challenge of language planning in the private sector: Welsh and Catalan perspectives*, unpublished PhD thesis, The University of Wales, Cardiff.

Rampton, B. (1995). *Crossing: Language and Ethnicity among Adolescents*, London: Longman.

Ricento, T. (2000). 'Historical and theoretical perspectives in language policy and planning', *Journal of Sociolinguistics* 4(2), pp. 196–213.

Robinson, J. (1999). 'Divisive cities: power and segregation in cities'. In Pile, S., Brook, C. & Mooney, G. (eds.), *Unruly Cities? Order/Disorder*, London: Routledge, pp. 149–200.

Robinson, T. (1996). *Setting Foot on the Shores of Connemara and Other Writings*, Dublin: Lilliput Press.

Rogers, A. & Tillie, J. (eds.) (2001). *Multicultural Policies and Modes of Citizenship in European Cities*, Aldershot, Ashgate.

Rogers, A. & Vertovec, S. (eds.) (1995). *The Urban Context: Ethnicity, Social Networks and Situational Analysis*, Oxford: Berg.

Romaine, S. (1984). 'The status of sociological models and categories in explaining linguistic variation', *Linguistische Berichte* 90, pp. 25–38.

Roosens, E. (1989). *Creating Ethnicity: The Process of Ethnogenesis*, London: Sage.

Sandercock, L. (1998). *Towards Cosmopolis: Planning for Multicultural Cities*, London: Routledge.

Sandercock, L. (2003). *Cosmopolis II: Mongrel Cities of the Twenty First Century*, London, Continuum.

Sassen, S. (1991). *The Global City: New York, London and Tokyo*, Princeton, NJ: Princeton University Press.

Sassen, S. (1996). 'Analytic borderlands: Race, gender and representation in the new city'. In King, A.D. (ed.), *Re-presenting the City: Ethnicity, Capital and Culture in the 21st Century Metropolis*, Houndmills: Macmillan, pp. 183–202.

Sennett, R. (1976). *The Fall of Public Man*, London: Faber.

Sennett, R. (1996). *The Uses of Disorder: Personal Identity and City Life*, London: Faber and Faber.

Sennett, R. (2002). 'Cosmopolitanism and the social experience of cities'. In Ver-tovec, S. & Cohen, R. (eds.), *Conceiving Cosmopolitanism: Theory, Context and Practice*, Oxford: Oxford University Press, pp. 42–47.

Shaw, S., Bagwell, S. & Karmowska, J. (2004). 'Ethnoscapes as Spectacle: Reimagining Multicultural Districts as New Destinations for Leisure and Consumption', *Urban Studies* 41(10), pp. 1983–2000.

Shikama, A. (2005). 'Japan as a host country: attitudes towards migrants', *International Journal of the Sociology of Language* 175/176, pp. 179–191.

Shuy, R.W., Wolfram, W.A. & Riley, W.K. (1968). *Field Techniques in an Urban Language Study*, Washington, DC: Center for Applied Linguistics.

Smith, A.D. (1986). *The Ethnic Origins of Nations*, Oxford: Blackwell.

Smith, A.D. (1995). *Nations and Nationalism in a Global Era*, Cambridge: Polity Press.

Smith, M.P. (2001). *Transnational Urbanism*, Oxford, Blackwell.

Spolsky, B. & Cooper, R.L. (1991). *The Languages of Jerusalem*, Oxford: Oxford University Press.

Stavans, I. (2001). *The Hispanic Condition: The Power of a People*, New York: HarperCollins.

Stavans, I. (2003). *Spanglish*, New York: Harper Collins.

Steiner, D. & Nauser, M. (1993) (eds.). *Human Ecology. Fragments of Anti-fragmentary Views of the World*, London: Routledge.

Stoker, G. (1995). 'Regime theory and urban politics'. In Judge, D., Stoker, G. & Wolman, H. (eds.), *Theories of Urban Politics*, London: Sage, pp. 54–61.

Stoker, G. (ed.) (2000). *The New Politics of British Local Governance*, Houndmills: Macmillan.

Suro, R. (2004). *Changing Channels and Crisscrossing Cultures: A Survey of Latinos on the News Media*, Washington, DC: The Pew Hispanic Centre.

Suro, R. & Singer, A. (2002). *Latino Growth in Metropolitan America: Changing Patterns, New Locations*, Washington, DC: The Brookings Institution and The Pew Hispanic Centre.

Suro, R. & Tafoya, S. (2004). *Dispersal and Concentration: Patterns of Latino Residential Settlement*, Washington, DC: The Pew Hispanic Centre.

Tafoya, S. (2004). *Shades of Belonging*, Washington, DC: The Pew Hispanic Centre.

Taylor, P.J. (1995a). 'Beyond containers: internationality, interstateness, interterritoriality', *Progress in Human Geography* 19(1), pp. 1–15.

Taylor, P. (1995b). 'World cities and territorial states: the rise and fall of their mutuality'. In Knox, P. & Taylor, P. (eds.), *World Cities in a World System*, Cambridge: Cambridge University Press, pp. 48–62.

Thomas, H. (2004). 'Identity building and cultural projects in Butetown, Cardiff', *City* 8(2), pp. 274–278.

Thomas, H. & Cowell, R. (2002). 'Managing nature and narratives of dispossession: reclaiming territory in Cardiff Bay', *Urban Studies* 39(7) pp. 1241–1260.

Thompson, G. (2000). 'Economic globalization?' In Held, D. (ed.), *A Globalizing World? Culture, Economics, Politics*, London: Routledge, pp. 85–125.

Thrift, N. (1983). 'On the determination of social action in space and time', *Environment and Planning D: Society and Space* 1, pp. 23–57.

Toribio, A.J. (2002). 'Spanish-English code-switching among US Latinos', *International Journal of the Sociology of Language* 158, pp. 89–119.

Tripp, A.M. (1999). 'Deindustrialization and the Growth of Women's Economic Associations and Networks in Urban Tanzania'. In Allen, J., Massey, D. & Pryke, M. (eds.), *Unsettling Cities: Movement/Settlement*, London: Routledge, pp. 263–266.

Trudgill, P. (1974). *The Social Differentiation of English in Norwich*, Cambridge: Cambridge University Press.

United Nations (UN) (1999). *The World at Six Billion*, New York: United Nations.

UN (2001). *Press Release 6th June 2001 'Urban Millennium'*, press release accessed from http://www.un.org/ (site accessed 10 June 2001).

United Nations – Habitat (2006). *State of the World's Cities 2006/2007. Urbanization: Mega and Meta Cities, New City States?* Report accessed from http://www.unhabitat.org (site accessed 1 June 2006).

United Nations Population Fund (UNPF) (2004). *State of World Population, 2004.* Report accessed from http://www.unfpa.org/ (site accessed 5 June 2005).

Van Der Merwe, I.J. (1993). 'The urban geolinguistics of Cape Town', *GeoJournal* 31, pp. 409–417.

Van Der Merwe, I.J. (1995). 'Language change in South Africa: a geographical perspective' *GeoJournal* 37, pp. 513–523.

Van Der Merwe, I.J. (1996). 'Geolinguistics of European minority groups in Cape Town', *Tijdschrift voor Economische en Sociale Geografie* 87(2), pp. 146–160.

Van Els, T.J.M. (2006). 'The European Union, its institutions and its languages: some language political observations'. In Baldauf, R.B. & Kaplan, R.B. (eds.), *Language Planning and Policy in Europe, volume 2: the Czech Republic, the European Union and Northern Ireland*, Clevedon: Multilingual Matters, pp. 202–256.

Vertovec, S. (1996). 'Multiculturalism, culturalism and public incorporation', *Ethnic and Racial Studies* 19(1), pp. 222–242.

Vertovec, S. (2001). *Transnational challenges to the 'new' multiculturalism* WPTC-01-06, paper presented to the ASA conference, the University of Sussex, 30 March–2 April 2001.

Vertovec, S. & Cohen, R. (eds.) (2002). *Conceiving Cosmopolitanism: Theory, Context and Practice*, Oxford: Oxford University Press.

Wardhaugh, R. (1992, 2nd ed.). *An Introduction to Sociolinguistics*, Oxford: Blackwell.

Wardhaugh, R. (1998, 3rd ed.). *An Introduction to Sociolinguistics*, Oxford: Blackwell.

Wardhaugh, R. (2001, 4th ed.). *An Introduction to Sociolinguistics*, Oxford: Blackwell.

Watson, S. (1999). 'City politics'. In Pile, S., Brook, C. & Mooney, G. (eds.), *Unruly Cities?Order/Disorder*, London: Routledge, pp. 201–245.

Weinstein, B. (1990). *Language Policy and Political Development*, Norwood NJ: Ablex Publishing.

Werlen, B. (1993). 'On regional and cultural identity: outline of a regional culture analysis'. In Steiner, D. & Nauser, M. (eds.), *Human Ecology: Fragments of Anti-fragmentary Views of the World*, London: Routledge, pp. 296–309.

Western, J. (2002). 'A divided city: Cape Town', *Political Geography* 21(5), pp. 711–716.

Whorf, B.L. (1956a). 'Linguistics as an exact science'. In Carroll, J.B. (ed.), *Language, Thought, and Reality: Selected Writings of Benjamin Lee Whorf*, Cambridge MA: MIT Press, pp. 220–232.

Whorf, B.L. (1956b). 'An American Indian model of the universe'. In Carroll, J.B. (ed.), *Language, Thought, and Reality: Selected Writings of Benjamin Lee Whorf* Cambridge MA: MIT Press, pp. 57–64.

Whyte, J. (1990). *Interpreting Northern Ireland*, Oxford: Clarendon Press.

Williams, G. (1992). *Sociolinguistics: A Sociological Critique*, London: Routledge.

Williams, C.H. & Van Der Merwe, I.J. (1996). 'Mapping the multilingual city: a research agenda for urban geolinguistics', *Journal of Multilingual and Multicultural Development*, 17(1), pp. 49–66.

Withers, C.W.J. (1984) *Gaelic in Scotland 1698–1981: The Geographical History of a Language*, Edinburgh: John Donald.

Wolfram, W. (1969). *A Sociolinguistic Description of Detroit Negro Speech*, Washington, DC: Center for Applied Linguistics.

Wolfram, W. & Fasold, R.W. (1974). *The Study of Social Dialects in American English*, Englewood Cliffs, NJ: Prentice Hall.

Woolgar, S. (2001). *Reflections on the Virtual Society?* Paper presented to ICUST 2001, Paris, 12–14 June 2001.

Worsley, P. (1984). *The Three Worlds: Culture and World Development*, London: Weidenfeld & Nicholson.

Wright, S. (2004). *Language Policy and Language Planning. From Nationalism to Globalisation*, Houndmills: Palgrave Macmillan.

Yağmur, K. (2004). 'Language maintenance patterns of Turkish immigrant communities in Australia and western Europe: the impact of majority attitudes on ethnolinguistic vitality and perceptions', *International Journal of the Sociology of Language* 165, pp. 121–142.

Yeoh, B. (2001). 'Postcolonial cities', *Progress in Human Geography* 25(3), pp. 456–468.

Young, I. (1989). 'Polity and group difference: a critique of the model of universal citizenship' *Ethnics* 99(2), pp. 250–274.

Young, I. (1990). *Justice and the Politics of Difference*, Princeton: Princeton University Press.

Zukin, S. (1991). *Landscapes of Power*, Berkeley: University of California Press.

Zukin, S. (1995). *The Cultures of Cities*, Oxford: Basil Blackwell.

Index

— Language Schools in Reading.
Landon Street.
— Enrolment presupposes subscription to an
order of hegemony.

— Contexts and appropriateness
of language, language attitudes,
language choice

"Sorry my English is poor"
Conveys a certain ideological leaning.
submissive, apologetic, totally as
structurally 'othered'. response/reaction

Cultural nucleus :
cultural epicentres :
Madjeski Stadium : Landmark.
Institute of sports.